In the SHADOW of FREEDOM

In the SHADOW of FREEDOM

The Enduring Call for Racial Justice

Alessandra Harris

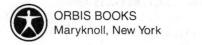

ORBIS BOOKS
Maryknoll, New York

Founded in 1970, Orbis Books endeavors to publish works that enlighten the mind, nourish the spirit, and challenge the conscience. The publishing arm of the Maryknoll Fathers and Brothers, Orbis seeks to explore the global dimensions of the Christian faith and mission, to invite dialogue with diverse cultures and religious traditions, and to serve the cause of reconciliation and peace. The books published reflect the views of their authors and do not represent the official position of the Maryknoll Society. To learn more about Maryknoll and Orbis Books, please visit our website at www.orbisbooks.com.

Library of Congress Cataloging-in-Publication Data

Names: Harris, Alessandra, author.
Title: In the shadow of freedom : the enduring call for racial justice / Alessandra Harris.
Other titles: Enduring call for racial justice
Description: Maryknoll, NY : Orbis Books, [2024] | Includes bibliographical references. | Summary: "Traces the roots of systemic anti-Black racism and police violence from 1619 to present-day mass incarceration"— Provided by publisher.
Identifiers: LCCN 2023049391 (print) | LCCN 2023049392 (ebook) | ISBN 9781626985421 (print) | ISBN 9798888660010 (ebook)
Subjects: LCSH: African Americans—Violence against. | African American prisoners—United States. | Racial profiling in law enforcement—United States. | Police brutality—United States. | Racism—United States. | United States—Race relations—Religious aspects—Christianity.
Classification: LCC E185.615 .H285 2024 (print) | LCC E185.615 (ebook) | DDC 305.800973—dc23/eng/20231114
LC record available at https://lccn.loc.gov/2023049391
LC ebook record available at https://lccn.loc.gov/2023049392

For America,
that you may one day be the land of the free.

Contents

Note to Readers

Content Warning: Please be advised that in describing historical and recent events, various chapters contain graphic details of violence, lynching, killing, executions, rape, infanticide, police brutality, and torture.

Introduction

> History, despite its wrenching pain,
> Cannot be unlived,
> but if faced with courage,
> need not be lived again.
> "On the Pulse of Morning,"
> Maya Angelou

In 2008, my oldest son was a first grader at a Catholic school. He had enjoyed his first year in kindergarten. As his second year at the school progressed, however, he started getting in trouble with his teacher. The young woman had a behavior system whereby she would hand out cards: green for good behavior, yellow as a warning, and red for bad behavior, which incurred a disciplinary measure. At first, my son's red cards meant he would not earn prizes in class, but they steadily progressed to his having to sit out some time at recess, then sitting out his whole lunch, and then having to meet with the principal.

I was a busy stay-at-home mom who had my fourth baby a few months after the school year started. So, after speaking with my son's teacher but not understanding exactly what the problem was, I asked the principal if a professional from outside the school could observe the class and report back what was happening. The principal agreed, and a school district psychologist came to my son's school and observed him at school and in the class over a period of weeks. Once she had completed her observation, we had a long phone conversation. The psychologist believed the teacher was biased against my son. The teacher was disciplining only my son for behavior that other kids were doing. The psychologist said she saw that a lot in her work with African American boys in particular.

The psychologist talked to the principal and reported to him the same information. The principal ignored the report and told other parents that there were problems at my home that were leading to my son's misbehavior. We made the decision to leave the school and enroll at a

1

small Christian school that was not Catholic and had a lot more diversity and specifically a larger Black student population. My son still had a lot of energy and at times would misbehave in class, all the way up until eighth-grade graduation. But the school had a philosophy of accepting that different kids have different needs and activity levels, and the teachers did not resort to punishment.

It wasn't until years later that I came across the statistic from the 2014 U.S. Department of Education Office for Civil Rights Data Collection that found that Black *preschoolers* represented 18 percent of preschool enrollment, but 42 percent of preschool students suspended at least one time, and 48 percent of students suspended more than once.[1] Black boys and teens are more heavily policed in the United States than any other group, and it begins at the earliest stages. The current prediction for lifetime incarceration for Black males born in 2001 is one in five (21.1 percent) and four times higher than white males born the same year.[2] The lifetime risk of incarceration is ten times higher for Black high schoolers who drop out than Black students who attend college.[3] As I discuss in chapter 5, for millions of predominantly Black and Latino students living in the poorest neighborhoods, schools are mirroring prisons and more often armed with cops than counselors, psychologists, or nurses. For a mom of four Black kids, this is not only unacceptable; it's unconscionable and one of the reasons I feel compelled to write this book.

In *Racial Justice and the Catholic Church,* Bryan Massingale wrote, "Racism functions as an ethos, as the animating spirit of U.S. society, which lives on despite observable changes and assumes various incarnations in different historical circumstances."[4] In 2002, sociologist Loïc Wacquant wrote that the United States has had four "peculiar institutions": slavery (1619–1865), Jim Crow (1865–1965), northern ghettos (1915–1968), and hyperghettos and prisons (1968–present). My book will discuss all four institutions and focus on the present period, which is characterized by "mass incarceration" and includes policing, the criminal legal system, incarceration, the multibillion-dollar prison-labor industry, and postincarceration social exclusion. Here's how Wacquant summarized mass incarceration's impact on Black people in this country:

> The astronomical overrepresentation of blacks in houses of penal confinement and the increasingly tight meshing of the hyper-

ghetto with the carceral system suggests that, owing to America's adoption of mass incarceration as a queer social policy designed to discipline the poor and contain the dishonoured, lower-class African-Americans now dwell, not in a society with prisons as their white compatriots do, but in the first genuine prison society in history.[5]

This new peculiar institution has become so ingrained in American society that its grotesque racism and brutality are not only ignored but justified. In chapter 3 I look at how the United States incarcerates two million people in its prisons and jails, which is the largest number of people both in absolute numbers and as a percentage of the population in the history of the world. Over the last forty years, the incarceration rate has increased by 500 percent.[6] *The New Jim Crow: Mass Incarceration in the Age of Colorblindness* by Michelle Alexander made the case that the war on drugs was disproportionately waged against the Black community, and specifically Black Americans living in concentrated poverty. Alexander argued that the drug war was not about drugs; it was the mechanism used to reinstate a caste system and control of the Black population after the civil rights movement ended Jim Crow segregation. Elizabeth Hinton's *From the War on Poverty to the War on Crime* documented that the groundwork for the overpolicing and overincarceration of Black people and neighborhoods was actually laid by President Lyndon B. Johnson and accelerated with the administration of President Richard Nixon. Other books, such as *Policing the Black Man: Arrest, Prosecution and Imprisonment,* with included contributions by Angela J. Davis, Bryan Stevenson, Marc Mauer, Bruce Western, and Jeremy Travis, and *Rise of the Warrior Cop,* by Radley Balko, demonstrate how the police have been trained and given billions of dollars to wage war against American citizens who are overwhelmingly Black.

According to the Sentencing Project, the American prison boom started in 1973 and lasted until 2009.

The prison expansion that commenced in 1973 reached its peak in 2009, achieving a seven-fold increase over the intervening years. Between 1985 and 1995 alone, the total prison population grew an average of eight percent annually. And between 1990 and 1995, all states, with the exception of Maine, substantially increased their prison populations, from 13% in South Carolina to as high as 130% in Texas. The federal system grew 53% larger during this five-year period alone.[7]

According to the study "A Generational Shift: Race and the Declining Lifetime Risk of Imprisonment," during the period of the prison boom, "the number of individuals incarcerated in prisons increased by more than 700%," with Black men born during my birth cohort of 1981–1984 most impacted, with one in three incarcerated. Incarceration during the prison boom years was so pervasive for African American males that Black men were more likely to go to prison than obtain a college degree, marry, or serve in the military.[8] As a result of this mass incarceration in the United States, nearly half of Americans report "that they have had an immediate family member in prison or jail, including more than 2 million children who currently have an incarcerated parent and 10 million children who have had a parent imprisoned at some point in their lives." Again, Black children are most affected, with one in four estimated to have a parent incarcerated by their teenage years, compared to one in ten Latino children and one in twenty-five white children.[9]

Though the rate of African Americans incarcerated declined every year under President Barack Obama's tenure, and the Black male incarceration rate has declined by 44 percent since 2019, America still spends more money on policing than any other country in the world, with Black men still disproportionately arrested, convicted, and incarcerated for the longest lengths of time. A 2019 Vera Institute report found that American law enforcement makes an arrest every three seconds. Over 80 percent of the arrests are for nonserious, low-level offenses such as drug abuse violations or disorderly conduct. Fewer than 5 percent of arrests are for serious violent offenses.[10]

In this book, I look at the millions of people criminalized for reasons that are completely out of their control, such as being born Black; living in a neighborhood with concentrated poverty; experiencing violence in the home or being sexually abused while growing up; or having an untreated mental health or substance use disorder. During the same period of astronomical growth of prisons and incarceration, the population of patients in psychiatric institutions shrank by 90 percent. The National Alliance for Mental Illness (NAMI) states that "jails and prisons have become America's de-facto mental health facilities."[11] Data from a 2004 survey of people incarcerated in state and federal prisons found that 38.1 percent identified as having a mental-health disorder, and in the year before their incarceration, 32.6 percent of people had an alcohol-use disorder and 43.6 percent had a substance use disorder.[12] The Prison Policy Initiative's data from the 2017 Substance Abuse and Mental Health Services Administration's National Survey on Drug Use and Health found that 62 percent of people who had been jailed three or more times in a twelve-month period had a substance use disorder.[13]

Because the reality of mass incarceration cannot be viewed in isolation, my book explores how America's original sin of slavery has shape-shifted after the Civil War and manifested itself as convict-leasing *neoslavery*, Jim Crow segregation enforced by racial terror such as lynching, and now the death penalty, imprisonment, and social exclusion postincarceration for millions of African Americans. For over four hundred years, African Americans have been subject to oppression and subjugation, which continues in the form of racial profiling, overpolicing, and extrajudicial police murders. What accompanied slavery was the white supremacist belief that Black people were inferior to white people, which morphed postbellum into the still-present stereotype of Black criminality.

Ironically, stating these facts and reading the above-mentioned books might *not* lead the average American who is not Black to reach the conclusion that there is a persistent racial problem in America; it may actually result in white Americans *approving even more* of the systems and policies that lead to such stark racial disparities. In a series of studies, researchers ran social experiments on white people throughout the country to determine their level of punitiveness based on the proportion of African Americans incarcerated.

In California, the researchers found the blacker the white people believed the prison population to be, the less willing registered voters were to take steps to reduce the severity of a three-strikes law they acknowledged to be overly harsh. In New York, though white participants thought their city's stop-and-frisk policy, which led to a disproportionate number of Black and Latino residents being stopped and frisked by police, was somewhat punitive, participants who viewed the prison population as more Black were significantly less willing to sign a petition to end the stop-and-frisk policy than were participants who were told the prison population was less Black. Similarly, "the more participants worried about crime, the less likely they were to say they would sign a petition to end the stop-and-frisk policy." The researchers concluded that the more white people were exposed to extreme racial disparities in the prison population, for example, believing more Black people were incarcerated, the heightened "their fear of crime and increased acceptance of the very policies that lead to those disparities. Thus, institutionalized disparities can be self-perpetuating."[14]

In the same vein, researchers at the University of Georgia psychology department reached similar conclusions related to the effect of disparate rates of severity of Covid-19 among Black people during the pandemic. When the pandemic first began, people believed all Americans were equally susceptible to the deadly virus; but when the "U.S. media began reporting on the dramatic racial disparities in COVID-19 infection and mortality rates—resulting from structural inequalities, persistent racial health disparities, and overrepresentation of people of color among essential workers—in April of 2020," white Americans' attitudes and public policy began to change. The researchers explained that in general, "people tend to have less empathy for members of social groups that they do not belong to," and "people show a dampened neural response when viewing racial outgroup (vs. ingroup) members in pain." So, two studies were conducted to test "whether White U.S. residents' perceptions of and exposure to information about COVID-19 racial disparities in the U.S. predict fear of COVID-19 and support for COVID-19 safety precautions."

The two studies found white residents who perceived there to be greater racial disparities in Covid-19 were less fearful of the virus; that reduced fear may decrease support for safety precautions that could limit the spread of Covid-19; and they had reduced empathy as well. The conclusions of the studies were in line with what happened in the country between late March and early June 2020: white Americans increased their support for reopening the economy despite the impact it would have on Black people and other essential workers of color.[15] The results were deadly for Black Americans.

White apathy to Black mortality backfired. In October 2022, the *Washington Post* reported that white Americans had become more likely to die from Covid. Their reduced fear of the virus and lack of support for precautions resulted in increased numbers of white people dying. So too, when it comes to mass incarceration; after decades of Black people being targeted for marijuana and crack-cocaine use and sales, the opioid crisis began leveling the playing field as more and more white Americans entered jails and prisons. Chapter 6 on the opioid crisis not only proves that the war on drugs was never about drug use, but it also demonstrates the hypocrisy in America's judicial system. More than six hundred thousand people in the United States and Canada have died from opioid overdoses, and not a single executive or owner of Purdue Pharma, the company that created OxyContin, has been sentenced to jail or prison, despite thousands of pages of court documents directly linking their drug, their false and aggressive marketing, and their pill-pushing to the start of the opioid crisis in America. In April 2021, the House Committee on Oversight and Reform reported that the Sackler family, which owns Purdue Pharma, had built an enormous fortune, valued at $11.1 billion, "in large part through the sale of OxyContin."[16] On the other hand, while incarceration rates have declined over the past two decades across every state and for almost every racial and ethnic group, white women are the only segment of the American population with an increase in rate of imprisonment—by 12 percent from 2000 to 2021, owing mainly to the opioid crisis.

In April 2022, a White House proclamation painted a dire picture faced by victims of the war on crime, the war on drugs, and the opioid epidemic. It stated that more than seventy million Americans have a criminal record that "creates significant barriers to employment, economic stability, and successful reentry into society. Thousands of legal and regulatory restrictions prevent these individuals from accessing employment, housing, voting, education, business licensing, and other basic opportunities."[17] In a 2021 interview with NPR, Reuben Jonathan Miller, author of *Halfway Home: Race, Punishment, and the Afterlife of Mass Incarceration*, stated, "Forty-five thousand federal and state laws regulate the lives of the accused. . . . In Illinois, there are over 1,400, including more than 1,000 employment regulations, 186 policies that limit political participation, 54 laws restricting family rights, and 21 housing statutes."[18] Miller, a sociologist, criminologist, social worker, and professor at the University of Chicago, was awarded a 2022 MacArthur Fellow Genius Grant for his work examining "the long-term consequences of incarceration on the lives of individuals and their families, with a focus on communities of color and those living in poverty."[19]

African Americans have been fighting for freedom, equality, and full citizenship in the United States for centuries. Black people have challenged the hypocrisy of a nation's founding document, the Declaration of Independence, which proclaimed that the unalienable rights of life, liberty, and the pursuit of happiness applied only to white men—not to the hundreds of thousands of people of African descent brutally enslaved and denied freedom at that time.

A country that claims to be a beacon of democracy must confront the truth that slavery was legal for 246 years, followed by Jim Crow segregation from 1877 until the 1950s and a current legal system that has created a new caste system whereby people are defined by their worst mistake, their untreated health crisis, their poverty, their race—and an overwhelming number of those people are permanently punished, excluded, and relegated to second-class citizenship.

All Black Americans could not freely vote until 1965. In the history of this country, the majority of Black people were shut out of democracy. And yet again today, as America is becoming more diverse racially, democracy itself is under attack by people more concerned with maintaining the status quo and white power.

An analysis by Reflective Democracy examined the often-not-discussed white male minority rule that dominates the United States. A study in 2021 found that white men hold 62 percent of all elected offices despite being just 30 percent of the population, exercising minority rule over 42 state legislatures, the House, the Senate, and statewide offices in this country. The political mechanizations of voter suppression to remove the power from voters, the January 6 insurrection, and the disenfranchisement of people who were incarcerated or have former felony convictions continue the shameful history of blocking a diverse body of people from fully participating in American civic life. Instead of the power structures rectifying these undemocratic practices, they attack and vilify

Black people for seeking full citizenship and call them unpatriotic, un-American, ungrateful traitors who should just "stay in their place" and be happy they live in this country.

One such African American who has received intense backlash is Nikole Hannah-Jones, who created the Pulitzer Prize–winning 1619 Project, published in the *New York Times Magazine* in 2019 to commemorate the four-hundredth anniversary of the beginning of American slavery. Hannah-Jones's aim was to reframe the country's history by placing the consequences of slavery and the contributions of Black Americans at the very center of the American national narrative. For far too long, Black Americans' historical importance has been a footnote in U.S. history. But the 1619 Project's forceful argument proved that Black people literally and figuratively helped build this country. And the profits from their forced labor and their innovation fueled the Industrial Revolution, creating what has become the richest and most powerful country today. According to Yale historian David W. Blight, "the nearly 4 million American slaves were worth some $3.5 billion—equivalent to $42 trillion today—making them the largest single financial asset in the entire U.S. economy, worth more than all manufacturing and railroads combined."[20]

Yet while Black Americans who are descendants of people who were enslaved make up 14 percent of the American population today, they only own 2 percent of the wealth in America. In contrast, white Americans, who make up 60 percent of the American population today, own 90 percent of the wealth.[21] The descendants of Black Americans who were brutally exploited and denied the fruits of their labor are now calling for what is rightfully owed to them. Like Martin Luther King Jr. said, "We refuse to believe that there are insufficient funds in the great vaults of opportunity of this nation. So we have come to cash this check, a check that will give us upon demand the riches of freedom and security of justice."

The 1619 Project has spawned a book and a Hulu docu-series. It has also produced a tremendous backlash that has resulted in states passing legislation to ban teaching it. Telling the truth about the history and ongoing impact of racism and discrimination is now considered "woke," "CRT," and dangerous to the stability of the country. Books that teach African American history or explore the roots of inequality are being banned, and teachers and professors teaching about anti-Black racism are being silenced. But this isn't just a political issue. In a 2020 *New Yorker* interview, Michelle Alexander stated, "the crisis of mass incarceration is not simply a legal or political problem to be solved, but it's a profound spiritual and moral crisis, as well. And it requires a reckoning, individually and collectively, with our racial history, our racial present, and our racial future."[22]

Weaving the threads of American slavery, apartheid-like Jim Crow segregation, and mass incarceration today with those spiritual and moral crises they spawned, my book argues that those who consider themselves Christian—or religious—must not only understand and acknowledge this history but root out white supremacy and anti-Blackness from their identity. Given the claims of Christianity, the counter-intuitive truth is that white American Christians harbor racist and intolerant positions at higher rates than nonbelievers. In *White Too Long: The Legacy of White Supremacy in American Christianity*, Robert P. Jones states:

> After centuries of complicity, the norms of white supremacy have become deeply and broadly integrated into white Christian identity, operating far below the level of consciousness. To many well-meaning white Christians today—evangelical Protestant, mainline Protestant, and Catholic—Christianity and a cultural norm of white supremacy now often feel indistinguishable, with an attack on the latter triggering a full defense of the former.[23]

The Catholic Church specifically must understand and reckon with its role in transatlantic slavery and its enduring effects in America, which is home to the second largest population of people descended from Africa outside of the African continent. Not only did the church provide a seminal role in blessing the slave trade launched by Portugal, but it was complicit, as three of the five major countries dominating the trade, Portugal, Spain, and France, were Catholic; and Catholic bishops, priests, religious orders, and laypeople throughout the world owned, sold, and profited from enslaved Africans. In *The 272: The Families Who Were Enslaved and Sold to Build the American Catholic Church*, Rachel L. Swarns writes, "For more than a century, the American Catholic Church relied on the buying, selling, and enslavement of Black people to lay its foundations, support its clergy, and drive its expansion. Without the enslaved, the Catholic Church in the United States, as we know it today, would not exist."[24]

While I write as someone informed by Christianity, this book is meant for a wider readership. It's for all people who want a better understanding of American history, African American history, and racial justice movements in this country, and for those who want to be part of making the United States more equitable, just, and democratic today. As an author and racial justice advocate, my aim is to bring together different fields of study across history, the sciences, politics, theology, and the humanities to synthesize the issues and highlight just and moral action as the appropriate response.

What is that just action? Jesus's parable in Matthew 25:37–40 brings together moral understanding and ethical action:

> Lord, when was it that we saw you hungry and gave you food, or thirsty and gave you something to drink? And when was it that we saw you a stranger and welcomed you, or naked and gave you clothing? And when was it that we saw you sick or in prison and visited you? And the king will answer them, "Truly I tell you, just as you did it to one of the least of these who are members of my family, you did it to me."

Today in America, because of the enduring legacy of slavery, segregation, and racism, African Americans, and specifically those living in neighborhoods of concentrated poverty, incarcerations, or with criminal convictions, continue to be "the least of these" in this country. The question isn't how people convicted of a crime should be treated in jail or prison. The question is, how would a Christian treat Jesus if he were in jail or prison? Jesus was arrested, condemned, tortured, spit on, and crucified. When we see incarcerated people, Christian tradition teaches us to see the face of Christ. And when we are complicit in the face of Americans routinely being beaten, raped, murdered, tortured, neglected, and exploited in our jails and prisons, we are defacing the image of God. When African Americans are targeted by the police, treated as less than human, and deprived of the same educational and economic opportunities as white Americans, Christian tradition calls us to see the face of Christ. Similarly, as people of faith who profess the importance of God's mercy, grace, and forgiveness, we are called to extend those same principles to people after they leave incarceration, allowing them full reentry into American society.

As I discuss in chapter 8, there are people, organizations, courts, and collectives working throughout the United States to implement restorative justice practices as a more life-giving response when people commit harm instead of our punitive criminal legal system. The faith formation guide *Harm, Healing, and Human Dignity* describes restorative justice as "a way of responding to harm that focuses on repairing relationships and healing all those who are impacted by crime. Beautifully aligned with Gospel values, rooted in indigenous traditions, and applicable in many areas of life, restorative justice offers an approach to crime and suffering that honors human dignity and gives way to redemption." Restorative justice, however, isn't just a "nice" or "feel-good" or "soft" way to approach crime. Longtime victim rights advocates Sandra Pavelka and Anne Seymour explain:

> Restorative practices integrate data and evidence from a number of disciplines and fields, i.e., education, psychology, social work, criminology, victimology, sociology and organizational development and leadership, in order to build safe communities, increase social capital, decrease crime and antisocial behavior, repair harm and restore relationships.[25]

A pilot restorative justice program in the San Francisco District Attorney's Office from 2013 to 2019 was found to be a successful way to reduce recidivism in youth and an effective alternative to traditional juvenile justice practices. The twelve-month rearrest rates among youth who completed the program was much lower (19.2 percent) than among those who enrolled but did not complete the program (57.7 percent).[26] Restorative justice practices implemented correctly as pretrial diversion have the potential not only to address offenses in a victim-centered way but also to prevent future offenses. Similarly, restorative justice practices implemented in educational settings have the potential to decrease student suspensions, arrests, and dropouts, all directly linked to a higher likelihood of incarceration later in life. In *The Little Book of Race and Restorative Justice*, Fania Davis explains how restorative justice practices implemented in schools in Oakland, California, had a profound effect:

> According to a 2015 implementation study of whole-school restorative justice in Oakland that compared schools with restorative justice to schools without, from 2011 to 2014, graduation rates in restorative schools increased by 60 percent compared to a 7 percent increase in nonrestorative schools; reading scores increased 128 percent versus 11 percent; and the dropout rate decreased 56 percent versus 17 percent. Harm was repaired in 76 percent of conflict circles, with students learning to talk instead of fight through differences at home and at school, and more than 88 percent of teachers said that restorative practices were very or somewhat helpful in managing difficult student behaviors.[27]

Systemic change within the United States is required to stop the institutional and personal harms committed against African Americans, and reparations must be discussed in order for true racial reconciliation to occur. For that to happen, unfiltered American history must be taught, African American stories must be told, and destructive policies like the war on drugs, mass incarceration, and overpolicing must be exposed and ended. It's time to reckon with the history of anti-Black racism in order to break its stronghold over the country and create a truly just society.

I know that the toil, resistance, sacrifice, and prayers of my paternal ancestors, some of whom were most likely enslaved in this country, have contributed to who I am today. Similarly, my maternal grandmother, May Brutus, and grandfather, Dennis Brutus, who was shot, imprisoned, and exiled from South Africa because of his resistance to apartheid in the 1960s, have instilled in me a passion for equality and justice.

For all the progress that has been made in America, though, including the elections of the first Black president and vice president, far too many African Americans do not experience true freedom because the threat or reality of racial discrimination, poverty, incarceration, and violence are ever present. Based on the racism and bullying my children have faced thus far in their lives while attending various private and public schools in the ethnically diverse San Francisco Bay area—from teachers overly punishing them and trying to place them unnecessarily in special education; to other students (mainly nonwhite) bullying them, excluding them, and calling them the N-word and other derogatory terms—it's clear anti-Black racism is no longer a white and Black issue. Anti-Black sentiment is grossly pervasive and crosses color lines in the twenty-first century, and the United States' growing more ethnically diverse will not alone result in less racism unless anti-Blackness is uprooted from society.

As a Black wife, mom, activist, and writer, I am advocating for changes in this country so I don't have to fear that the people in my life may be targeted for arrest and imprisonment because of their skin color or that the police will be called on them or that they will be killed because their mere presence is threatening. I don't want Black women, including my daughter, to face the highest maternal mortality and infant mortality rates in this country. I want to live in a country where my children have an equal chance at gainful employment, economic stability, and home ownership. And I want to be part of a Christian faith that believes and practices that our lives as Black people are just as important and deserve as much protection as any other person in this country. In order for lasting change to occur in the criminal legal system and American society, common ground must be reached, and hearts and minds must change. My hope is that this book will foster dialogue and spur action in order for those changes to occur.

Chapter 1

Slavery and Neoslavery

> How lonely sits the city
> that once was full of people!
> How like a widow she has become,
> she that was great among the nations!
> She that was a princess among the provinces
> has become a vassal.
>
> Lamentations 1:1

In the year 1441, the European Christian slave trade in Africa began what Dwight N. Hopkins called "the largest displacement, forced migration, and genocide in human history."[1] In 1452, Pope Nicholas V legitimized the Portuguese slave trade with the issuance of the papal bull *Dum Diversas*, and the 1455 papal bull *Romanus Pontifex* gave Portugal the right to enslave all Africans they encountered south of Cape Bojador on the coast of Western Sahara and hold them in perpetual slavery.[2] Nicolas V commended Prince Henry of Portugal "for his devotion and apostolic zeal in spreading the name of Christ" and gave him the "authorization to conquer and possess distant lands and their wealth."[3]

In 1492, Catholic Spain's King Ferdinand and Queen Isabella commissioned Christopher Columbus to "discover, conquer, and subdue foreign lands" and gave him the authority to "punish any persons who would disobey his command." When a conflict arose and Portugal protested Columbus's commission, Pope Alexander VI issued papal bulls on May 3 and May 4, 1493, in favor of Spain and assured Ferdinand and Isabella that they had the right to any islands or mainlands "discovered." He specified that land to the west of an imaginary line running through the eastern part of present-day Brazil belonged to the Spanish kingdom, and everything to the east belonged to the Kingdom of Portugal. Hopkins explains, as "theological justification, the pope draws on the authority of 'Almighty God,' the 'vicarship of Jesus Christ,' the tradition of 'apostolic power,' and the premier role of Peter."[4]

Fifteen months before Columbus's first voyage, on May 3, 1491, King Nzinga a Nkuwu of Kongo converted to Christianity and adopted the name Joâo I. The Kingdom of Kongo covered an area of nearly sixty thousand square miles in what is present-day Angola and the Democratic Republic of Congo. Its first contact with Europeans occurred in 1483 when a Portuguese explorer named Diogo Câo landed on the southeast shores of an estuary of the Congo River and sent emissaries with gifts to the capital to begin relations. Câo kidnapped several of the Kongolese and took them back to Portugal, then returned to Kongo two years later with more gifts and the hostages, who could now serve as translators and witnesses of the Portuguese kingdom.[5]

After Joâo I's conversion, he sent youth from Kongo to Europe for "literacy and education in matters of faith, setting in motion the adoption of the Portuguese language by the kingdom for official correspondence, diplomacy, and record keeping, which would have far-reaching consequences."[6] Before his death in 1509, Joâo I had his first son by his principal wife baptized Catholic and gave him the Christian name Afonso I. After Joâo I's death, both Afonso I and his half-brother, Mbanza Kongo, sought to succeed their father. Lore has it, however, that with the assistance of the sudden manifestation of St. James the Apostle, Afonso was able to defeat his half-brother and ascend the throne.[7]

Cyprian Davis's *The History of Black Catholics in the United States*, published in 1990, was the first full-length book discussing the Black Catholic experience. It remains one of the few modern English resources, along with Howard French's *Born in Blackness: Africa, Africans, and the Making of the Modern World, 1471 to the Second World War*, to discuss the Kingdom of Kongo's conversion to Catholicism. According to Davis, Afonso, known as Afonso the Good, ruled from 1506 to 1543 and had two main concerns. He wanted his people to convert to Catholicism and profit from the "technological knowledge of the Europeans," and he tried to control the "rapacious appetite of the Portuguese for riches and especially slaves."[8]

As French explains, upon Afonso's ascent to the throne, the ruler ordered the destruction of idols and the construction of a new church dedicated to Our Lady of Victory. Afonso dispatched Kongolese elite to Portugal and other European cities, including thirty-five of his own off-spring and clan kinsmen. One of Afonso's sons, Henrique, was ordained a priest in Portugal and in 1518 was named "bishop in *partibus infide-lum*, meaning presiding over pagan territories in Africa." French further details, "for the 1530s, and for a period stretching across the next century, Kongo frequently sent missions to the Vatican, reflecting the kingdom's keen understanding of the institutional power and political centrality of the Catholic Church in Europe." However, Afonso's petitions for Rome to grant Kongo its own episcopal see were denied after Portugal lobbied against it.[9]

Afonso initially accepted Portugal's request to trade Africans who were enslaved, which resulted in the trafficking of four thousand African people a year by the middle of the sixteenth century. He acquired many of the Africans by trade with another kingdom, Tio, and he would supplement the trade with copper and other items such as wax, ivory, and palm cloth. French notes, "by the 1560s, according to one estimate, captive human beings had essentially become the only 'currency' that the Portuguese would readily accept in exchange for their coveted goods."[10]

According to Davis, "slavery meant the undoing of all that Afonso had tried to accomplish." The king realized that the Portuguese demand for Africans to be sold into slavery knew no bounds, including the Portuguese's seizing Afonso's own people and even members of his family. Afonso had written the Portuguese King João III sometime in 1529 stating he wished to stop the sale of the enslaved people because it was depopulating his country. João threatened that if the slave traffic ceased, so too would most of Portugal's trade with Kongo.[11]

João's threat apparently worked, and another correspondence in 1540 revealed Afonso had a change of mind. In a letter Afonso sent to his Portuguese counterpart, he ensured that his kingdom, even more than any other African nation-state, could supply Portugal the Africans to be traded into slavery.[12] Over the duration of the transatlantic slave trade, 1.3 million captives were generated by Portugal's colony in Africa, Luanda, which made it the most prolific single source of enslaved people for the American trade. Consequently, a large number of Kongolese who were kidnapped and trafficked to the Americas were baptized Catholics.[13]

In the 1625 Virginia colony census, of the twenty-one Africans listed, the only person with an age recorded was thirty-year-old John Pedro, who was believed to have been a practicing Catholic from a prominent family in Kongo. By early 1650s, John Pedro was freed, but he was later executed in Maryland for his involvement in a Catholic dissident faction.[14] Though the Kingdom of Kongo would remain staunchly Catholic for over two hundred years, Davis states, "it was the curse of the slave trade that drove many of Afonso's subjects against the church after his death."[15]

In *Black and Catholic: The Challenge and Gift of Black Folk*, Jamie T. Phelps, O.P., explains that "Columbus and subsequent explorers and missionaries from Spain, Portugal, France, and England came to these shores not as emissaries of their Queens and Kings but as 'instruments of God' with a divine mission and gospel mandate to 'go out all over the world and preach the gospel to all creation.'"[16] As the reality of the relationship between the Kingdom of Kongo and Portugal and Rome reveals, however, colonial expansion served the economic and political expansionist interests of Europeans only under the guise of evangelization. Unlike American stereotypes of people from Africa who were forced into slavery in the Americas as primitive pagan heathens who had no history, agency, or culture, the Kingdom of Kongo and the majority of African nation-states had well-formed societies, religious practices, valuable skills, and lifestyles before European powers exploited them for people to enslave.

So, too did Indigenous people in the Americas have their own sacred traditions, stewardship of their land, and complex societies before Europeans colonized them. French notes that the "waves of epidemic and expiration that followed the arrival of whites became part of what has been described as a hemisphere-wide Great Dying." As many as "56 million people, or roughly 90 percent of the overall hemispheric population of indigenous Americans" were killed "between the time of first European contact and the start of the seventeenth century."[17] While European settlers killed off huge numbers of people in conflicts, more victims of colonization were killed by Eurasian diseases such as smallpox, influenzas, or measles than by either the gun or the sword.[18] A study by scientists at University College London also citing the genocide of approximately

56 million Indigenous people found that "European colonization of the Americas resulted in the killing of so many native people that it transformed the environment and caused the Earth's climate to cool down," resulting in a "Little Ice Age."[19]

According to the Trans-Atlantic Slave Trade Database, between 1525 and 1866, 12.5 million people were captured in Africa and trafficked to the Americas. About 10.7 million survived the Middle Passage and were enslaved in North America, the Caribbean, and South America.[20] French adds the following to the human toll slavery inflicted on the continent of Africa and people of African descent:

> Lost in this atrocious but far too neat accounting is the likelihood that another 6 million Africans were killed in or near their homelands during the hunt for slaves, before they could be placed in chains. Estimates vary, but between 5 and 40 percent perished during brutal overland treks to the coast, or while being held, often for months, in barracoons, or holding pens, as they awaited embarkation on slave ships. . . . When one considers that Africa's total population in the mid-nineteenth century was probably around 100 million, one begins to gauge the enormity of the demographic assault that the slave trade represented.[21]

In August 1619, the English who settled Jamestown, Virginia, brought with them twenty to thirty enslaved Angolan Africans bought from pirates who had stolen them from a Portuguese slave ship. This marked the beginning of slavery in the colonies that would become the United States of America, and it would last for more than two centuries.[22]

In order to justify the brutal conquest of Indigenous peoples and the enslavement of Africans, Phelps explains the dehumanization of non-Europeans that took place.

> The personhood and culture of Native Americans and Africans were ignored and denied. The isolation of Native Americans on reservations and their genocide during the period of Western expansion was justified by denying their full humanity, by denying their land rights, and by fear of their retaliatory violence.

The genocide of Africans during the slave trade of the Middle Passage, and their brutal treatment as slaves, were similarly justified by denying their full humanity, by denying them any human rights, and the fear of their retaliatory violence.[23]

In *The 1619 Project*, Nikole Hannah-Jones argues that the United States "is a nation founded on both an ideal and a lie." The Declaration of Independence, approved on July 4, 1776, was drafted by white men who did not believe that the hundreds of thousands of Black people in America were "created equal" to white men nor did they possess the unalienable rights of "Life, Liberty, and the pursuit of Happiness."[24] Thomas Jefferson, a founding father, the principal author of the Declaration, and the third president, not only enslaved over six hundred people throughout his lifetime but also had six children with enslaved Sally Hemings. Jefferson began a sexual relationship with Hemings when she was only fourteen years old. In a *Farm Book*, Jefferson kept detailed information about farming activities, livestock, and the people he enslaved, including his own children.[25]

On July 5, 1852, Frederick Douglass, the African American who had escaped slavery and became a world-renowned orator, author, and leader in the abolitionist movement, gave a speech at an event commemorating the signing of the Declaration of Independence titled, "What to the Slave Is the Fourth of July?" He lamented the hypocrisy of the nation that celebrated freedom while keeping the African American population enslaved in bondage.

This Fourth [of] July is yours, not mine. You may rejoice, I must mourn. . . . Fellow-citizens; above your national, tumultuous joy, I hear the mournful wail of millions! whose chains, heavy and grievous yesterday, are, to-day, rendered more intolerable by the jubilee shouts that reach them. . . . What, to the American slave, is your 4th of July? I answer: a day that reveals to him, more than all other days in the year, the gross injustice and cruelty to which he is the constant victim. To him, your celebration is a sham; your boasted liberty, an unholy license; your national greatness, swelling vanity; your sounds of rejoicing are empty and heartless; your denunciations of tyrants, brass fronted impudence; your shouts of liberty and equality, hollow mockery; your prayers and hymns, your sermons and thanksgivings, with all your religious parade, and solemnity, are, to him, mere bombast, fraud, deception, impiety, and hypocrisy—a thin veil to cover up crimes which would disgrace a nation of savages. There is not a nation on the earth guilty of practices, more shocking and bloody, than are the people of these United States, at this very hour.[26]

In the Pulitzer Prize–winning book *Slavery by Another Name: The Re-Enslavement of Black Americans from the Civil War to World War II*, Douglas A. Blackmon explains that in early colonial America, categorizing humans by race and color was foreign to the European tradition, which identified people by nationality and place of origin. Beginning in the 1650s, however, colonial legislatures, especially in Virginia, South Carolina, and Georgia, began to define residents by their lineage and skin color. Blackmon states this change served a twofold purpose:

> to create the legal structure necessary for building an economy with cheap slave labor as its foundation, and . . . to reconcile bondage with America's revolutionary ideals of intrinsic human rights. Blacks could be excluded from the Enlightenment concepts that every man was granted by God individual freedom and a right to the pursuit of happiness because colonial laws codified a less-than-fully human status of any person carrying even a trace of black or Indian blood.[27]

According to British inheritance and kinship law, a child's social status was passed down through the father. But in 1662 colonial America, the colonists passed a statute that asserted that "all children borne in this country shall be held bond or free only according to the condition of the mothers." In *The 1619 Project*, Dorothy Roberts states this was done because of the "political and economic disadvantages of classifying children born to Black women as white" when the child's father, who was often the enslaver, was white. If the traditional British convention were adopted in the colonies, it would "expand the pool of human beings who were entitled to the privileges of whiteness, and it would decrease the pool of human beings who could be enslaved." This law helped to invent the meaning of race in America as a natural identity and inherited condition the mother passed down to her child. As a result of this and a similar Maryland Colony law passed in 1663, enslavement became a "heritable condition across colonial America."[28]

Roberts explains that there is no way to definitively answer the question of how often white men sexually assaulted the Black girls and women that they enslaved, though there is documentation:

> An analysis by historian Thelma Jennings of 514 narratives of formerly enslaved people found that 12 percent of the female authors referred to experiences of coerced sex by white men. Of those women, 35 percent had fathers who were white men or had given birth to children fathered by white men. Jennings noted that the numbers were likely far larger, given the reluctance of recently freed Black women to discuss such private matters with their white interviewers. Census records show that in 1850, roughly 11 percent of the enslaved population was classified as mulatto.[29]

A 2020 study sampling DNA conducted by Joanna Mountain, the senior director of research at 23andMe, has also reinforced the historical record. The research included the DNA of fifty thousand people, including thirty thousand people with African ancestry whose grandparents were born in a region touched by the transatlantic slave trade.

> The researchers found that although a majority of the more than 12 million enslaved people who arrived in the Americas were men, enslaved women contributed more to the current gene pool. The genetic contribution of European men to the ancestry of African Americans is three times greater than that of European women. This means that enslaved men were more likely to die before they were able to have children and that enslaved women were often raped by white men and forced to bear their children.[30]

Unlike the many white men who forcibly fathered children with Black enslaved women and viewed their own flesh and blood as less than human and suitable to a life of slavery, Thomas Jefferson freed the four children he fathered with Sally Hemings who lived to be adults. That was the exception and not the rule. Two of the most prominent African American male voices who were born into slavery and fought for Black rights after freedom, Frederick Douglass and Booker T. Washington, both had Black mothers and white fathers, whose identities they did not know.

In *Sisters in the Wilderness*, Dolores Williams details how Black mothers could receive a penalty for the offense of telling their children the identity of their white fathers. Williams relays the story of an octoroon woman named Louisa Picquet whose mother told her that her slave master was her father. "For this 'offense' of telling the child about her parentage, the slave mother was sold away from her child."[31]

Generations of Black people were born and held in bondage in perpetuity and considered property of white enslavers. As Hannah-Jones writes, "Over time the enslavers created a network of laws and customs, astounding in both their precision and their cruelty, designed to strip the enslaved of every aspect of their humanity."[32]

In the essay "Slave Patrols, 'Pack of Negro Dogs' and Policing Black Communities," Larry H. Spruill explains that enslaved Black people, motivated by the innately human instinct to resist their enslavement and the enslavers' barbaric and dehumanizing treatment, were the primary threat to whites from every socioeconomic class. The desire of people of African descent to change their social status and upset the slavocracy was the primary rationale for white people to label the enslaved as inherently dangerous and criminal.[33]

Laws known as slave codes emerged, varying by state, and restricted every aspect of the lives of Black Americans in order for white people to exert total control over them. The slave codes stated the enslaved people were "property"; they were unable to enter into any contract, including legal marriage; prohibited from leaving the plantation where they were forced to labor without a pass; prohibited from learning how to read and write; prohibited from assembling unsupervised with others who were enslaved; and even prohibited from practicing religion.

To enforce these laws of white domination and Black subordination, Spruill describes how slave patrols, slave hunters, and "negro dogs" were employed. The idea of a slave-patrol system was imported from Barbados to South Carolina in 1704 and later used in all slaveholding colonies and states in the South.

> Patrollers policed all movement and unsupervised activity through passes, detainments, interrogations, unrestrained search and seizures of slave quarters, legally sanctioned on-the-spot violent punishment for the slightest infringement of slave laws and customs. The use of "negro dogs" to intimidate and control slaves, as well as pursue, punish, and recapture runaways, was also introduced from the West Indies. Patrollers carried out their duties on foot and horseback, both day and night, armed with guns, "negro whips" and given the situation, bloodhounds. They addressed white concerns that blacks were the foremost threat to their way of life. Authorized by county courts, slave patrols scrutinized every aspect of black lives with the power to spontaneously mete out corporal punishment.[34]

While Black people were incessantly policed, white enslavers could rape, beat, murder, torture, and impregnate the people they held in captivity. Frederick Douglass pointed out that the state of Virginia had seventy-two crimes that, if committed by a Black person, were punishable by death, yet only two of the same crimes committed by a white person would merit the same punishment.[35]

The same white supremacist views that argued people of African descent were inherently inferior, both intellectually and morally, also fetishized Black women. As Hannah-Jones describes, "The legal system that countenanced sexual violence against Black women and girls had required a moral excuse for its barbarism—especially in a nation that espoused ideals of female chastity and male civility. . . . Whether free or enslaved, Black women were portrayed as sexually licentious, always consenting, and therefore unrapeable."[36] This belief was solidified by a jury finding a Black woman named Celia guilty in 1855 of murdering the man who enslaved and repeatedly raped her and punishing her with death by hanging.

Celia had been purchased at the age of fourteen to be a sexual partner for a white Missouri farmer named Robert Newsom, whose wife had died less than a year before. Newsom first raped Celia on the trip to his home. He housed Celia in a cabin on his farm and raped her repeatedly over the course of five years, resulting in two children, and a third pregnancy at the time of Newsom's death. Celia's defense attorneys argued that she was sick during her third pregnancy and pled with Newsom not to sexually violate her. When Newsom entered Celia's cabin to rape her, Celia struck him on the head with a large stick multiple times, then threw his body into her fireplace and later disposed of the ashes. Celia's attorneys used the defense of an 1845 Missouri statute against coercing any woman to have sexual intercourse, and they argued Celia had a right to protect herself. The statute stated, "homicide shall be deemed justifiable, when committed by any person resisting an attempt to commit any felony upon him or her." The jurors rejected the defense's argument and instead found Celia guilty of first-degree murder. "She was considered chattel, personal property, without legal rights to defend herself against sexual abuse, whereas her owner, Robert Newsom, was within his legal rights to determine the boundaries of their relationship, even if it included rape." After she gave birth to her third baby, who was stillborn, Celia was hanged, and her two children were sold.[37]

Celia's conviction was representative of the larger hypocrisy in the legal system. Enslaved Black people had no civil or legal rights that protected *them* from violence and other crimes committed against them; yet the courts treated them as persons and prosecuted them to the fullest extent of the law when they violated the rights of *others*.[38]

Not only were the enslaved not afforded legal protection under the law, they also were hindered by the law from protecting their family members and keeping their families together. Wives and husbands could be separated, as well as parents and their children. A man named John S. Jacobs, who was born into slavery in North Carolina and later escaped to freedom, reflected on the destitution he felt as a man held in bondage.

To be a man, and not to be a man—a father without authority—a husband and no protector—is the darkest of fates. Such was the condition of my father, and such is the condition of every slave throughout the United States: he owns nothing, he can claim nothing. His wife is not his; his children are not his; they can be taken from him, and sold at any minute, as far away from each other as the human fleshmonger may see fit to carry them. Slaves are recognised as property by the law, and can own nothing except by the consent of their masters. A slave's wife or daughter may be insulted before his eyes with impunity. He himself may be called on to torture them, and dare not refuse. To raise his hand in their defence is death by the law. He must bear all things and resist nothing. If he leaves his master's premises at any time without a written permit, he is liable to be flogged. Yet, it is said by slave holders and their apologists, that we are happy and contented.[39]

Advocates of slavery argued that Black people were intellectually and morally inferior to white people, and therefore suited to enslavement by "benevolent" white people who provided for their needs. In *Slave Breeding: Sex, Violence, and Memory in African American History*, proponents of slavery, according to Gregory D. Smithers, argued the institution was "in keeping with the 'republican' ideals and humanitarian impulses embedded in American society." Southern paternalism portrayed a white enslaver providing for his white wife and children, as well as the people he enslaved, who were attached to their white master and mistress and committed to working for the family as laborers.[40]

The majority of white American Christians supported slavery, and theologians argued that Africans being brought to the Americas was providential because they were introduced to true religion, which would lead to eternal salvation. A "slave bible" published in 1807 was constructed to help Christian missionaries emphasize slaves' obedience to their masters and removed all Scripture passages about equality under God or liberation. It excluded 90 percent of the Old Testament, such as the Exodus story of God freeing the Israelites from Egyptian bondage, and about half of the New Testament. Christian slavery apologists also preached the myth created by Europeans in the fifteenth century that Africans were the children of Ham who were cursed to live in slavery.[41]

In *White Too Long: The Legacy of White Supremacy in American Christianity*, Robert P. Long argues that white American Christianity didn't just tolerate or support slavery; it was even more deeply involved in the inhumane practice.

> The "garb of Christianity" and the church covered the injustices of slavery in the social realm, and Christian theology gave "religious sanction" to punishment and cruelty in the personal realm. The churches conferred respectability, and even elevated esteem, on white Christian slaveholders; and the theological blessing of slavery paradoxically lobotomized white Christian consciences, severing what natural moral impulses there may have been limiting violence and cruelty.[42]

In contrast, Black Christians were motivated by their faith to seek freedom. The Stono Rebellion in 1739 was such early proof that the enslaved people from the African continent had their own spirituality that propelled them to resist domination, and, in some instances, fight for their liberation. The Spanish colony St. Augustine was established in 1565 in what is now northern Florida, primarily as a military outpost to protect the Spanish holdings from the threat of the English and French. Both free and enslaved people of African descent lived there. Spanish authorities invited the enslaved in the English settlements in the Carolinas and Georgia to escape slavery and find refuge in Florida. The enslaved people were promised they would receive their freedom if they converted to Catholicism. From the end of the seventeenth century to 1763, many people escaped slavery and found a home in a free Black settlement just to the north and east of the town of St. Augustine and its fort, the Castillo de San Marcos.[43]

At the time of the Stono Rebellion, the number of enslaved Africans in South Carolina outnumbered the free population by almost two to one. Many of the newer people enslaved were born in Africa, and of those, almost all were Kongolese and Catholic. A year before, twenty-three people had escaped slavery and found refuge in St. Augustine. On September 9, a group led by a man named Jemmy set their plot to attain freedom in motion. About twenty Africans raided a store near Wallace Creek, a branch of the Stono River. They took guns and weapons and killed two shopkeepers. After they displayed the shopkeepers' heads on pikes, they marched south toward the Spanish settlement. As they marched, the armed group played drums, flew white flags, and chanted, "Liberty!" On the way, they attacked plantations and gathered more followers, but a white militia mobilized and stopped the rebellion. Forty of the Black people were executed. To make an example of them, the white enslavers lined the road with their decapitated heads. Sixty people died during the rebellion, the largest in British North America.[44]

The only successful slave insurrection that resulted in independence for people of African descent was led by Black Catholic Toussaint Louverture in 1791 on the French colony of Saint Domingue—present-day Haiti; it caused ripples of fear among American enslavers and even greater repression for the enslaved people. The British slave trade was abolished in 1807, and the United States ended the international slave trade in 1808; however, domestic slavery was still legal and widely practiced in the United States. And African Americans continued to resist it.

Nat Turner was an enslaved African American whose Christian faith propelled him to lead a revolt against captivity on August 21, 1831. Though the revolt was unsuccessful and Turner and many others were executed, Turner had opportunity to speak in depth prior to his execution about his life, spiritual experiences, and motivation for the revolt in a jailhouse interview given to Thomas Ruffin Gray, later published as *The Confessions of Nat Turner*.

Born on a plantation in Virginia in 1800, Turner possessed spiritual gifts that were recognized early on by his family. When he was only three or four years old, his mother overheard him telling playmates something that had occurred before he was born. His mother believed he would become a prophet because the Lord had shown him something that happened previously. Both his parents told him he "was intended for some great purpose."[45] His deeply spiritual grandmother instructed Turner in the faith, and he was very religious. His parents taught him to read and write, and he spent much time reading the Bible, praying, fasting, and later preaching.[46]

Turner had experiences with the "Spirit" speaking to him, whom he explained was the same "Spirit that spoke to the prophets in former days." He believed God ordained him for a great purpose. When he was twenty-one, he ran away like his father and remained in the woods for thirty days. He had a spiritual vision from God that instructed him to return to the service of his "earthly master," so he returned to the plantation, though the other Black people thought he was foolish for coming back.[47]

Turner continued to have spiritual revelations and mystical experiences that deepened his faith. He described one such experience that occurred on May 12, 1828:

> I heard a loud noise in the heavens, and the Spirit instantly appeared to me and said the Serpent was loosened, and Christ had laid down the yoke he had borne for the sins of men, and that I should take it on and fight against the Serpent, for the time was fast approaching when the first should be last and the last should be first. . . . And on the appearance of the sign (the eclipse of the sun last February), I should arise and prepare myself, and slay my enemies with their own weapons.[48]

On May 20, Turner and other men on the plantation devised a plan of attack that was carried out the following day. First, they murdered their enslaver and his family, including a nine-year-old son and an infant, and then they collected the slaveowner's guns and ammunition before they continued the rebellion. As many as sixty white men, women, and children may have been killed as Turner and the other men swept through the countryside. Close to seventy-five other Black people joined the uprising, which lasted two days, before hundreds of federal troops and thousands of militiamen caught those who had rebelled, with the exception of Turner, who hid in the woods for two months. Fifty of the Black men who took part in the revolt were convicted and executed, and white mobs lynched additional enslaved people who took no part in the uprising. Some historians have estimated that the white mobs killed between forty and two hundred enslaved people out of retaliation.

After his capture and arrest, Turner stood trial and was convicted in the small town of Jerusalem, Virginia. He was hanged from a tree on November 11, 1831.[49] After both the Stono Rebellion and Nat Turner's revolt, even harsher laws were enacted to restrict the lives of the enslaved in order to prevent further insurrections from occurring.

Eight years after Nat Turner's execution in 1839, and after centuries of the Catholic Church blessing and participating in the slave trade, Pope Gregory XVI condemned the slave trade in the apostolic letter *In Supremo Apostolatus Fastigio* stating:

> [We] do . . . admonish and adjure in the Lord all believers in Christ, of whatsoever condition, that no one hereafter may dare unjustly to molest Indians, Negroes, or other men of this sort; or to spoil them of their goods; or to reduce them to slavery; or to extend help or favour to others who perpetrate such things against them; or to exercise that inhuman trade by which Negroes, as if they were not men, but mere animals, however reduced into slavery, are, without any distinction, contrary to the laws of justice and humanity, bought, sold, and doomed sometimes to the most severe and exhausting labours.[50]

Nonetheless, many Catholic organizations, clergy, and families were slaveholders, and most white Catholics were apologists for slavery. In spite of Gregory's condemnation of the slave trade, American enslavers and the religious hierarchy argued that his position did not apply to domestic slavery in the United States and continued the practice unabated.[51]

As a result of the boom in the cotton industry, there was a mass transfer of the population of enslaved people from the Upper South (Arkansas, North Carolina, Tennessee, and Virginia) to the Lower South (Alabama, Florida, Georgia, Louisiana, Mississippi, South Carolina, and Texas).[52] According to the Equal Justice Initiative's (EJI) "Slavery in America" report, an "estimated one million enslaved people were forcibly transferred from the Upper South to the Lower South between 1810 and 1860."[53]

There were four million African Americans in the South counted in the 1860 census. Out of this number, 250,000 were free Black people living in the slave states. There were a small number of free Black people who were also slavers. But millions of people who were enslaved lived under the control of a minority of white slavers in the area known as the Black Belt, which stretched from South Carolina through Georgia and Alabama, then across to Mississippi and Louisiana.[54]

Douglas A. Blackmon states, "The South's highly evolved system of seizing, breeding, wholesaling, and retailing slaves was invaluable in the final years before the Civil War, as slavery proved in industrial settings to be more flexible and dynamic than even most slave owners could have otherwise believed."[55] In the early 1860s, industrial slavery became commonplace in the most intensive commercial farming in Mississippi and parts of Alabama. It was different and more brutal than plantation work, consisting of mainly young, strong Black men driven mercilessly by overseers. Under this form of slavery, Black mortality was high, and Blackmon quotes a white planter named James H. Ruffin who observed, "The Negroes die off every few years, though it is said that in time each hand also makes enough to buy two more in his place."[56]

Antebellum abolitionists took aim at the domestic slave trade and "slave breeding," which Smithers states they defined as "the coercive reproduction of new generations of slave laborers for sales and resale . . . that highlighted the immoral commodification of reproductive sexuality in Caribbean and North American plantation societies."[57] Smithers explains that prominent Black female abolitionists such as Sojourner Truth, Margaretta Forten, Susan Paul, and Sarah and Grace Douglass were motivated by their faith in God to call out slavery's "licentious excesses."

> Scores of formerly enslaved women provided firsthand testimonies of slave owners interfering in the sexual, reproductive, and "married" lives of slaves. Nancy Howard, an escaped Maryland slave, remembered calling on God's help to see her through enslavement. She described her life in slavery as "one of the blackest, the wickedest things that ever were in the world."[58]

The EJI report estimates that "more than half of all enslaved people held in the Upper South were separated from a parent or child through sale, and a third of all slave marriages were destroyed by forced migration."[59]

The reverse migration of an enslaved Black man named Dred Scott from a slave state to a free state and free territory then back to a slave state resulted in one of the most notorious Supreme Court decisions in United States history. Scott was born into slavery around the turn of the nineteenth century. In 1834, Scott was enslaved by Dr. John Emerson, a surgeon in the United States Army who traveled to work at different military posts. Scott traveled with Emerson to the state of Illinois, where they were stationed for nearly three years. Illinois was governed by the Northwest Ordinance of 1787, which prohibited slavery in regions between the Mississippi and Ohio Rivers and the Great Lakes, except as punishment for crimes. The state constitution had also prohibited slavery since 1818.[60]

In May 1836, Emerson was transferred to Fort Snelling, which was located in the newly created Wisconsin Territory on the west bank of the Mississippi River. The territory was under the conditions of the 1820 Missouri Compromise, which "prohibited slavery north of 36° 30' except within the boundaries of the state of Missouri." Emerson and Scott stayed there until 1838, and during that time, Scott met and married Harriet Robinson, who was also enslaved and subsequently sold to Emerson as well. The Scotts would have two daughters.[61]

The Scotts traveled with Emerson to St. Louis and Louisiana before being moved to Missouri, where Emerson died in 1843. On April 6, 1846, the Scotts petitioned for their freedom in court, stating they were entitled to their freedom based on their history of residing in the free state of Illinois and the free Wisconsin Territory. Missouri had a statute that allowed anyone held wrongfully in slavery to sue for their freedom. An 1824 Missouri Supreme Court decision, *Winny v. Whitesides*, had a mandate of "once free, always free," which became standard judicial practice.[62]

The Scotts case went all the way to the U.S. Supreme Court, and Chief Justice Roger Taney issued a stunning blow not only to the Scotts but to all African Americans in the United States. The first question Taney addressed was:

Can a negro, whose ancestors were imported into this country, and sold as slaves, become a member of the political community formed and brought into existence by the Constitution of the United States, and as such become entitled to all the rights, and privileges, and immunities, guaranteed by that instrument to the citizen? One of which rights is the privilege of suing in a court of the United States in the cases specified in the Constitution.

Taney answered by stating,

> We think they are not, and that they are not included, and were
> not intended to be included, under the word "citizens" in the
> Constitution, and can therefore claim none of the rights and
> privileges which that instrument provides for and secures to
> citizens of the United States. On the contrary, they were at that
> time considered as a subordinate and inferior class of beings, who
> had been subjugated by the dominant race, and, whether emanci-
> pated or not, yet remained subject to their authority, and had no
> rights or privileges but such as those who held the power and the
> Government might choose to grant them.

The opinion further declared that the unalienable rights in the Declaration of Independence did not intend to include the "enslaved African
race" nor did the founders believe Americans were to "embrace the negro
race, which, by common consent, had been excluded from civilized Governments and the family of nations, and doomed to slavery."[63]

Nikole Hannah-Jones describes how this notion of Black inferiority
informed Abraham Lincoln during his presidency, when the country was
at war with itself. "Like many white Americans, he opposed slavery as a
cruel system at odds with American ideals, but he also opposed Black
equality." Lincoln believed that free Black people were "incompatible
with a democracy intended only for white people." So, he decided in 1862
that at the same time he would emancipate the enslaved African American population in the Confederate states, he would also call for them to
voluntarily leave the United States and resettle in another country.[64]

> This idea, known as "colonization," had been circulating since
> the 1790s, and counted among its proponents presidents such as
> Jefferson and James Monroe. In 1816, a group of white enslavers
> and politicians in Washington, D.C., created the American Col-
> onization Society (ACS) to promote the removal of free Black
> people, who would be encouraged to leave the United States and
> resettle in West Africa. The ACS soon had chapters in much of
> the country, alongside other local organizations. It drew many

adherents who were fearful of the growing population of free Black people following the American Revolution. They believed colonization could rid the nation of free Black people while protecting the institution of slavery. But some who opposed slavery embraced colonization, too. Many white Americans across the political spectrum believed Black people held no place in American society as free citizens, and some abolitionists—Black and white—did not think free Black people would ever know real freedom here.[65]

On August 14, 1862, Lincoln brought five highly esteemed free Black men to the White House to sell the idea of colonization. He informed the men that Congress had appropriated $600,000 to ship the Black people he would free to another country. In his address, he explained his justification for the resettlement:

Why should they leave this country? This is, perhaps, the first question for proper consideration. You and we are different races. We have between us a broader difference than exists between almost any other two races. Whether it is right or wrong I need not discuss, but this physical difference is a great disadvantage to us both, as I think your race suffer very greatly, many of them by living among us, while ours suffer from your presence. In a word we suffer on each side. If this is admitted, it affords a reason at least why we should be separated. . . . Your race are suffering, in my judgment, the greatest wrong inflicted on any people. But even when you cease to be slaves, you are yet far removed from being placed on an equality with the white race. You are cut off from many of the advantages which the other race enjoy. The aspiration of men is to enjoy equality with the best when free, but on this broad continent, not a single man of your race is made the equal of a single man of ours. Go where you are treated the best, and the ban is still upon you.[66]

The month after the meeting, Lincoln issued a "preliminary Emancipation Proclamation that advocated colonization."[67]

That same month, in September 1962, Frederick Douglass, who was not invited to the White House meeting, published in *Douglass' Monthly* a scathing rebuke of Lincoln's colonization plan.

> In this address Mr. Lincoln assumes the language and arguments of an itinerant Colonization lecturer, showing all his inconsistencies, his pride of race and blood, his contempt for Negroes and his canting hypocrisy. How an honest man could creep into such a character as that implied by this address we are not required to show. The argument of Mr. Lincoln is that the difference between the white and black races renders it impossible for them to live together in the same country without detriment to both. Colonization, therefore, he holds to be the duty and the interest of the colored people. Mr. Lincoln takes care in urging his colonization scheme to furnish a weapon to all the ignorant and base, who need only the countenance of men in authority to commit all kinds of violence and outrage upon the colored people of the country. Taking advantage of his position and of the prevailing prejudice against them he affirms that their presence in the country is the real first cause of the war, and logically enough, if the premises were sound, assumes the necessity of their removal.[68]

Douglass rebukes Lincoln's assertion that the presence of Black people caused the war, stating, "Mr. Lincoln knows that in Mexico, Central America and South America, many distinct races live peaceably together in the enjoyment of equal rights, and that the civil wars which occasionally disturb the peace of those regions never originated in the difference of the races inhabiting them." Instead, Douglass blames the evils of the institution of slavery for causing white hatred of Black people.

Douglass further excoriates Lincoln's duplicity.

> Illogical and unfair as Mr. Lincoln's statements are, they are nevertheless quite in keeping with his whole course from the beginning of his administration up to this day, and confirm the painful conviction that though elected as an anti-slavery man by Republican and Abolition voters, Mr. Lincoln is quite a genuine

representative of American prejudice and Negro hatred and far more concerned for the preservation of slavery, and the favor of the Border Slave States, than for any sentiment of magnanimity or principle of justice and humanity.[69]

The final version of the Emancipation Proclamation, issued on January 1, 1863, did not include the mention of colonization, and it allowed Black men to enlist in the Union Army, which contributed to the Union's success.[70] British historian Sebastian R. Page claims Black colonization "was almost doomed" from the start. It lacked backing from legislators, who would have to fund the plan, support from host states that would accept Black American emigres, and African Americans who rejected the idea and often had deeper familial roots in the United States than white people who had immigrated more recently from Europe. A botched colonization experiment that sent 450 African Americans to Île-à-Vache, "a small island of about twenty square miles off the southwestern coast of Haiti," in April 1863, just months after the Emancipation Proclamation was issued, failed miserably and resulted in the U.S. government providing resettlement back to America for those who survived, in March 1864.[71]

The Civil War would be fought beginning in 1861 until the Union claimed victory in 1865 before all African Americans were granted freedom. The Emancipation Proclamation, signed by President Abraham Lincoln on January 1, 1863, granted freedom only to enslaved Black people in Confederate states outside Union control and did not immediately abolish slavery. But it made emancipation an irrevocable war aim and changed the course of the war by authorizing the enlistment of African Americans in the Union armed forces. Some two hundred thousand African Americans would fight for the Union Army, with forty thousand losing their lives. "By fighting and dying for the Union, black soldiers staked a claim to citizenship in the reconstructed nation that would emerge from the Civil War."[72]

In 1866, the Fourteenth Amendment to the U.S. Constitution was ratified by the requisite twenty-eight states, though three of the four slaveholding border states—Delaware, Maryland, and Kentucky—did not ratify the amendment until 1901, 1959, and 1976, respectively. The Fourteenth Amendment superseded the Dred Scott decision, and it added birthright citizenship to "all persons born or naturalized in the United States," including African Americans.[73]

The Thirteenth Amendment, passed by Congress on January 31, 1865, and ratified on December 6, 1865, abolished slavery with a caveat having repercussions felt to this day: "Neither slavery nor involuntary servitude, *except as a punishment for crime whereof the party shall have been duly convicted,* shall exist within the United States, or any place subject to their jurisdiction."[74]

As Blackmon states, "The Civil War settled definitively the question of the South's continued existence as a part of the United States, but in 1865 there was no strategy for cleansing the economic and intellectual addiction to slavery." White southerners could not accept the free African Americans as fully human and equal because it challenged "the legitimacy of their definition of what it was to be white."[75]

So, beginning in the late 1860s, *neoslavery* emerged in the South to re-enslave African Americans in order both to reinforce Black subordination to whites and to continue to exploit Black labor for enormous profits. Convict leasing began in 1866 in states such as Texas, Mississippi, and Georgia before spreading throughout all the southern states. It was the system of "selling the labor of state and local prisoners to private interests for state profit" that "utilized the criminal justice system for the exploitation and political disempowerment of black people."[76]

Every southern state enacted an array of "Black codes" intended to criminalize Black life. While conducting research, Blackmon uncovered thousands of arrests of Black people for inconsequential charges or for violations of laws such as "changing employers without permission, vagrancy, riding freight cars without a ticket, engaging in sexual activity—or loud talk—with white women."[77] The Black codes hampered newly freed Black people's ability to assert independence, freely work, and earn a living by making it illegal to be hired without their current employer's approval. "Vagrancy" was so vaguely defined that almost any Black person not working for a white man could be arrested for it. Though it wasn't explicitly stated in the laws, it was widely understood that these laws applied only to Black people and would rarely, if ever, be enforced on unemployed or employed white southerners.[78] After the collapse of Reconstruction (detailed in the following chapter), southern governments slashed an array of public service benefits in order to prevent African Americans from benefitting from them.[79] In addition to being arrested for petty infractions, African American men were also routinely rounded up for no reason at all, taken into custody, and sold as convict laborers.

After arrest and conviction, Black people, and a small minority of white people, were trapped into the convict leasing system. Blackmon estimates that the total number of African Americans caught in this new form of bondage totaled more than one hundred thousand, and possibly twice that figure.

It was a form of bondage distinctly different from that of the antebellum South in that for most men, and the relatively few women drawn in, this slavery did not last a lifetime and did not automatically extend from one generation to the next. But it was nonetheless slavery—a system in which armies of free men, guilty of no crimes and entitled by law to freedom, were compelled to labor without compensation, were repeatedly bought and sold, and were forced to do the bidding of white masters through the regular application of extraordinary physical coercion.[80]

According to Ellen Terrell's blogpost on the Library of Congress website, "The Convict Leasing System: Slavery in Its Worst Aspects," much of the United States' infrastructure, "encompassing roads, railroads, buildings, and levees," was built with the use of the exploitive and abusive convict leasing system. "Torture and beatings were common, and countless individuals perished from abuse; poor and dangerous working conditions; communicable diseases, such as tuberculosis, malaria, and pneumonia; and from environmental conditions like contaminated water." Not only were the people forced to labor affected, but all laborers seeking to make a living in the South felt the impact since convict leasing undermined competition in the labor markets and decreased the standard of living by a reduction in wages and employment rates. The majority of "free" African Americans in the South were subject to sharecropping, debtor's servitude, and peonage.[81]

In the pamphlet *The Crime of Crimes; or, The Convict Leasing System Unmasked*, published in 1907, Clarissa Olds Keeler worked to expose the horrors of the convict leasing system. She described life for people forced to labor as "convicts" in Tennessee, Alabama, Georgia, Mississippi, Florida, Virginia, the District of Columbia, Kentucky, Louisiana, and Arkansas. The Tennessee Coal, Iron and Railroad Company (TCI) was "one of the original 12 companies listed in the Dow Jones Industrial Index" and "one of the largest users of prison laborers, mostly comprised of African Americans convicted of petty crimes." After United States Steel, which was the largest corporation in the world at that time, acquired TCI in 1907, even more people were entrapped into the convict lease system and forced to work for the company, enriching it and its owners.[82] According to Olds Keeler:

> The life of a Tennessee convict whether he is worked in a coal mine, or on railroad construction, as the Tenn. Coal, Iron and Railroad Company worked some of them, has been short and terrible. A writer in the *New York Sun* of Sept. 11, 1891, in giving a description of some of the convicts said in part: "They are herded about from place to place like wild animals. No life could be more horrible. The company counts upon the guards to get a certain amount of work out of each convict. As the guards are from the lowest sort of white men in the State, the treatment of the wretches can easily be imagined. . . . The guard curses, kicks, clubs or kills at pleasure. The company asks no questions; the State has meagre chance of finding the truth and would be slow to act unless public indignation should be aroused. To make a dash for liberty is simply a way of committing suicide; convicts frequently court death by making this bold dash. The rifle rings out its challenge. The convict runs on a bit, then his striped and ragged legs begin to totter, and then he sinks down. A hole is dug and the dead zebra is put out of sight speedily. Any guard can tell you many a tale and the chances are he will boast and laugh a good deal.[83]

Olds Keeler also quoted Mr. Carmichael, the president of the Convict Board, who lamented the injustice of people not even convicted of serious offenses or any offense at all, being reduced to the status of "beasts" to profit the wealthy white men, companies, and government coffers. Carmichael declared:

> The operation of the fee system is a blot upon civilization. The poor and unfortunate are often made to suffer for the greed of the official; men and women too, white as well as black are caught in the meshes of the drag net and imprisoned on the most frivolous charges. Men, women and little children give up their lives seemingly to increase the fees of some official. The county convicts have no safeguard thrown around them; they are leased and delivered per capita to the highest bidder, regardless of the work they are able to perform. These unfortunates are now no more than the beasts of the field.[84]

Particularly distressed by the treatment of girls and women forced into the convict leasing system, Olds Keeler decried that females often lived in unsanitary and inhumane camps with males and as a result would become impregnated against their will by other convicts or guards. Those who were not raped and impregnated also faced inhumane treatment like beatings and murder. Olds Keeler described the fate of a young Black girl named Sarah Nealy in Alabama in 1903.

> It seems she had been convicted on some trumped up charge by some "crime hunter" and put in confinement with a gang of men held in involuntary servitude by a wealthy planter. The next day after her arrival at the camp she was stretched across a log, her clothing drawn up and while her hands and feet were held by negroes, the white guard who was the son of the planter, gave her one hundred lashes with a buggy trace. She was then handcuffed, her feet tied together, a rope put around her neck when she was drawn up until her toes barely touched the ground. In this condition she was kept from 10 a.m. until 12 o'clock, when she was released and she crawled away. She was afterward ordered to go to work but being unable the guard beat her on the head and jumped upon her stomach. Before three o'clock she was dead.[85]

Unlike for the duration of slavery when enslaved people were the valuable "property" of enslavers, imprisoned Black people faced extremely dire outcomes. In Alabama, for example, nearly 20 percent of prisoners died in the first two years, 35 percent in the third year, and nearly 45 percent were killed by the fourth year of prison labor.[86] In addition to the wealth created for the white men using forced Black labor, Blackmon states, "revenues from the neo-slavery poured the equivalent of tens of millions of dollars into the treasuries of Alabama, Mississippi, Louisiana, Georgia, Florida, Texas, North Carolina, and South Carolina—where more than 75 percent of the black population in the United States then lived." Most "ominous" to Blackmon was his realization that white Americans postbellum, in spite of the protestations of Black leaders and Black southerners, came to believe that African Americans in the South would have to "accept the end of their freedom."[87]

In 1903, President Theodore Roosevelt directed Secret Service agents and later the Department of Justice to investigate, and subsequently indict and charge, white landowners for holding Black Americans against their will, forcing them to work, and treating them inhumanely and at times sadistically. The federal investigations found tens of thousands of such cases throughout the South. The overwhelming majority of white men indicted for crimes against Black workers, however, were given symbolic monetary fines, and after the criminal cases had concluded, they continued the practice of holding Black people in slavery-like conditions. In 1905, the U.S. Supreme Court overturned a Georgia court's order against the convict leasing system and found that the federal courts "had no jurisdiction to dismantle the system of obtaining and selling prisoners." As a result, the arrest and sale of Black men continued to grow. In 1927, 37,701 men were arrested on misdemeanor charges, which amounted to one out of every nineteen Black men over the age of twelve forced into neoslavery, just in Alabama alone. In 1930, 4.8 million African Americans, which was roughly half of the Black population in the United States, lived in the Black Belt region of the South and were almost certainly "trapped in some form of coerced labor." As Blackmon concluded, "Certainly, the great record of forced labor across the South demands that any consideration of the progress of civil rights remedy in the United States must acknowledge that slavery, real slavery, didn't end until 1945. . . ."[88]

Generations of "free" Black people suffered under conditions that were in some ways arguably worse than endured during slavery. Bryan Stevenson argues that even more enduring from this period was the mythology of Black criminality, which persists to this day. "The presumptive identity of black men as 'slaves' evolved into the presumptive identity of 'criminal,' and we have yet to fully recover from this historical frame."[89]

History that is forgotten is ripe to be repeated. When we shed light on the neglected and often forgotten history of slavery and the racist and exploitative penal system that emerged after emancipation, we see how the foundation was laid to understand how new forms of racial exclusion and punishment were recreated and inflicted on generations of African Americans since 1619, and, as we'll see, they continue to the present.

Chapter 2

The Evolution from Lynching to the Death Penalty

The slave went free; stood a brief moment in the sun; then moved back again toward slavery.

—W. E. B. Du Bois,
Black Reconstruction in America

On May 16, 1918, in South Georgia, a Black man named Sidney Johnson shot and killed his white employer, Hampton Smith, known for beating and cheating his employees. After Johnson refused to work one day, Smith whipped Johnson, who then retaliated by shooting Smith dead, then shooting and injuring Smith's pregnant wife. Though multiple sources later confirmed that Johnson had worked alone, Mrs. Smith identified Sidney Johnson and another Black man as the attackers who were on the run. The local papers placed three men at the scene and claimed the men had also raped the pregnant Mrs. Smith and ransacked the house.

A white mob gathered, intent on hunting the killers and any other Black people they considered complicit. Hayes Turner, a Black man, was arrested and charged with conspiracy to kill Hampton Smith. When a county superintendent led Turner to a car leaving the jail, a mob of forty to fifty armed and masked white men surrounded the car and demanded Turner be handed over to them. The men hanged Turner from a tree with his hands cuffed behind his body.

The mob next turned on Hayes Turner's pregnant wife, Mary Turner, who was accused of "talking back" and threatening to press charges against the men who had lynched her husband. Walter White, investigating what were called the Brooks-Lowndes lynchings for the NAACP in June 1918, described Mary Turner's fate:

> At the time she was lynched, Mary Turner was in her eighth month of pregnancy. Her ankles were tied together and she was hung to the tree head down. Gasoline was taken from the cars and poured on her clothing which was then fired. When her clothes had burned off, a sharp instrument was taken and she was cut open in the middle, her stomach being entirely opened. Her unborn child fell from her womb, gave two cries, and was then crushed by the heel of a member of the mob. Her body was then riddled with bullets from high-powered rifles until it was no longer possible to recognize it as the body of a human being.

The recorded count of family and friends of Sidney Johnson murdered by white mobs was eleven, though rumors placed it at eighteen.[1]

Walter White, in his first year with the NAACP, was extremely effective in his role as an investigator. With his fair skin and straight hair, he could "pass" for white and gain access to white spaces in order to gather otherwise inaccessible information about lynchings and race riots. From 1918 to 1927, White investigated forty-one lynchings.[2]

Though the brutal lynching and murder of Mary Turner and her baby is an extreme account, racialized terrorism inflicted by white people on Black communities after slavery ended was not uncommon. Since 1989, when the Equal Justice Initiative was founded, led by its executive director, Bryan Stevenson, years and thousands of hours have been spent researching documented lynchings in the United States. The initiative found almost 6,500 racial terror lynchings documented between the end of the Civil War and 1950.[3]

The Reconstruction era that followed the Civil War lasted from 1865 to 1877 and was led by the government and intended to enforce and exercise the new rights granted to African Americans in the United States. The federal government sent troops to southern states to maintain a military presence, as millions of freedmen attempted to claim their rights. General William T. Sherman's Special Field Order No. 15, issued on January 16, 1865, ordered the redistribution of four hundred thousand acres of land to the newly freed Black population.[4] Black men were elected to local and state office, including the Senate, opening a path to political power. Congress established the Freedmen's Bureau, which "provided food, housing, legal assistance, and medical aid to newly anticipated citizens," and founded the "building of thousands of schools for Black children and young people." During this time, a number of historically Black colleges and universities (HBCU) were founded, including Morehouse College, Fisk University, and Howard University. A savings bank was also founded with the goal of helping four million Black people who had been enslaved gain financial freedom.[5]

General Sherman's order, however, was overturned in the fall of 1865 when Andrew Johnson became president after Lincoln's assassination. Johnson returned the confiscated lands to the white planters who originally owned them.[6]

By January 1867, all the Black Union troops were removed from the South, and in their absence, white people terrorized the Black population in the southern states in what historian Annette Gordon-Reed called "a slow motion genocide." In one area of Texas, more than one thousand Black people were murdered by whites between 1865 and 1868. More African Americans were massacred in Memphis; New Orleans; Hamburg, South Carolina; and Colfax, Louisiana. Any time Black people tried to assert their autonomy, either by leaving an employer, demanding payment for their labor, or even traveling to visit family, they were at risk of being killed, imprisoned, or violently attacked.[7]

Though more than sixty thousand African Americans had deposited over $3 million into the savings bank created by the Freedman's Bureau, in 1874 the bank failed and depositors lost a majority of their savings.

After the disputed presidential election of 1876, the Compromise of 1877 led to the installation of Rutherford B. Hayes as president and the federal withdrawal of Union troops from the South, ending the short-lived Reconstruction era. In 1883, the U.S. Supreme Court "ruled that the Civil Rights Act of 1875, the one federal law forcing whites to comply with the provisions of the Fourteenth and Fifteenth amendments— awarding voting and legal rights to blacks—could be enforced only under the most rare circumstances. Civil rights was a local, not federal issue, the court found." By 1901, nearly every southern state had passed legislation taking away the African American right to vote.[8]

In 2011, theologian and Black liberation theology scholar James H. Cone wrote his seminal work, *The Cross and the Lynching Tree*. He outlined the rise of white mob violence and torture following the end of Reconstruction in 1877. "The black dream of freedom turned into a nightmare 'worse than slavery' initiating what black historian Rayford Logan called the 'nadir' in black history." For the majority of white southerners, allowing Black people to be viewed as equals and granted full citizenship under the law was considered an intolerable affront. Therefore, whites turned to lynchings and other forms of violence to enforce white supremacy and keep African Americans subservient.[9]

> Assured of no federal interference, southern whites were now free to take back the South, to redeem it from what they called "Negro domination," through mob violence—excluding blacks from politics, arresting them for vagrancy, forcing them to work as sharecroppers who never got out of debt and creating a rigid segregated society in which being black was a badge of shame with no meaningful future. A black person could be lynched for any perceived insult to whites.[10]

An infamous opinion by the justices of the U.S. Supreme Court would become the legal basis for the segregation of white and Black people under the Constitution in the case *Homer Adolph Plessy v. John Ferguson*. Homer Plessy was seven-eighths white and only one-eighth Black but considered Black under Louisiana law. In 1892, Plessy was working in accord with the Comité des Citoyens (Committee of Citizens), a group of New Orleans residents who wanted to repeal Louisiana's Separate Car Act, which required separate railway cars for Blacks and whites. Plessy sat in a "whites only" car of a Louisiana train, refused to leave when told to, and was arrested. At trial, Plessy's lawyers argued that the Separate Car Act violated the Thirteenth and Fourteenth Amendments, but the judge ruled in favor of Louisiana and Plessy was convicted. In 1896, the Supreme Court upheld the constitutionality of racial segregation under the "separate but equal" doctrine.[11]

When justifying its opinion that racial segregation did not violate the Fourteenth Amendment, which forbids states "from making or enforcing any law which shall abridge the privileges or immunities of citizens of the United States, or shall deprive any person of life, liberty, or property without due process of law, or deny to any person within their jurisdiction the equal protection of the laws," Justice Henry Billings Brown argued the following:

> The object of the amendment was undoubtedly to enforce the absolute equality of the two races before the law, but, in the nature of things, it could not have been intended to abolish distinctions based upon color, or to enforce social, as distinguished from political, equality, or a commingling of the two races upon terms unsatisfactory to either. Laws permitting, and even requiring, their separation in places where they are liable to be brought into contact do not necessarily imply the inferiority of either race to the other, and have been generally, if not universally, recognized as within the competency of the state legislatures in the exercise of their police power. The most common instance of this is connected with the establishment of separate schools for white and colored children, which has been held to be a valid exercise of the legislative power even by courts of States where the political rights of the colored race have been longest and most earnestly enforced.[12]

Billings Brown further opined that segregation does not create Black inferiority, and if Blacks are considered inferior to whites socially, there is no legal remedy for that.

> We consider the underlying fallacy of the plaintiff's argument to consist in the assumption that the enforced separation of the two races stamps the colored race with a badge of inferiority. If this be so, it is not by reason of anything found in the act, but solely because the colored race chooses to put that construction upon it. The argument necessarily assumes that if, as has been more than once the case and is not unlikely to be so again, the colored race

should become the dominant power in the state legislature, and should enact a law in precisely similar terms, it would thereby relegate the white race to an inferior position. We imagine that the white race, at least, would not acquiesce in this assumption. The argument also assumes that social prejudices may be overcome by legislation, and that equal rights cannot be secured to the negro except by an enforced commingling of the two races. We cannot accept this proposition. If the two races are to meet upon terms of social equality, it must be the result of natural affinities, a mutual appreciation of each other's merits, and a voluntary consent of individuals. . . . Legislation is powerless to eradicate racial instincts or to abolish distinctions based upon physical differences, and the attempt to do so can only result in accentuating the difficulties of the present situation. If the civil and political rights of both races be equal, one cannot be inferior to the other civilly or politically. If one race be inferior to the other socially, the Constitution of the United States cannot put them upon the same plane.[13]

The decision upheld and strengthened segregation throughout the country and Jim Crow laws across the South. As a result, African Americans were relegated to second-class citizenship, denied equal access to the fruits of American society, and were physically punished for crossing the color line.

African Americans, however, organized and tried to resist the violence inflicted upon them. Among them was Ida B. Wells-Barnett, a trailblazing Black journalist, civil rights advocate, wife, mother of four, and suffragist, who became an international spokesperson against lynching. Born into slavery in Holly Springs, Mississippi, on July 16, 1862, Wells assumed care of her five siblings at the age of sixteen after her parents died from yellow fever. Later, Wells moved to Memphis, Tennessee, and began writing for Black newspapers and periodicals concerning issues of race and politics. She went on to become the first Black woman to co-own a newspaper, *The Free Speech and Headlight*, in a major city. For Wells, a turning point occurred in 1892 when a close friend of hers and two other Black men were lynched in Memphis.[14]

At the time, whites held a widespread belief that lynching was a just response of white men getting retribution after Black men raped white women. Yet as Wells examined the reality of lynching, she discovered it was a form of racial violence used against Black men in cases of consensual relationships with white women, failure to pay debts, or challenges to white economic dominance. Three friends of Wells, Thomas Moss, Calvin McDowell, and Henry Stewart, owned and operated a successful grocery store that rivaled the store of a local white grocer. Their success gained the man's ire, eventually resulting in their arrest and murder.[15]

Wells also uncovered how Black women were targets of lynching as well. In several editorials, Wells forcefully spoke out against lynching and urged Black residents to leave Memphis, where so many lynchings had taken place. As a result of her activism, Wells's newspaper office was burned and threats against her life were made, leading to her permanent exile from the state. Even so, her voice carried strength and had an effect, as close to 20 percent of the Black population of Memphis left the city, causing an economic impact on white business owners and residents.

Wells relocated to Chicago, where she continued writing for different newspapers and publishing anti-lynching pamphlets. She also toured the northern states, the United Kingdom, and Scotland to raise awareness about, and speaking against, lynching.

Wells was also one of the sixty founders of the National Association for the Advancement of Colored People (NAACP), which emerged in 1909 as a civil rights organization with the aim, among other things, of fighting against racial violence and specifically lynching, which disproportionately targeted Black people. A lynching, according to the NAACP, is a public killing of an individual who was not given any due process. Though the term "lynching" evokes images of a Black person hanging from a tree, Black people were lynched in other brutal ways, involving torture, mutilation, burning, decapitation, castration, drowning, and desecration.[16]

W. E. B. Du Bois, known as one of the foremost Black intellectuals of his era, became the NAACP's director of publicity and research and launched the organization's official journal, *The Crisis*, in 1910. Du Bois, the first Black American to earn a PhD from Harvard University, published widely and wrote his seminal work on the plight of African Americans, *The Souls of Black Folk,* in 1903. He used *The Crisis* to draw attention to the widespread practice of lynching and pushed for nation-wide legislation to end it. One article he wrote in 1915 documented over twenty-seven hundred lynchings within three prior decades. By 1920, the journal reached one hundred thousand subscribers, helping attract supporters to the NAACP and earning the organization the reputation for being the leading protest organization for African Americans.[17] In a December 1916 issue, Du Bois published a painting titled *Christmas in Georgia*, which Cone later described as depicting "a black man, held up with the silhouette image of Christ, while an angry mob of white men hoist the victim with a rope. On the tree on which the black man hangs there is a sign that reads, 'Inasmuch as ye did it unto the least of these, My brethren, ye did it unto Me.'"[18]

On July 28, 1917, between eight thousand and ten thousand African Americans came to New York to protest lynchings in what was called a Silent Protest Parade. Black Boy Scouts handed out to passersby leaflets titled "Why Do We March" and listed the civil rights violations: "Segregation, Discrimination, Disenfranchisement, LYNCHINGS." The leaflet explained:

> We march because we want to make impossible a repetition of Waco, Memphis, and East St. Louis by arousing the conscience of the country, and to bring the murderers of our brothers, sisters, and innocent children to justice. We march because we deem it a crime to be silent in the face of barbaric acts.

The leaflet referenced two mob lynchings that had occurred in Waco and Memphis and the race riot in East St. Louis that had killed nearly forty Black people and displaced thousands more. Three hundred Black children led the march down Fifth Avenue, followed by nearly five thousand women, then men, some of whom wore military uniforms. The march underscored the hypocrisy of Black men risking their lives to fight in World War I to promote democracy abroad even as they were being treated as second-class citizens and unprotected from white mob violence at home.[19]

Another method of protesting the racial violence in the South was relocation. What has been termed "The Great Migration" was the exodus of approximately six million Black people from the South to northern, midwestern, and western states starting roughly in the 1910s and continuing through the 1970s. It happened in two waves and together forms one of the largest migration movements of people in U.S. history as Black Americans fled racial violence to pursue better economic and educational opportunities, and freedom from the oppression of Jim Crow.[20]

In contrasting African American resistance to racial violence and white toleration of lynchings, James Cone describes how lynchings were a source of spectacle and entertainment.

> Lynching became a white spectacle, in which prominent newspapers, like the *Atlanta Constitution*, announced to the public the place, date, and time of the expected hanging and burning of black victims. Often as many as ten to twenty thousand men, women, and children attended the event. It was a family affair, a ritual celebration of white supremacy, where women and children were often given the first opportunity to torture black victims—burning black flesh and cutting off genitals, fingers, toes, and ears as souvenirs. Postcards were made from the photographs taken of black victims with white lynchers and onlookers smiling as they struck a pose for the camera. They were sold for ten to twenty-five cents to members of the crowd, who then mailed them to relatives and friends, often with a note saying something like this: "This is the barbeque we had last night."[21]

Cole Blease, who served as the governor of South Carolina from 1911 to 1915, and as a senator from 1925 to 1931, proclaimed that lynching was a "divine right of the Caucasian race to dispose of the offending blackamoor without the benefit of a jury." The opinion that white southerners were entitled to engage in extrajudicial forms of violence against the Black community, Cone wrote, was "grounded in the religious belief that America is a white nation called by God to bear witness to the superiority of 'white over black.'"[22]

In contrast to Cole Blease, on July 26, 1918, President Woodrow
Wilson issued a proclamation condemning lynching and bolstering the
work of the NAACP and multiple anti-lynching groups.[23] In it Wilson
stated,

> There have been many lynchings, and every one of them has been
> a blow at the heart of ordered law and humane justice. No man
> who loves America, no man who really cares for her fame and
> honor and character, or who is truly loyal to her institutions, can
> justify mob action while the courts of justice are open and the
> governments of the States and the Nation are ready and able to
> do their duty. We are at this very moment fighting lawless pas-
> sion. . . .
>
> We proudly claim to be the champions of democracy. If we
> really are, in deed and in truth, let us see to it that we do not dis-
> credit our own. I say plainly that every American who takes part
> in the action of a mob or gives it any sort of countenance is no
> true son of this great democracy, but its betrayer. . . .
>
> I therefore very earnestly and solemnly beg that the gover-
> nors of all the States, the law officers of every community, and,
> above all, the men and women of every community in the United
> States, all who revere America and wish to keep her name with-
> out stain or reproach, will cooperate—not passively merely, but
> actively and watchfully—to make an end of this disgraceful evil.
> It can not live where the community does not countenance it.[24]

In spite of Wilson's anti-lynching statement, 1919 would become one
of the most violent years on record in the United States because of racial
violence. At least twenty-six cities across the country experienced white
mobs attacking Black people and communities during an outbreak of
racial terror that author James Weldon Johnson labeled "Red Summer"
because of the bloodshed. The causes of the "crime" varied by city, but
what they all had in common was white racial hatred toward Black people, who they believed transgressed the invisible color line. Will Brown
in Omaha was falsely accused of assaulting a white woman while she
walked with her boyfriend. In Longview, Texas, the offense was a Black

man's newspaper story about a Black and white love affair. A Black man in Washington, DC, was accused of taking a white woman's umbrella. In Chicago, a Black teenager was drowned after he floated to the "white side" of a designated swimming area in Lake Michigan. Throughout the country, thousands of Black people were murdered, often being lynched on trees and burned alive. White mobs burned to the ground hundreds of Black-owned businesses and homes, resulting in the loss of millions of dollars of Black generational wealth.[25]

Bryan Stevenson's research revealed the six most common motivations of lynchings between the Reconstruction era and World War II: (1) allegations of interracial sex between a Black male and white female (including consensual sex and rape); (2) casual social transgressions; (3) allegations of serious crime; (4) for purposes of public spectacle; (5) violence intended to intimidate and suppress the entire Black community; and (6) targeting of sharecroppers, ministers, and other community leaders who resisted mistreatment. Whatever the reason, lynching ultimately was used as a means to enforce Jim Crow laws and racial segregation with the purpose of victimizing the entire African American community.[26]

As the title of his work *The Cross and the Lynching Tree* suggests, Cone compared the violence committed against Black Americans to Jesus's crucifixion and death. Calling out the irony of white Christians who did not see the contradiction in their behavior, he argued his case in undeniable terms.

> As Jesus was an innocent victim of mob hysteria and Roman imperial violence, many African Americans were innocent victims of white mobs, thirsting for blood in the name of God and in defense of segregation, white supremacy, and the purity of the Anglo-Saxon race. Both the cross and the lynching tree were symbols of terror, instruments of torture and execution, reserved primarily for slaves, criminals, and insurrectionists—the lowest of the low in society. Both Jesus and blacks were publicly humiliated, subjected to the utmost indignity and cruelty. They were stripped, in order to be deprived of dignity, then paraded, mocked and whipped, pierced, derided and spat upon, tortured

for hours in the presence of jeering crowds for popular entertainment. In both cases, the purpose was to strike terror in the subject community. It was to let people know that the same thing would happen to them if they did not stay in their place.[27]

In the face of racial violence, those African Americans who fought back were met with even greater force, including from white militias and National Guards. Cone describes the helplessness many African Americans felt in the face of lynching and terror.

> Blacks knew that violent self-defense was tantamount to suicide; even affirming blackness in a world defined by white power took great courage. Whites acted in a superior manner for so long that it was difficult for them to even recognize their cultural and spiritual arrogance, blatant as it was to African Americans. Their law was not designed to protect blacks from lynching, especially when blacks acted as if they were socially equal to whites. Should a black in the South lift his hand or raise his voice to reprimand a white person, he would incur the full weights of the law and the mob. Even to look at white people in a manner regarded as disrespectful could get a black lynched. Whites often lynched blacks simply to remind the black community of their powerlessness.[28]

When one African American community resisted lynching, it resulted in the destruction of one of the most prosperous Black communities in the United States, known as Black Wall Street, located in the Greenwood neighborhood of Tulsa, Oklahoma. Between 1910 and 1920, the African American population in Tulsa County had increased from 2,754 to 10,903. People migrated there for the increased employment opportunities. Though segregation restricted African American opportunities, in Greenwood the opportunity for people to put money back into their community created financial autonomy for the Black community. By 1920, the community businesses in Greenwood included restaurants, hotels, movie theaters, billiard halls, and car repair shops. There was also a large professional population, with nineteen Black physicians/surgeons, eight lawyers, six pharmacists, and three dentists. White newspapers often derogatorily referred to the African American district as "Little Africa" or "Niggertown."[29]

On the morning of May 30, 1921, Dick Rowland, a nineteen-year-old Black teenager who worked at a shoeshine stand in front of the Drexel Building in Tulsa, rode the elevator to the third floor with a seventeen-year-old elevator operator named Sarah Page to use the restroom.[30] Different rumors circulated about what occurred on the elevator, and the following day Rowland was arrested and accused of assaulting Page. A white newspaper published sensational claims about the assault on the front page, and a mob of thousands of white people gathered at the courthouse where Rowland was held. Fearing he would be lynched, Black residents also gathered at the courthouse, and a single gunshot was fired. What ensued was one of the bloodiest racial attacks in U.S. history. Tulsa police deputized white men and armed them with guns, multiplying the police force overnight.[31]

In the early morning of June 1, 1921, all hell broke loose as white law enforcement and residents unleashed their fury on the Black Greenwood district.

Biplanes dropped fiery turpentine bombs from the night skies onto their rooftops—the first aerial bombing of an American city in history. A furious mob of thousands of white men then surged over Black homes, killing, destroying, and snatching everything from dining room furniture to piggy banks. Arsonists reportedly waited for white women to fill bags with household loot before setting homes on fire. Tulsa police officers were identified by eyewitnesses as setting fire to Black homes, shooting residents and stealing. Eyewitnesses saw women being chased from their homes naked—some with babies in their arms—as volleys of shots were fired at them. Several Black people were tied to cars and dragged through the streets.

Black residents valiantly fought back but were outmanned and out-armed. The governor declared martial law and called in the National Guard.[32] Though not a single white person was arrested, over six thousand Black residents were detained and held, some for as long as eight days. As a result of the mob violence, thirty-five city blocks of the African American district were burned to the ground, including an estimated 1,256 homes, along with virtually every business and community structure—including churches, schools, businesses, a hospital, and a library. More than eight hundred people were injured, as many as three hundred people died, and thousands remain unaccounted for. The white city officials designated the violence and destruction a "race riot," preventing insurance companies from their requirement of having to pay benefits to the Black people of Greenwood whose homes and businesses were destroyed.[33] Ten thousand residents became homeless.[34]

The grand jury that was formed to investigate the cause of the riot laid blame on Greenwood's Black community, which had acted to protect one of its residents from lynching.

> We find that certain propaganda and more or less agitation had been going on among the colored population for some time. This agitation resulted in the accumulation of firearms among the people and the storage of ammunition, all of which led them as a people to believe in equal rights, social equality and their ability to demand the same.[35]

Walter White from the NAACP came to Tulsa after the massacre to investigate. He perceived that the Black district posed an economic threat to the white residents, concluding that the Black prosperity of Greenwood contributed to the riot, writing, "The fact has caused a bitter resentment on the part of the lower order of whites, who feel these colored men, members of an 'inferior race,' are exceedingly presumptuous in achieving greater economic prosperity than they who are members of a divinely ordered superior race."[36]

In *The Cross and the Lynching Tree*, Cone wrote that the majority of white Christians did not call out the evil of lynchings, but he also pointed out white ministers who did, such as Episcopalian Quincy Ewing, one of the founders of the NAACP; Andrew Sledd, a professor at Emory College; and John E. White, an Atlanta minister.[37] Another person who spoke out against the terror was Katherine Drexel, a white Catholic born into a wealthy and prestigious banking family. She spent much of her fortune evangelizing and supporting the education of Indigenous and Black communities. Among other projects, she founded the Sisters of the Blessed Sacrament for Indians and Colored People and also Xavier University of Louisiana, which still remains the only Catholic HBCU. She and her sister, Louise Drexel Morell, were vocal supporters of the NAACP's anti-lynching campaign.[38]

With public support of lynchings decreasing in the United States, and with the acknowledgment that white mob violence against African Americans was tarnishing the country's reputation abroad, white America had to change. Nonetheless, executions of Black Americans did not end; they became sanctioned by the state. The "decline of lynching in America," Bryan Stevenson explains, "relied heavily on the increased use of capital punishment following court trials and accelerated unreliable legal process in state courts. The death penalty's roots are clearly linked to the legacy of lynching."[39]

By the end of the 1930s, court-ordered executions outpaced lynchings in the former slave states for the first time ever. Two-thirds of those executed that decade were black, and the trend continued: as African Americans fell to just 22 percent of the southern population between 1910 and 1950, they constituted 75 percent of those executed in the South in those years.[40]

Similarly, during the time period 1930 through 1967, 455 men were killed by capital punishment for rape. In all, 405 of the executed were Black men, and almost all of the rape victims were white women.[41] (Only in 1977 did the Supreme Court declare the death penalty for rape unconstitutional.) Following the pattern of the convict lease system replacing slavery in the southern states, the white-controlled legal system of arrest, conviction by all-white juries, and the death penalty took the place of lynchings and white mob violence and disproportionately killed African American men. Though the public lynchings were declining in the 1950s, Cone wrote that "there were many legal lynchings as state and federal governments used the criminal justice system to intimidate, terrorize, and murder blacks."[42]

In 1940, Thurgood Marshall founded the NAACP's Legal Defense Fund (LDF) and served as its first director-counsel. He aggressively worked to challenge *Plessy v. Ferguson* and the legal doctrine of "separate but equal." Marshall successfully argued *Brown v. Board of Education* before the Supreme Court in 1952 and 1953, which led to the groundbreaking verdict against school segregation in 1954.

When Marshall was chosen to serve on the Supreme Court in 1967, he was the first African American to do so. In 1974, Marshall would be one of five justices to strike down the death penalty and halt national executions in the case *Furman v. Georgia*, which was brought by the LDF. The court held that carrying out the death penalty in the three cases brought before the court constituted cruel and unusual punishment under the Eighth and Fourteenth Amendments.[43] In his opinion statement, Justice Marshall wrote:

> In striking down capital punishment, this Court does not malign our system of government. On the contrary, it pays homage to it. Only in a free society could right triumph in difficult times, and could civilization record its magnificent advancement. In recognizing the humanity of our fellow beings, we pay ourselves the highest tribute. We achieve "a major milestone in the long road up from barbarism" and join the approximately 70 other jurisdictions in the world which celebrate their regard for civilization and humanity by shunning capital punishment.[44]

When the Supreme Court reinstated the death penalty four years later in the case *Green v. Georgia*, as Bryan Stevenson notes, the court capitulated "to the claim that legal executions were needed to prevent vigilante mob violence."[45] With executions resumed, so, too, did disproportionate racial violence against African Americans continue. "More than eight in ten American lynchings between 1889 and 1918 occurred in the South, and more than eight in ten of the more than 1,400 legal executions carried out in this country since 1976 have been in the South," Stevenson wrote.

In 1987 the LDF brought another case, *McCleskey v. Kemp*, representing an African American man who had been sentenced to die after killing a white police officer in 1978. The LDF argued that Georgia administered the punishment of death in a racially discriminatory and unconstitutional manner. To prove its argument, the LDF provided empirical evidence and introduced a study by University of Iowa law professor David Baldus, who examined over two thousand Georgia murder cases between 1973 and 1979 that resulted in a sentence of death. The study found that defendants who killed white victims were eleven times more likely to be sentenced to death than when the victim was Black; killers of white victims were sentenced to death at a rate that was 4.3 times higher than a convicted killer of a Black victim; prosecutors sought the death penalty for 70 percent of Black defendants with white victims but only 19 percent of white defendants with Black victims, and "no factor other than race explained these results."[46] The LDF made it undeniably clear that racial bias "permeated the Georgia capital punishment system."[47]

In its opinion, the court acknowledged but ultimately dismissed the Baldus report. "At most, the Baldus study indicates a discrepancy that appears to correlate with race. Apparent disparities in sentencing are an *inevitable part of our criminal justice system*." In order for McCleskey to prove that the Equal Protection Clause had been violated, the Supreme Court held he "must prove that the decisionmakers in his case acted with discriminatory purpose," and he failed to offer evidence specific to his own case that racial consideration played a part in his sentencing.[48] Therefore, in a 5–4 decision, the court ruled against McCleskey and affirmed his death sentence. The racial disparities in Georgia's capital punishment system would stand.[49]

Anthony G. Amsterdam, University Professor Emeritus at New York University, decried the Supreme Court ruling, arguing it harkened back to the Dred Scott decision:

McCleskey is the Dred Scott decision of our time. It is a declaration that African-American life has no value which white men are bound to respect. It is a decision for which our children's children will reproach our generation and abhor the legal legacy we leave them. One inherent evil of the death penalty is that it extends the boundaries of permissible inhumanity so far that every lesser offense against humanity seems inoffensive by comparison, leading us to tolerate them relatively easily. McCleskey extends the boundaries of permissible discrimination and hypocrisy in that same measure. Accept McCleskey, and race discrimination in matters less momentous than life or death can be shrugged off. Accept McCleskey, and any hypocrisy with less than lethal consequences can be viewed as trivial in a legal system where the highest tribunal sits in a building bearing the proud motto "Equal Justice Under Law" on its west facade and ignores it.[50]

Later, Justice Powell admitted to his biographer that if he had the chance, he would change his vote in *McCleskey*. But hindsight could not prevent the calamitous effects of the decision on Black Americans.[51]

After the *McCleskey* decision, single state studies examining racial disparities and the death penalty from Florida, Missouri, Arizona, Ohio, California, North Carolina, Illinois, Maryland, South Carolina, Colorado, and Connecticut all found that defendants convicted of murdering white victims had the greatest chance of being condemned to death. A multistate study in 2004 analyzing data from 1977 through 1999 in thirty-one states found that Black murders of whites received the harshest penalties. In eight states, the ratio of death sentences for those type of murders ranged from 2.9 to 23.2 times higher than death sentences for Black murders of other Blacks.[52]

Unlike South Africa in the case of the Truth and Reconciliation Commission, Germany in the Nuremberg trials after the Holocaust, or the National Unity and Reconciliation Commission after the Rwandan genocide, the United States has not only been unwilling to confront its history of racism, but it continues to perpetuate it. As Stevenson argues, "America has never systemically and publicly addressed the effects of racial violence, the criminalization of African Americans, and the critical role these phenomena have played in shaping the American criminal justice system."

To address and remedy this collective forgetting, the Equal Justice Initiative opened the National Memorial for Peace and Justice in Montgomery, Alabama, on April 26, 2018. Set on a six-acre site, the memorial uses sculpture, art, and design to contextualize racial terror. It is the "nation's first memorial dedicated to the legacy of enslaved Black people,

people terrorized by lynching, African Americans humiliated by racial segregation and Jim Crow, and people of color burdened with contemporary presumptions of guilt and police violence." A memorial square on the site displaying eight hundred six-foot monuments symbolizes the thousands of victims of lynching in the United States.[53]

In the preface to the 2013 edition of Sister Helen Prejean's book *Dead Man Walking*, Archbishop Desmond Tutu stated,

> At the height of apartheid, South Africa had the third highest judicial execution rate in the world, killing 1,109 people on death row between 1980 and 1989. Then a moratorium was declared, and a year after Nelson Mandela became president, in 1995, we abolished the death penalty. . . . People around the world were making the same connections about the death penalty—how racist, unfair, and broken it is—and slowly a new global movement for the abolition of the death penalty began.[54]

Archbishop Tutu commended Sr. Prejean, the leading American activist advocating for ending capital punishment. *Dead Man Walking* was made into a major motion picture in 1995, topped the *New York Times* bestsellers' list for eight months, was translated into ten languages, and sparked an international debate about the death penalty.

Prejean, a white Catholic who was raised in Baton Rouge and joined the Congregation of the Sisters of St. Joseph in the late 1950s, had an awakening to social justice in the 1980s when she moved to the predominantly African American St. Thomas housing development in New Orleans. *Dead Man Walking* was her account of being a spiritual adviser to two men on death row, which led to her advocacy for the abolition of the death penalty. Describing her moral position, Prejean stated:

> Jesus Christ, whose way of life I try to follow, refused to meet hate with hate and violence with violence. I pray for the strength to be like him. I cannot believe in a God who metes out hurt for hurt, pain for pain, torture for torture. Nor do I believe that God invests human representatives with such power to torture and kill. The paths of history are stained with the blood of those

who have fallen victim to "God's Avengers." Kings and Popes and military generals and heads of state have killed, claiming God's authority and God's blessing. I do not believe in such a God.[55]

In *Dead Man Walking*, Prejean documented the vast opposition to her anti-death penalty stance. She also acknowledged the suffering felt by the victims' families, something she originally neglected while counseling the first man she befriended on death row. Now Prejean made sure to always reach out to the families who were impacted by her spiritual advisees' crimes, founding SURVIVE to help families of victims of murder and related crimes, predominantly African American.

Prejean believed the public's fear of the rising crime rate in the 1990s fueled public support for state-sanctioned murder. Support for execution dropped to 43 percent when the public was presented with data that capital punishment did not deter crime and when offered an alternative such as life imprisonment.[56]

Today, the average American has little interaction with the reality of the death penalty and the cruelty inflicted on the people subjected to it. The Death Penalty Information Center (DPIC) estimates that 3 percent of executions that have occurred in the United States were botched, including people "catching fire while being electrocuted, being strangled during hangings (instead of having their necks broken), and being administered the wrong dosages of specific drugs for lethal injections." DPIC lists thirty-nine cases of botched lethal injection cases where the misadministration of the drugs led to the person's execution lasting, in some cases, over two hours.[57]

The medical examination of autopsies of people executed by lethal injection have stirred new debate about exactly how much pain the condemned persons experienced before their deaths. Dr. Joel Zivot, an anesthesiologist at Emory University Hospital in Atlanta, and his colleague, Dr. Mark Edgar, an anatomical pathologist, identified that in more than three-quarters of more than thirty-six autopsy reports, the lungs of the dead men were filled with "a mixture of blood and plasma and other fluids," and "froth and foam in the airways," which indicated they had a severe form of pulmonary edema, indicating high levels of pain before death. National Public Radio (NPR) expanded the doctors' investigation, reviewing more than two hundred autopsies across different states and across the different drug protocols used, with evidence of pulmonary edema in 84 percent of the cases.[58]

In 2018 in Ohio, Magistrate Judge Michael Merz reviewed the arguments brought against a drug known to cause pulmonary edema. He wrote, "All medical witnesses to describe pulmonary edema agreed it was painful, both physically and emotionally, inducing a sense of drowning and the attendant panic and terror, much as would occur with the torture tactic known as waterboarding." He therefore ruled that it constituted "cruel and unusual punishment."[59]

Prejean's next book, published in 2006, *The Death of Innocents: An Eyewitness Account of Wrongful Executions*, recounts her experience with two executed men who she believed were innocent. The DPIC, which was founded in 1990, has documented that 189 people who were executed by capital punishment have been exonerated of all charges related to their conviction since 1973. Out of the 189 exonerations, 103 of the men were Black. Further, the center details the cases of 20 people who were executed who had a high probability of being innocent.[60]

The National Registry of Exonerations, founded in 2012, is a project of the University of California Newkirk Center for Science & Society, the University of Michigan Law School, and Michigan State University College of Law. It has tracked the number of people who have been exonerated from the conviction of a crime they did not commit between largely 1989 and the present, with limited earlier figures. In 2022, it passed the milestone of three thousand exonerations. That means a combined twenty-five thousand years of innocent lives were lost to incarceration due to falsely made convictions.[61]

A 2017 report for the National Registry of Exonerations, "Race and Wrongful Convictions," found that 47 percent of people exonerated as of October 2016 were Black, though African Americans made up only 13 percent of the U.S. population. Black people were seven times more likely to be wrongfully convicted of murder than white people. Of those convicted of murder, African Americans were 50 percent more likely to be innocent than other racial groups. Black people were twelve times more likely to be wrongfully convicted of drug possession than white people, and 3.5 times more likely to be wrongfully convicted of sexual assault than white people. Black people also made up the greatest majority of exonerees of the more than eighteen hundred innocent people who were framed and convicted of crimes in fifteen large-scale police scandals where crimes did not actually occur.[62]

These racial discrepancies may explain what African Americans already know and why only a third (36 percent) of African Americans polled in 2019 supported the death penalty,[63] compared to 60 percent support among all Americans in 2021.[64]

In 2018, Pope Francis revised the *Catechism of the Roman Catholic Church*, a doctrinal manual used for teaching the Catholic faith, a revision that reflected a change in the church's position on the death penalty.

> There is an increasing awareness that the dignity of the person is not lost even after the commission of very serious crimes. In addition, a new understanding has emerged of the significance of penal sanctions imposed by the state. Lastly, more effective systems of detention have been developed, which ensure the due protection of citizens but, at the same time, do not definitively deprive the guilty of the possibility of redemption.
>
> Consequently, the Church teaches, in the light of the Gospel, that the "death penalty is inadmissible because it is an attack on the inviolability and dignity of the person," and she works with determination for its abolition worldwide.[65]

On October 3, 2020, Pope Francis issued *Fratelli Tutti,* an encyclical that went a step further:

> The arguments against the death penalty are numerous and well-known. The Church has rightly called attention to several of these, such as the possibility of judicial error and the use made of such punishment by totalitarian and dictatorial regimes as a means of suppressing political dissidence or persecuting religious and cultural minorities, all victims whom the legislation of those regimes consider "delinquents." All Christians and people of good will are today called to work not only for the abolition of the death penalty, legal or illegal, in all its forms, but also to work

for the improvement of prison conditions out of respect for the human dignity of persons deprived of their freedom. I would link this to life imprisonment. . . . A life sentence is a secret death penalty. Let us keep in mind that, "not even a murderer loses his personal dignity, and God himself pledges to guarantee this."[66]

By the end of 2021, according to Amnesty International, 108 countries had completely abolished the death penalty, more than two-thirds of the world's countries. The United States is one of the 55 countries that still retains the death penalty and is the only country that recorded all eleven executions in the Americas, as the rest of the neighboring countries remained execution-free for the thirteenth consecutive year.[67]

According to Krisanne Vaillancourt Murphy, executive director of Catholic Mobilizing Network, "today, the U.S. death row population is 41 percent Black—almost 30 points higher than the national population."[68] African Americans have endured centuries of violence inflicted upon them, yet the history of lynchings and mob violence and their ties to the death penalty today are seldomly acknowledged or discussed. An institution like the death penalty, which has roots so deeply connected to the horror of racial terror lynchings, cannot be justified and practiced unabated. Instead, a moral revolution must take place whereby American citizens demand their state and federal governments cease the barbaric practice of executions and instead pursue a path of justice, safety, and healing for victims' families and true accountability and reparations for those who have taken another's life.

In the next chapter, I will delve into how after the civil rights movement mass incarceration became a new form of social control for African Americans who were largely uneducated, unemployed, and living in poor, segregated neighborhoods.

Chapter 3

From the War on Crime to the War on Drugs: The Creation of Mass Incarceration

> Mass incarceration will be halted only by a moral awakening. Citizens nationwide must refuse to remain silent while entire communities are stigmatized, targeted, and destroyed by a system preying on the least of these.
>
> Dominique DuBois Gilliard,
> *Rethinking Incarceration:*
> *Advocating for Justice That Restores*

In 2008, Fate Vincent Winslow was a homeless Black father living in Shreveport, Louisiana. When an undercover officer approached Winslow and asked him for a sex worker, Winslow declined to find him one. The man then asked Winslow for marijuana. Winslow rode his bike and bought two dime bags of marijuana from a white drug supplier for $10 each, which he sold to the undercover officer for $20. Winslow made $5 from the transaction as the middle man, which he intended to use for food. After the sale, Winslow was arrested, though the white supplier who was found with the marked $20 bill was not.

At his trial, ten white jurors found Winslow guilty of marijuana distribution. Though two Black jurors found him not guilty, and the state of Louisiana does not require a unanimous jury to convict, and Winslow was sentenced to mandatory life without parole as a fourth strike offender. Winslow's three other convictions were for simple burglary at the age of seventeen, simple burglary at age twenty-seven when he was convicted of opening an unlocked car door and rummaging inside (he stole nothing), and possession of cocaine, though he maintained that he did not purchase the cocaine an undercover officer tried to sell him.[1]

Winslow served twelve years at Louisiana State Penitentiary, a notorious prison complex better known as Angola, which sits atop a former slave plantation. The last job he held in the prison before his release was cleaning dorms, for which he made 80 cents a week. After Louisiana changed a law related to postconviction sentencing, the Innocence Project New Orleans took on his case. A judge ruled in favor of Winslow, that he had inadequate legal representation at his original trial, and resentenced him to twelve years, time he had already served. So, Winslow was freed from prison in December 2020, reuniting with his daughter and meeting his grandson for the first time. Tragically, Winslow had very little time to enjoy his freedom after spending over a decade imprisoned for selling $20 of marijuana. In May 2021 he was shot and killed by an unknown assailant.[2]

Winslow's story is not an anomaly. According to the 2021 Sentencing Project report, 3,974 people throughout the country are serving life sentences for a drug-related offense. Thirty-eight percent of those people are incarcerated in the federal prison system, which abolished parole in 1987.[3]

In a 2013 report examining life without parole sentences (LWOP) for nonviolent offenses, the ACLU estimated that, nationwide, 65.4 percent of prisoners serving LWOP for nonviolent offenses are Black, 17.8 percent are white, and 15.7 percent are Latino.[4] A 2022 report examining all people sentenced to life, including for violent and nonviolent offenses, found that Black people account for 46 percent of people serving a life sentence and 55 percent of those serving LWOP.[5]

The United States leads the world in incarcerations, with the highest number of people in its prisons and jails in world history—two million—and the highest rate of incarceration. Over the last forty years, the incarceration rate has increased by 500 percent.[6] Not only does America have the highest incarceration rate in the world, but currently "every single U.S. state incarcerates more people per capita than virtually any independent democracy on earth."[7] A Prison Policy Initiative report, "Visualizing the Racial Disparity in Mass Incarceration," found that although African American males make up about 7 percent of the U.S. population, they make up 43 percent of the male prison population and 46 percent of those held in solitary confinement.[8]

According to a report by Lila Kazemian, professor in the Department of Sociology at John Jay College of Criminal Justice, comparing the United States to the rest of the world, the United States is an outlier in the length of incarceration of offenders. The United States holds 40 percent of the globe's people serving life sentences as well as the majority (83 percent) of individuals sentenced to LWOP. Kazemian notes, "analysis of U.S. states suggests that sentencing laws may be a response to the size of the Black population and racial differences in support for more punitive policies, and that White public support influences policy adoption."[9] In the year 2004 during the prison boom that lasted from 1970 through 2010, the rate of incarceration in the United States (the number of people in prison or jail on a given day per one hundred thousand of the population) was seven hundred in one hundred thousand, seven times higher than the Western European penal systems, which averaged one hundred per one hundred thousand.[10]

A long line of historians, lawyers, and civil rights activists have concluded that the nation did not become the world's largest incarcerator by accident. Similar to the slave codes that applied to enslaved African Americans and the Black codes that applied only to African Americans, the war on crime and the war on drugs proved to disproportionately target and criminalize the Black community after the civil rights movement.

David Garland first used the term "mass imprisonment" in 2000, a term now often referred to as "mass incarceration." Here he explains the term and its context:

What are the defining features of mass imprisonment? There are, I think, two that are essential. One of sheer numbers. Mass imprisonment implies a rate of imprisonment and a size of prison population that is markedly above the historical and comparative norm for societies of this type. The US prison system clearly meets the criteria. The other feature is the social concentration of imprisonment's effects. Imprisonment become *mass imprison-*

ment when it ceases to be the incarceration of individual offenders and becomes the systematic imprisonment of whole groups of the population. In the case of the USA, the group concerned is, of course, young black males in large urban centres. For these sections of the population, imprisonment has become normalized. It has come to be a regular, predictable part of experience, rather than a rare and infrequent event.[11]

In *Fratelli Tutti*, Pope Francis writes about the "existential foreigner"—people who are born in a country and have citizenship yet are treated like foreigners. "Racism is a virus that quickly mutates and, instead of disappearing, goes into hiding and lurks in waiting."[12] For African Americans, especially those who are low-income and segregated in economically depressed neighborhoods, the war on crime and war on drugs, which will be explained further, were a reappearance of racialized oppression and terror akin to enslavement and Jim Crow segregation. To understand the connection, we must revisit both the civil rights movement and the Black protests in the form of uprisings that occurred after it in order to understand the white backlash that led to the creation of vast carceral systems of oppression against Black people and new forms of social control through policing and incarceration.

The civil rights movement, also referred to as the freedom movement, lasted from 1954 until 1968. Nikole Hannah-Jones frames the twentieth-century campaign for Black liberation in *The 1619 Project:*

This was the second mass movement for Black civil rights, after Reconstruction. As the centennial of slavery's end neared, Black people were still seeking the rights they had fought for and won after the Civil War: the right to be treated as full citizens before the law, which was guaranteed in 1868 by the Fourteenth Amendment; the right to vote, which was guaranteed in 1870 by the Fifteenth Amendment; and the right to be treated equally in public accommodations, which was guaranteed by the Civil Rights Act of 1875. In response to Black demands for these rights, white Americans strung them from trees, beat them and dumped their bodies in muddy rivers, assassinated them in their front yards, firebombed them on buses, mauled them with dogs, peeled back their skin with fire hoses, and murdered their children with explosives set off inside a church.[13]

Led by Martin Luther King Jr., the civil rights movement became the twentieth century's largest mass movement for racial reform and civil rights. King, who grew up in Atlanta, Georgia, entered Morehouse College at the age of fifteen. Graduating in 1954, first in his class from a predominately white seminary, Crozer Theological, he went on to become a pastor like his father and grandfather.[14] That same year the landmark *Brown v. Board of Education* was decided, and fewer than one hundred thousand Black men were incarcerated in either prison or jail.[15]

Then on December 1, 1955, Rosa Parks refused to give up her seat for a white person on a Montgomery, Alabama, bus. Four days later, twenty-six-year-old King was unanimously elected president of the Montgomery Improvement Association, to lead the Montgomery Bus Boycott. Under his leadership the boycott lasted for 381 days, during which time 90 percent of Black riders participated, cutting revenue for the bus company by 65 percent. By November 13 of the following year, the U.S. Supreme Court affirmed Montgomery's three-judge federal court ruling that Alabama's state and local laws requiring segregation were unconstitutional, and Montgomery's buses were integrated on December 21, 1956.[16]

In 1955, King completed his doctorate in systematic theology at Boston University[17] and went on to lead the national movement with the philosophy of nonviolent direct action. In protest after protest, "Between autumn 1961 and 1963, twenty thousand men, women, and children had been arrested. In 1963 alone, another fifteen thousand were imprisoned, and one thousand desegregation protests occurred across the region, in more than one hundred cities."[18] With their rights denied since the nation's founding, African Americans protested for equal participation in American society. King rooted the moral justification for protests, boycotts, and sit-ins in the teachings of nonviolent leaders such as Mahatma Gandhi as well as those of Protestant and Catholic theologians:

One may well ask, "How can you advocate breaking some laws and obeying others?" The answer is found in the fact that there are two types of laws: there are *just* and there are *unjust* laws. I would agree with Saint Augustine that "An unjust law is no law at all."

Now what is the difference between the two? How does one determine when a law is just or unjust? A just law is man-made code that squares with the moral law or the law of God. An unjust law is a code that is out of harmony with the moral law. To put it in the terms of Saint Thomas Aquinas, an unjust law is a human law that is not rooted in eternal and natural law. Any law that uplifts human personality is just. Any law that degrades human personality is unjust. All segregation statutes are unjust because segregation distorts the soul and damages the personality. It gives a segregator a false sense of superiority, and the segregated a false sense of inferiority.[19]

Although protests, marches, and boycotts were held in southern states like Alabama, North Carolina, Georgia, and Tennessee, segregation and racial discrimination were not only southern problems; they were entrenched in federal and business policy throughout the country. After the Second World War, American manufacturing soared, and a large number of African Americans and white working-class men migrated from the South to the Upper Midwest for union-wage jobs in the auto and steel industries. Black workers began to organize for both better working conditions and an end to racial segregation and oppression there as well.[20] In *The Color of Law: A Forgotten History of How Our Government Segregated America*, Richard Rothstein explains that "when African Americans who left the South entered a northern labor market, federal, state, and local governments collaborated with private employers to ensure they were paid less and treated worse than whites."

Social Security, minimum wage protection, and the recognition of labor unions all excluded from coverage occupations in which African Americans predominated: agriculture and domestic service. State and local governments behaved similarly. . . .

The first national New Deal program, the Federal Emergency Relief Administration, adopted in 1933, disproportionately spent its funds on unemployed whites, frequently refused to permit African Americans to take any but the least skilled jobs, and even in those, paid them less than the officially stipulated wage.[21]

Labor unions, such as the American Federation of Labor, denied membership to African Americans or only allowed them to be hired in janitorial or other low-wage positions. During World War II, most unions, such as the Marine Laborers Union, which had thirty thousand members, and the Steamfitters Union, which had seventeen thousand members, had National Labor Relations Board–certified agreements "that companies could not hire without a union referral, and the unions would not refer African Americans." In the instance of the International Brotherhood of Boilermakers, Iron Shipbuilders and Helpers, when there were not enough white workers to fill shipyard positions, the boilermakers "established segregated auxiliary union chapters," whose Black members had to pay dues but could not "file grievances or vote in union elections. They received fringe benefits worth about half what white members received" but could not supervise whites or receive union support to advance to better-paying jobs. For thirty years the government recognized segregated unions and tolerated white unions that denied membership to African Americans until President Kennedy banned the practice in 1962.[22] The civil rights movement was a response to American society's glass ceiling that kept the majority of Black Americans from full participation and benefit in civic and social life. Yet, as will be seen, a new glass ceiling was instituted in the form of mass incarceration that would literally trap a sizeable portion of the Black population in cages.

Though the unemployment rates of Black and white Americans were roughly equal in 1940 at 11 percent and 9 percent, respectively, by the 1960s the African American unemployment rate became twice as large as the white rate. Due to racism and segregation, which prevented the majority of Black Americans from holding high-wage jobs, many African Americans were either underemployed, unemployed, or stagnant in low-wage positions and unable to build wealth.

John F. Kennedy's administration was concerned about the high unemployment rate of Black youth. Arthur J. Goldberg, the administration's secretary of labor, called the lack of jobs available to Black urban youth "potentially the most dangerous social condition in America today." According to her 2016 book, *From the War on Poverty to the War on Crime,* Yale University historian Elizabeth Hinton shows that leading (mainly white) social scientists of the time placed the blame on cultural and behavioral deficiencies that they claimed led to the problems plaguing the Black urban communities—and not the historical and continued systemic racism that left working-age Black Americans in segregated neighborhoods, segregated unions (if any at all), and largely outside of the American economy. As Hinton stated, Kennedy's administration and public policy officials "aimed to change the psychological impact of racism within individuals rather than the impact of the long history of racism within American institutions."[23]

In 1963, the centennial of the Emancipation Proclamation, African Americans were organizing to protest the high levels of unemployment and underemployment in low-paying jobs, systemic disenfranchisement, and continued racial segregation. A. Philip Randolph telegraphed Martin Luther King Jr. and asked for his support to hold a major action. The leaders of prominent civil rights organizations set a date and stated their goals for the protest in a letter to President Kennedy. On August 28, 1963, more than two hundred thousand demonstrators descended on the National Mall for the March on Washington for Jobs and Freedom. Participants and sponsors included the NAACP, National Urban League, the National Catholic Conference for Interracial Justice, the National Council of the Churches of Christ in America, the United Auto Workers, and many more. King took the podium toward the end of the event and delivered his "I Have a Dream" speech. The march effected a change, exerting pressure on the Kennedy administration.[24]

Kennedy responded and sent the Civil Rights Act of 1963 to Congress, expressing his hope that his administration would complete the work begun by President Lincoln and fully emancipate the descendants of Africans, who he believed were not yet free from the bonds of injustice.[25] After initiating a series of staff studies on poverty and Black unemployment in the summer of 1963, Kennedy declared he wanted to make the eradication of poverty a legislative goal in 1964. Though Kennedy didn't live to see that happen, President Lyndon B. Johnson picked up the mantle. During Johnson's State of the Union address in 1964, he called for an "unconditional war on poverty."[26] Later that year, on July 2, 1964, Johnson signed into law the Civil Rights Act of 1964, the most sweeping civil rights legislation since Reconstruction. It formally dismantled the Jim Crow system of segregation by prohibiting discrimination in public places, calling for the integration of schools and other public facilities, and made employment discrimination illegal.[27]

The next month, Johnson signed into law the Economic Opportunity Act of 1964 as one of the landmarks of his War on Poverty and Great Society domestic programs. Hinton describes it as the "most ambitious social welfare program in the history of the United States, making an investment of nearly $1 billion to fight poverty." Coming from that legislation was the newly created Office of Economic Opportunity, which provided funding to programs such as Head Start and grassroots community organizations.

With this funding, communities began to disrupt racial hierarchies and exercise their right to self-determination. One such organization, Mobilization for Youth, "confronted public school administrators, unresponsive landlords, the New York City Department of Welfare, and the police department," Hinton wrote. "Similarly, the Syracuse Development Corporation supported low-income residents in protests, rent strikes, and sit-ins." However, mayors of cities with residents organizing for their rights, congressional Republicans, and southern Democrats pushed back on the government funding these groups received and began calls for law and order to maintain the status quo.[28] Those calls for law and order would later become the bedrock of the justification for mass incarceration.

In January 1965, King traveled to Selma, Alabama, where neoslavery had ended only decades earlier. As scholar Douglas Blackmon described the state at that time, it was a place "of desolate black powerlessness and unchecked white brutality," where the white people controlled virtually all the land. Black people were still tenants and sharecroppers, and the Black vote had not been allowed there in the twentieth century.[29] King then held a mass meeting and declared that they would bring a voting bill into the streets of Selma.

Leading to that time, the Student Nonviolent Coordinating Committee (SNCC) had been organizing in the South and registering people to vote. After twenty-six-year-old Jimmie Lee Jackson was shot and killed by Alabama state trooper James Fowler on February 26 during a peaceful protest, Rev. James Bevel of the Southern Christian Leadership Conference (SCLC) called for activists to march the fifty-four miles to Montgomery, the state capital, to call on the governor to listen to their demand for equality. While King offered his support for the march, SNCC refused to support it, concerned with the potential for danger from violent white resistance. SNCC's president, John Lewis, though, determined to participate with six hundred other marchers on March 7. When the protesters tried to cross the Edmund Pettus Bridge, they were met by Alabama state troopers, Dallas County sheriff's deputies, and city and county police armed with billy clubs and wearing white helmets and gas masks.

Law enforcement beat and gassed the unarmed marchers, as television cameras captured the entire assault. That night, ABC interrupted their programming of *Judgment at Nuremberg*—the movie that explored the war crimes and events in Nazi, Germany, during the Holocaust—to air the footage of civil rights supporters being beaten. The nearly fifty million Americans who saw the images and footage were shocked to witness the brutality against American citizens seeking equal rights.[30]

After what became known as "Bloody Sunday," many white people throughout the country were moved with sympathy. Soon eight hundred volunteers from twenty-two states arrived to join the demand for the rights of Black people in Selma. When on Thursday, March 25, King led a now-even-larger number of protesters on a successful march to Montgomery, the efforts urged President Lyndon Johnson and other members of Congress to commit to a federal voting rights bill.[31]

But even with the changes at the federal level, violence followed. Jonathan Daniels, a young white Episcopalian seminarian galvanized by Martin Luther King Jr.'s call for civil rights, had been among those who came to Alabama to march; he was brutally shot and killed on August 20 by Deputy Sheriff Tom Coleman. Six weeks later Coleman was acquitted of murder by an all-white jury. Coleman had also shot Rev. Richard Morrisroe, a Catholic priest from Chicago, in the back, but Morrisroe survived. Daniels was only one of twenty-six civil rights workers killed in the South during that time.[32] Another was Medgar Evers, the first field officer for the NAACP in Mississippi, who was killed in 1963 by an avowed white supremacist.

Civil unrest wasn't taking place only in the South. Two weeks after President Johnson signed the Civil Rights Act, a riot in Harlem occurred after a New York City police officer murdered a fifteen-year-old Black high school student. Similar incidents occurred in Philadelphia and Chicago. In Hinton's book, she explains that the uprisings brought to the light the existing tensions between law enforcement and Black residents in segregated neighborhoods. "They also brought to the fore the unanswered legacy of Emancipation: despite civil rights reform and the unprecedented War on Poverty Johnson had recently declared, monumental federal actions had failed to resolve entrenched inequality and everyday racism within America institutions, North and South."[33]

While most Americans are aware that the Voting Rights Act of 1965 was passed, expanding the vote to all Americans, what is more often buried in the history is the line of change followed by the beginning of President Johnson's "war on crime," ultimately part of what led to the mass incarceration of Black men. In March of that year, Johnson called for the war on crime and proposed the Law Enforcement Assistance Act to Congress. In the wake of the riots in Black communities, Johnson's administration proposed a federal law enforcement program focused on "national punitive measures" that would be "primarily directed at black Americans living in urban neighborhoods that had high rates of crime."[34]

In 1964 a report came out titled "One Third of a Nation: A Report on Young Men Found Unqualified for Military Service"; it was delivered to Johnson and drew connections between poverty, low literacy, and national security, and argued that federal intervention was needed in urban and rural areas—places where Black and white low-income families were concentrated. The task force behind the report believed that the young men who failed the army's mental test had inherited poverty from their parents; and job training, counseling, and literacy programs were needed in order to break the cycle, so that poverty wouldn't be transmitted to the next generation of children. Without changes being made, the task force believed a third of the nation would face a lifetime of recurrent unemployment.[35]

Daniel Patrick Moynihan, who served as the assistant secretary of labor to President Kennedy, focused his attention on poverty among African Americans. His harmful theories about Black people would greatly influence the stance President Johnson took toward the Black community. Those prejudicial theories still persist in the American conscience today. In Moynihan's highly controversial study of African Americans, "The Negro Family: The Case for National Action," he wrote, "At the heart of the deterioration of the fabric of Negro society is the deterioration of the Negro family. It is the fundamental source of the weakness of the Negro community at the present time." He differentiated between middle-class Black families that he believed focused more on stability and conserving family resources, and the "increasingly disorganized and disadvantaged lower class group."

Moynihan gathered statistics that pointed to an increase in Black children born out of wedlock, increase in divorce among Black couples, increase in households headed by women without a father present, and an increase in Black children and women receiving Aid to Families with Dependent Children (AFDC). He argued that the chattel slavery practiced in America, which he described as "profoundly different from, and in its lasting effects on individuals and their children, indescribably worse than any recorded servitude, ancient or modern," Jim Crow segregation, and racial violence such as lynchings had the lasting effect of fracturing the African American family and disrupting Black men's sense of identity as men and husbands.

Moynihan also pointed to the high unemployment rate of Black males (in January 1965, the unemployment rate for Black teenagers was 29 percent) and additional statistics to show that male unemployment was "clearly" correlated with family separation and divorce.

The conclusion from these and similar data is difficult to avoid: During times when jobs were reasonably plentiful (although at no time during this period, save perhaps for the first two years, did the unemployment rate for Negro males drop to anything like a reasonable level) the Negro family became stronger and more stable. As jobs became more and more difficult to find, the stability of the family became more and more difficult to maintain.

Moynihan believed both middle-class and lower-income youth were in danger of what he termed a "tangle of pathology." He argued that at the center of the pathology was the weakness of the Black family structure, which was more matriarchal than white American families and society, which were patriarchal. This pathology was the "principal source of most of the aberrant, inadequate, or antisocial behavior that did not establish, but now serves to perpetuate the cycle of poverty and deprivation."

Blaming this pathology without absolute evidence and without any background in the fields of psychology and sociology that he was claiming competence in, Moynihan used his platform to state that Black people commit the majority of crimes such as rape, murder, and aggravated assault. His recommendation at the end of the "report"—and the president's response—reverberated through each subsequent decade. Moynihan's recommendation was not to improve schools in Black communities, increase access to jobs, or end the segregation of African Americans in economically depressed neighborhoods; rather, he stated that in order for Black Americans to have full and equal responsibilities and rewards of citizenship, federal government programs should be designed to effect, directly or indirectly, the stability and resources of the Black family.[36]

According to Hinton, President Johnson rejected Moynihan's arguments for federal responsibility for financially shoring up the Black family and instead embraced ideas of Black pathology. Moynihan's report provided Johnson's administration an understanding of the crisis facing urban cities and gave it a "rationale for directing domestic programs specifically at the plight of black men while removing itself from accountability for the de facto restrictions, joblessness, and racism that perpetuated poverty and inequality." Similarly, the report's assertion of Black juvenile crime led to federal policy that encouraged "patrol, surveillance, and confinement as means of exerting social control in neighborhoods of segregated poverty."[37] The report directly planted the seeds for the overpolicing and overincarceration of Black males that reached a peak during the prison boom and still occurs today.

A subsequent federal report on African American unrest, referred to as the Kerner Commission Report, directly contradicted Moynihan's. President Johnson announced to the nation on July 29, 1967, an executive order forming the National Advisory Commission on Civil Disorders, chaired by former Illinois governor Otto Kerner. The announcement came after the Watts, Los Angeles, riot in August 1965, eleven major riots in the summer of 1966, and twenty-five major riots in 1967. Johnson said he wanted to know the answer to three main questions: (1) what happened, (2) why did it happen, and (3) what can be done to prevent it from happening again, along with other questions about understanding why riots occurred and who suffered when they did.

In stark contrast to Moynihan's report, which relied on hypotheses, prejudices, and statistics taken out of context and attributed the problems faced by Black Americans to their "pathology" and breakdown of the family, the Kerner Commission spent months interviewing mayors, community leaders, business owners, and African Americans directly affected by the riots. As a result, the commission issued a report that placed the blame of Black inequality, unemployment, and poverty squarely on anti-Black racism that permeated all facets of American life. "This is our basic conclusion: Our Nation is moving toward two societies, one black, one white—separate and unequal." Further, it stated, "Segregation and poverty have created in the racial ghetto a destructive environment totally unknown to most white Americans. What white Americans have never fully understood—but what the Negro can never forget—is that white society is deeply implicated in the ghetto. White institutions created it, white institutions maintain it, and society condones it."[38]

The Kerner Commission challenged the term "rioting" and instead believed what was happening in Black communities was a political response to racial oppression. The top three main grievances of the African Americans interviewed by the commission were listed as unfair police practices that targeted Black Americans, unemployment, underemployment, and inadequate housing.

The report noted that for Black people living both in areas that had a riot and outside of them, they were severely disadvantaged compared to white people in the same cities or counties, twice as likely to be unemployed, three times as likely to be working a service job that required little skill, and more than twice as likely to be living in poverty. The subemployment rate was 33 percent or 8.8 times greater for Black Americans than overall U.S. workers. This disadvantage, the report held, was based on pervasive discrimination and segregation Black people faced in employment, education, and housing; the white exodus from cities when Black people moved in; and the government-backed creation of Black "ghettos" that were impoverished and filled with deteriorating facilities, crime, drug addiction, and in lieu of job opportunities, a dependence on welfare. About 16 to 20 percent of Black people in the central cities lived in "squalor and deprivation."

The report also found that rioters "appeared to be seeking fuller participation in the social order and the material benefits enjoyed by the majority of American citizens. Rather than rejecting the American system, they were anxious to obtain a place for themselves in it." The commission believed the programs required to remedy the situation faced by African Americans in urban communities would require "unprecedented levels of funding and performance," but there should be "no higher priority for national action and no higher claim on the Nation's conscience."[39]

The key recommendations the Kerner Report suggested included consolidating and concentrating employment efforts so every city had an agency to coordinate "all manpower programs, including employment service, community action agencies, and other local groups"; strengthening equal opportunity on the federal, state, and local levels; enforcing anti-discrimination laws; providing job training; and increasing the federal minimum wage—"a 3-year program aimed at creating 250,000 new public service jobs in the first year and a total of 1 million over the three-year period"; creating one million new private sector jobs in three years; a guaranteed minimum income; decreasing segregation in schools and year-round education for low-income students; fully funding education for all schools; removing barriers to higher education, including loan forgiveness; "production of 600,000 low and moderate housing units next year and 6 million units over the next 5 years"; and changing the police operations to end misconduct and provide more adequate police protection in Black neighborhoods.[40]

President Johnson, dissatisfied with the commission's findings and the call on the government to be at the forefront of change for Black communities, made the decision to ignore the report. Not once did he publicly mention the report or its findings and recommendations. Facing a tough reelection, ultimately Johnson did not believe he had the political capital to stand behind the solutions the report called for, especially the $80 million it recommended his administration spend to remedy the inequality faced by much of the Black community.

In addition to the recommendations for spending on social programs, the Kerner Commission also identified five basic problem areas within urban police departments and offered suggestions for improvements. Its fifth recommendation, which was to try and develop community support for law enforcement, including hiring more Black police officers, was the only policy recommended by the commission adopted by the federal government. The report pinpointed the negative impact of majority white law enforcement forces policing Black communities:

> The police are not merely a "spark" factor. To some Negroes police have come to symbolize white power, white racism, and white repression. And the fact is that many police do reflect and express these white attitudes. The atmosphere of hostility and cynicism is reinforced by a widespread belief among Negroes in the existence of police brutality and in a "double standard" of justice and protection—one for Negroes and one for whites.[41]

Two months after the report was released, Martin Luther King Jr. was assassinated, and riots erupted in over 125 cities across the country. Amid white concern of Black uprisings and a growing Black population, Johnson decided to end the roughly three decades of progressive federal legislation and instead moved forward with the war on crime's major crime control intervention for the remainder of his presidency. That decision was the genesis of the mass incarceration crisis faced today. To this day, the amount of federal funding the Kerner Commission recommended has never been infused in Black neighborhoods and communities to remedy the scourge of inequality, discrimination, and poverty; instead, trillions of dollars have been directed to police forces and to incarcerate Black Americans over the past half century.

Richard Nixon complained that the Kerner Commission report blamed "everybody for the riots except the perpetrators of the riots" and promised as president "he would meet force with force, if necessary, in the cities."[42] After Nixon won election and took office in 1969, he continued his law-and-order rhetoric and pushed back on the previous eight years of the Kennedy and Johnson Democratic administrations and civil rights gains for African Americans.[43] In addition to the rise in urban unrest, beginning in the 1960s and lasting a decade, crime rates also rose in the United States, with reported street crime increasing by four times and the homicide rate nearly doubling.[44]

Nixon criticized his predecessors for focusing on inequality as a cause of crime and instead argued criminals were not being held accountable for their own actions in breaking the law. He pushed for tougher policing and incarceration. And it was not all crime that Nixon was concerned with; it was crime committed by African Americans. According to Hinton,

> From the perspective of Nixon's Advisory Council, his closest aides, and Nixon himself, at the heart of the crime problem lay the *street* crime problem, seen as a black, urban issue. "You have to face the fact that the whole problem is really the blacks," Nixon's chief of staff, H. R. Haldeman, quoted Nixon as saying in Haldeman's diary entry from April 1969. "The key is to devise a system that recognizes this while not appearing to." In a direct and systematic way, Nixon recognized that the politics of crime control could effectively conceal the racist intent behind his administration's domestic programs.[45]

Nixon's administration and federal policymakers began to actively plan for a large growth in the penal system. Five million dollars was allotted for the expansion of prisons, as outlined in the "Long-Range Master Plan" that had been created by the Bureau of Prisons in 1970 pursuant to the president's orders. Nixon officials did not believe in the efficacy of rehabilitation for people who committed crime but instead envisioned violators being incarcerated for long periods of time in order to protect society.

Federal spending for prisons increased from $69.5 million in 1969 to $176.3 million by 1972, and within the first five years, 1,600 beds were added to prisons throughout the United States. Though the Kerner Commission had encouraged investment in treatment centers, halfway houses, and other community-based forms of rehabilitation, Nixon's administration did not support funding such measures and instead prioritized the construction of maximum-security penal facilities. By mid-1970s, "only 10 percent of the billions of dollars federal and state authorities spent on corrections went to rehabilitation measures for prisoners."[46]

Nixon's administration persuaded Congress to impose the goals of the Long-Range Master Plan on governors, and federal block grants and discretionary funding were given to states to strengthen the penal system. Between 1895 and 1975, the federal prison population increased tenfold from twenty-five hundred to twenty-five thousand, and the state prison population increased fourfold from fifty thousand to two hundred thousand. The African American prison population across the country skyrocketed. In Pennsylvania, the Black population was less than 10 percent but made up 62 percent of inmates in state jails. In Florida, Black people were 15 percent of the state's population but 55 percent of the prison population. In Alabama, Black residents were 26 percent of the population but made up 60 percent of the state's prisoners.

Black people were not incarcerated at higher rates because they committed more crimes; they were incarcerated more often because they were Black and overwhelmingly poor. Hinton gives the examples of Hawaii and Colorado, "which had high crime rates but relatively few Black and Latino residents, and in both states incarceration rates were low."[47]

With the Kerner Commission recommendations to remedy inequality and urban poverty completely ignored, the socioeconomic situation for many low-income and working-class African Americans only deteriorated more in the 1970s when the U.S. economy began to decline. As Marcus Mauer explains in "The Endurance of Racial Disparity in the Criminal Justice System," "With an initial shift to Latin American workforces and later a move to Asian nations, the once-robust high-wage production jobs in the United States began a precipitous decline that contributed in large part to the expansion of a lower-wage service economy and growing inequality."[48]

Due to globalization and the offshoring of industrial factories located in inner cities, manufacturing jobs that provided gainful employment to African Americans, and especially African American males with low levels of formal education, disappeared. A report published in the *Annals of the American Academy of Political and Social Science* found that in 1970, more than 70 percent of African Americans working in the metropolitan areas of Baltimore, Boston, Chicago, Cleveland, Detroit, New York, Philadelphia, St. Louis, and Washington, DC, held blue-collar jobs. Between 1972 and 1982, however, the U.S. censuses of manufacturers show dramatic losses in manufacturing jobs: New York City lost 30 percent, Detroit lost 41 percent, and Chicago lost 47 percent. In the same period, the white population drastically declined—by 1.4 million in New York, 700,000 in Chicago, and 420,000 in Detroit—while the Black population rose substantially in all three.[49]

As white residents left cities and relocated their business establishments to the suburbs, the exodus "further weakened the labor markets for lower-skilled consumer and personal services that, along with goods-processing industries, had employed the largest numbers of urban blacks." By 1987, the industrial employment of Black men sunk to 28 percent.[50]

Higher-earning African Americans also left poor, inner-city Black neighborhoods during this time. Before the end of Jim Crow segregation, a large swath of African Americans could not live in white, redlined neighborhoods. After the civil rights legislation in the 1960s, the Black middle class had expanded, and Black student enrollment in college increased by 85 percent between 1964 and 1968. During the 1970s and 1980s, with many barriers of racial segregation lifted, a significant number of middle- and upper-class African Americans migrated out of Black, inner-city neighborhoods to the suburbs for economic and social reasons. As a result of their absence, there was an increase in high-poverty Black neighborhoods.[51]

With a severe shortage of jobs, well-funded public schools, and community programs, the unemployment rate for Black youth in deindustrializing urban areas climbed to between 40 and 60 percent. There were few opportunities for formal employment in the cities, which the factories, white-owned businesses, white residents, and higher-earning and more educated Black people had abandoned. In turn, some residents turned to "pimping, prostituting, gambling, fencing stolen goods, stealing, robbing, and drug dealing—employment options of last resort that became known during this period as 'hustling.'"[52]

The economic devastation in Black inner-city communities in the late 1970s and early 1980s coincided with the launch of the war on drugs.

In a formal announcement made in 1971, Richard Nixon officially called for a "war on drugs," claiming illegal drugs were "public enemy number one." He blamed the rising crime rate on the "breakdown in lawfulness, morality, and social stability in the wake of the Civil Rights Movement."[53]

In *Locking Up Our Own: Crime and Punishment in Black America*, James Foreman Jr. describes, during this period of time, pressure mounting in African American communities hard hit by drugs and crime for tougher law enforcement involvement to clean up the open-air drug markets operating freely and for the imposition of longer sentences of incarceration to stop the "revolving door" of drug dealers coming in and out of jail without ending their illegal activity. "This argument arose from a central paradox of the African American experience: the simultaneous over- *and* under-policing of crime."[54] Black residents were certain that police would not ignore blatant drug sales and drug activity in white suburban communities, and they didn't want it overlooked in theirs either. Violence as a result of the illicit economy and desperation was rising within Black neighborhoods, and in the mid-'70s, the Black homicide rate was seven to eleven times higher than the white homicide rate.[55]

In Washington, DC, guns poured in from gun-friendly neighboring states such as North Carolina, South Carolina, and elsewhere. With both the scourge of drug use and sales as well as the violent crime committed within their neighborhoods, Black Americans understood that the root causes of economic oppression, subpar housing, lack of well-paying employment, and adequate health care services needed to be addressed and remedied. Living in constant fear of violence and of having massive drug markets overtake their communities, Black people desired immediate solutions.

In 1976, the District of Columbia passed one of the nation's strictest gun control laws, requiring gun owners to register their handguns and prohibiting residents from acquiring new ones. Foreman summed up the failure of the gun control laws alone: "Prohibiting gun possession in majority-black communities like D.C., while failing to curb the vibrant national gun market or to address crime's root causes, had led to the worst of all possible worlds. Guns—and gun violence—saturate our inner cities, while the people who go to prison for possessing guns are overwhelmingly black and brown."[56]

While Nixon may have called for the war on drugs, President Ronald Reagan set it in motion during his presidency, which lasted from 1981 to 1989. Having run his campaign on the major themes of crime and welfare, Reagan subtly used highly racialized appeals that pitted poor and working-class white people against Black people with new founded rights that placed them in nearer proximity to one another. After his election, the Justice Department announced it would "cut in half the number of specialists assigned to identify and prosecute white-collar crime and to shift its attention to street crime, especially drug-law enforcement."[57]

Reagan turned from the government policies of the 1960s and 1970s that funded social investments like schools, job training programs, and welfare. Instead, he called mainly for punitive crime measures in Black communities that were hardest hit by massive job losses as more American corporations moved factories overseas. During his first year in office, Congress passed legislation that changed the formulas for entitlement programs, which resulted in a nearly 2 percent increase in the rate of poverty and most affected African Americans.[58]

As Michelle Alexander writes in *The New Jim Crow: Mass Incarceration in the Age of Colorblindness*, Reagan shifted the federal budget to launch a full-scaled war against drug use and drug crime while cutting funds for drug prevention and treatment:

Practically overnight the budgets of federal law enforcement agencies soared. Between 1980 and 1984, FBI antidrug funding increased from $8 million to $95 million. Department of Defense antidrug allocations increased from $33 million in 1981 to $1,042 million in 1991. During that same period, DEA antidrug spending grew from $86 to $1,026 million, and FBI antidrug allocations grew from $38 to $181 million. By contrast, funding for agencies responsible for drug treatment, prevention, and education was dramatically reduced. The budget of the National Institute on Drug Abuse, for example, was reduced from $724 million to $57 million from 1981 to 1984, and antidrug funds allocated to the Department of Education were cut from $14 million to $3 million.[59]

By 1984, the Black unemployment rate had nearly quadrupled since the 1950s. In 1985, crack cocaine made its way to the economically depressed Black neighborhoods, and there was an increase in both violence as unemployed residents fought to control the drug-distribution channels and drug dependency as people became addicted to the new drug.

Foreman describes the devastation caused when crack inundated Black neighborhoods:

> This drug was seen as so damaging because it created so many addicts so quickly, and because its damage couldn't be contained: not just the addict, but his or her children, family, friends, and neighbors went down as well. Crack also spawned violent drug markets the likes of which American cities had never seen. In their fight for territory, heavily armed gangs turned urban neighborhoods into killing fields.[60]

The federal response to crack cocaine was not to find and stop the manufacturers of the new drug in order to prevent its sales in Black communities. The focus became the elimination of the Black dealers and users from their communities. In the introduction to *The New Jim Crow's* tenth-year edition, Alexander writes in retrospect that the actions of Reagan's administration overseas actually contributed to the drug scourge:

> The CIA admitted in 1998 that guerilla armies it actively supported in Nicaragua were smuggling illegal drugs into the United States—drugs that were making their way onto the streets of inner-city black neighborhoods in the form of crack cocaine. The CIA also admitted that, in the midst of the War on Drugs, it blocked law enforcement efforts to investigate illegal drug networks that were helping to fund its covert war in Nicaragua.[61]

The health, safety, and economic concerns of African Americans facing the crack-cocaine crisis, especially in inner-city neighborhoods, were not met with compassion but social stigma and stringent punishment. In 1985, the new director of the Drug Enforcement Agency, Robert Stutman, sought to draw journalists' attention to crack cocaine spreading throughout Black communities in an effort to build public support for Reagan's drug war. A year later, that strategy paid off. "The Social Construction of the Crack Epidemic in the Print Media," by Donna M. Hartman and Andrew Golub, explains:

> In 1986, the media's frenzied attention turned to crack cocaine. This coverage followed a now classic formula in which exaggerated claims are supported by carefully selected cases. The media focus led to a resurgent concern about drug abuse nationwide. In 1986, 3% of Americans reported drug abuse as the nation's most important problem; by 1989 this number had increased to 64%.[62]

Hartman and Golub's study of the newsmagazines *Time, Newsweek,* and the *New York Times* posits that the news coverage "made it easy to dismiss the disadvantages experienced by minority, urban poor as self-inflicted matters of individual choice and self-indulgence as opposed to recognizing them as matters of economic history, social structure, and racial inequality."

While crack was used more broadly in both large and small metropolitan areas of the country, the media coverage had a clear racial subtext and almost exclusively focused on urban areas (88 percent of the *New York Times,* 95 percent of *Time,* and 100 percent of *Newsweek* coverage from the years 1985 through 1995). The majority of sensational claims in the articles proved to be false for the most part. Crack cocaine is not more dangerous than other forms of the drug, such as powder, which is more often used by white people, nor is it instantly addictive.

"Crack babies" were a sensationalized myth, even as studies showed "cocaine dependence has not been shown to be directly transmitted from mother to child." The reality of babies born to mothers who used crack cocaine is more damning against poverty, with studies indicating "the abnormalities observed among babies born to crack addicts are similar to those prevailing among babies born to otherwise impoverished women who have had poor diets and received no prenatal care."[63]

One reason the media coverage proved to be so erroneous was that the "most commonly cited sources, in order, were law enforcement, public office holders, and street interviews; the least commonly cited sources were hospitals, academics, and surveys." In hindsight, law enforcement and public officials stood the most to gain from the media-induced public panic; and African Americans had the most to lose.[64]

In 1986, Congress passed a law to establish mandatory minimum sentences for drug trafficking offenses, which treated crack and cocaine powder offenses using a one-hundred-to-one ratio. Under this policy, a person convicted for selling as small an amount as five grams of crack would incur the same severe minimum sentence as someone who sold five hundred grams of powder cocaine. According to Foreman, "this distinction was based on racialized fear, not science.... Because the hundred-to-one ratio had so little to justify it, and because African Americans were more likely to be involved in the crack trade, the law's harsher treatment of crack defendants became one of the most grotesque examples of racial discrimination in the criminal justice system."[65]

As the prison system was becoming big business, the government continued to create an avalanche of punishment through each sector of society. In 1988, Congress passed the Anti-Drug Abuse Act, which "authorized public housing authorities to evict any tenant who allows any form of drug-related criminal activity to occur on or near public housing premises and eliminated federal benefits, including student loans, for anyone convicted of a drug offense." Draconian mandatory minimum sentences were imposed for people convicted of drug offenses, including a mandatory five-year sentence for people in possession of a cocaine base without intending to sell it. Before the new legislation, the maximum sentence for drug possession of any amount was one year of imprisonment.[66]

When George H. W. Bush won the 1988 presidential election, he did so with a campaign that exploited the fear of crime. In a racially loaded television ad, Bush highlighted Willie Horton, a Black man on furlough from a Massachusetts prison who raped and stabbed a white woman. He claimed the Democratic nominee, Michael Dukakis, was soft on crime, and attacked Dukakis's opposition to the death penalty and affiliation with the ACLU. As president, Bush appointed William Bennett to the position of drug czar. In *Rise of the Warrior Cop*, Radley Balko states that Bennett's "main contribution to the drug war was to infuse it with morality." He embedded his morality approach to drug prohibition with an effort to dehumanize drug users. As Balko explains:

Bennett demanded that drug warriors in the administration stop talking about addicts as "sick" and stop referring to addiction as a health problem. Going forward, the federal government would simply view them as bad people. Fundamentally bad people aren't cured or mended. The only real question is how best to remove them from the good people.[67]

Bennett described himself as a person who did not believe the "first purpose of punishment is rehabilitation." Instead for him, "The first purpose is moral, to exact a price for transgressing the rights of others."[68]

Over the next ten years, from 1988 through 1998, the budget increased for federal drug enforcement efforts. "$2 billion of federal money snowballed into $16 billion by 1998 while the prison population doubled, then tripled, in size and became increasingly dominated by Blacks."[69] The U.S. prison population ballooned from around three hundred thousand in the 1970s to more than two million in less than thirty years, largely due to the war on drugs. Alexander dispels two common misconceptions about the drug war: that the war's aim was to rid the nation of drug kingpins, and that the war mainly targeted dangerous drugs. Instead, the vast majority of those arrested were charged with relatively minor crimes, and arrests for simply possessing marijuana accounted for nearly 80 percent of the growth in drug arrests in the 1990s.[70] The law enforcement focus on marijuana had begun under the Reagan administration, who targeted the drug under the disputed theory that it was a "gateway" drug. In Washington, DC, for example, marijuana arrests had increased from 334 in 1968 to 3,002 in 1975, which was a 900 percent increase. In 2010, Black people in DC were arrested for marijuana possession at eight times the rate for white people, and police arrested 5,393 people for the offense, which amounted to nearly fifteen arrests a day.[71]

According to the ACLU, between 2001 and 2010, there were 8,244,943 marijuana arrests, of which 7,295,880, or 88 percent, were only for marijuana possession.[72] In an updated report released in 2020, the ACLU found, "While marijuana arrests were down by 18% overall since 2010, law enforcement still made more than 6.1 million such arrests over the past eight years." In 2018 alone, "there were almost 700,000 marijuana arrests, which accounted for more than 43% of all drug arrests. In fact, in 2018, police made more marijuana arrests than for all violent crimes combined, according to the FBI."[73]

What is even more damning when examining the impact of the war on drugs is that recreational marijuana is now legal in twenty-two states, Washington, DC, and Guam. State governments and businesses are now profiting from the sale of the drug that resulted in the incarceration of scores of Black Americans like Fate Winslow. In August 2022, the Arizona Board of Executive Clemency declined to shorten the sixteen-year prison sentence of Trent Bouhdida, an African American, who had been convicted of selling an undercover cop an ounce of marijuana. Three of the four board members who made the decision to keep Bouhdida incarcerated were previously employed in law enforcement careers. When Bouhdida was only fifteen years old, he had pled guilty to armed robbery, though he did not actively participate in the robberies at issue. That previous case led the board members to conclude at the hearing that his sentence of sixteen years was appropriate. Overlooking the progress Bouhdida had made while incarcerated to improve himself, such as taking college classes and working as a GED tutor, as well as letters of support from family members, the board, with disregard, moved forward. One letter of support was written by Bouhdida's brother George, appalled at the hypocrisy. "The fact that there are three stores in a three-mile radius of my house where any citizen with identification can purchase the same product that has Trent incarcerated is ludicrous. People and the state are benefiting and making a living off the exact substance that has him incarcerated."[74]

A 2000 Human Rights Watch report confirmed the racial bias inherent in the war on drugs and who it targeted and criminalized:

> In seven states, African Americans constitute 80 to 90 percent of all those sent to prison on drug charges. In at least fifteen states, blacks are admitted to prison on drug charges at a rate from twenty to fifty-seven times greater than that of white men. In fact, nationwide, the rate of incarceration for African Americans convicted of drug offenses dwarfs the rate of whites. When the

War on Drugs gained full steam in the mid-1980s, prison admissions for African Americans skyrocketed, nearly quadrupling in three years, and then increasingly steadily until it reached in 2000 a level more than twenty-six times the level in 1983.[75]

Dispelling a common misconception that African Americans are arrested for drugs more often because they use drugs more often, the National Institute on Drug Abuse's study first published in 1995, and revised in 1998 and 2003, had different findings: whites, nonwhite Hispanics, and African Americans had recently used illegal drugs at a percentage (6.4 percent) indistinguishable from one another when surveyed.

For youth, it was found that Black Americans used drugs at a lower rate than whites and Hispanics for all illegal drugs but marijuana, which was the same for white children and Black children. This means white and Hispanic youth used inhalants, crack cocaine, heroin, and other opioid drugs *more often* than Black youth. And at virtually every grade level, Black students had lower drug usage than white and Latino students. Between 1977 and 2000, it was Black high-school seniors who were estimated to have the lowest probability of being an illegal drug user.[76]

What *was* different between African American drug users and dealers in inner cities and white drug users and dealers in the suburbs and rural areas was the concentration of high and extreme levels of poverty in Black neighborhoods, lack of formal employment, and the number of police patrolling the neighborhoods.

The picture drawn by the ethnographic research is of poor neighborhoods, chronically short of legitimate work and embedded in a violent and illegal market for drugs. High rates of joblessness and crime, and a flourishing street trade in illegal drugs, combined with harsher criminal penalties and intensified urban policing to produce high incarceration rates among young unskilled men in inner cities. In the twenty-five years from 1980, the incarceration rate tripled among white men in their twenties, but fewer than 2 percent were behind bars by 2004. Imprisonment rates for young black men increased less quickly, but one in seven were in custody by 2004.[77]

A study by Lauren J. Krivo and Ruth D. Peterson published in *Social Forces* in December 1996 examined the connection between race, crime, violence, and poverty, and offered empirical evidence contradicting the media and the narrative perpetuated by the Moynihan report and Nixon administration that Black people were inherently criminal and prone to violence.

The researchers examined predominantly Black neighborhoods and predominantly white, high poverty neighborhoods in Columbus, Ohio, using census data from 1990 and reported crime data in 1994 from the Columbus Police Department. At the time, there were a total of 215 census tracts in Columbus, with 26 that were at least 70 percent Black and 122 that were at least 70 percent white. The percentage of Black tracts with "extremely high" levels of poverty was 38.5 percent, compared to only 7.4 percent of white tracts; and the rate of "extreme" poverty was nearly identical for the white and Black tracts.[78]

The authors concluded that "extremely disadvantaged communities have qualitatively higher levels of crime than less disadvantaged areas, and that this pattern holds for both black and white communities." It was also found that "persons experience much lower levels of violent crime living in black communities with low levels of disadvantage than in either black or white communities with extreme levels of disadvantage." The causes for the increase in crime were linked to both the *lack* of positive social influences such as professionals in the communities, high-income earners, and resources in the community, and the *increased* presence of negative social influences such as poverty and high male joblessness. The higher rates of crime in Black urban neighborhoods, they concluded, were due mainly to the fact that they were "structurally more disadvantaged."[79]

As the war on drugs gained momentum, measures were not created to reduce the disadvantage faced by African Americans in low-income communities in order to reduce crime. Instead, punitive measures of policing, arrest, and incarceration, which began during the war on crime, only further escalated during the war on drugs. This led to the racial disparity in incarceration growing substantially from the 1970s, before peaking in the late 1990s. According to Bruce Western and Christopher Wildeman, leading sociologists and scholars on mass incarceration, poverty and unemployment in Black neighborhoods directly correlated to increased incarceration.

> Variation in imprisonment is closely linked to variation in wages and employment. Weekly earnings for young low-education men declined through the 1980s and 1990s while imprisonment rates were rising. Among black men, unemployment increased steeply with declining education. One study estimates that if wages and employment had not declined among low-education men since the early 1980s, growth in prison admission rates would have been reduced by as much as 25 percent by 2001....
>
> The urban deindustrialization that produced the raw material for the prison boom was as much a failure of institutions as a failure of markets. Large job losses in the mid-1970s and early 1980s were concentrated in unionized industries. De-unionization thus joined manufacturing decline to drive down the incomes of unskilled inner city workers. Besides unemployment insurance, which provided only temporary assistance, few social programs were available to supplement the incomes or retrain or mobilize young able-bodied men into new jobs. The welfare system was also poorly equipped to handle the social problems linked to male unemployment. Drug addiction, petty offending, and public idleness all afflicted the neighborhoods of concentrated disadvantage.[80]

In *Dead Man Walking*, Sr. Helen Prejean brought her firsthand accounts of scores of young Black men being abused, harassed, arrested, and even killed by the police in the low-income St. Thomas projects while the government cut funding for social programs.

> I watch Reagan slash funds for prenatal and child care, low-income housing, employment training, and food subsidies. And as social programs are slashed, new prisons are built. Between 1975 and 1991 Louisiana expanded its adult prisons from three to twelve, with prison populations increasing by 249 percent. Throughout the 1980s Louisiana ranked first, second, or third

in the nation as the state incarcerating the greatest number of its residents—at an annual cost per inmate of $15,000, and that doesn't include the cost of prison construction, about $50,000 for the average prison bed. Louisiana's exponential prison expansion is part of a national trend. In 1980 about 500,000 Americans were behind bars; in 1990, 1.1 million—the highest confinement rate in the world. And if parole and probation systems are included, in 1990 the United States had in its criminal justice system 1 of every 43 adults, 1 of every 24 men, and 1 of every 162 women, at the cost of $20 billion a year. Between 1981 and 1991 the federal government cut its contribution to education by 25 percent (in real dollars) and increased its allocation for criminal justice by 29 percent.[81]

Throughout the 1990s, African Americans were about seven times more likely to be incarcerated than whites.[82] A report by the ACLU found that in "the states with the worst disparities, Blacks were on average over six times more likely to be arrested for marijuana possession than whites. In the worst offending counties across the country, Blacks were over 10, 15, even 30 times more likely to be arrested than white residents in the same county."[83]

It was not just Republican administrations that created policies during the drug war that harmed the Black community. Under President Bill Clinton's tenure, from 1993 to 2001, devastating public policies such as the 1994 Crime Bill were implemented that detrimentally impacted African Americans convicted of crimes, serving sentences, and released from prison, who overwhelmingly lived in neighborhoods with concentrated extreme and extremely high poverty levels. According to Bruce Western, at the end of Clinton's presidency in 2000, "among non-college black men, aged 22 to 30, the jobless rate (one minus the employment ratio) stood at 29.9 percent, in comparison to the adjusted rate of 42.1 percent that includes the prison and jail population."[84]

As Alexander explains, Clinton replaced AFDC with the block grants to states called Temporary Assistance to Needy Families (TANF), which imposed a "five-year lifetime limit on welfare assistance, as well as a permanent, lifetime ban on eligibility for welfare and food stamps

for anyone convicted of a felony drug offense—including simple possession for marijuana." By 1996, twice as many federal dollars went toward
the penal budget as to welfare or food stamps. The federal government
"slashed funding for public housing by $17 billion (a reduction of 61 per-
cent) and boosted corrections by $19 billion (an increase of 171 percent),
'effectively making the construction of prisons the nation's main housing
program for the urban poor.'"[85]

The punitive measures of overpolicing, arrest, and incarceration of the
African American communities that began under the Johnson administration and poured billions of dollars into waging war against Black
Americans did not result in safer streets or less crime. Instead, divestment
in social programs to remedy the root causes of poverty resulted in even
more devastation and violence in low-income communities. According
to Foreman, the Department of Justice "would later estimate that in the
mid-1990s, a black American male faced a 1-in-35 chance of being murdered over his lifetime—a risk that was eight times higher than a white
man's, whose chances were 1 in 251."[86]

Likewise, exchanging direct aid to low-income mothers for work
requirements in order to receive financial assistance did not elevate more
Black families out of poverty.

Women, especially women of color, were disproportionately
affected by the dismantling of welfare. In 2014, the poverty rate
was 14.8 percent, but for families headed by women, it was 39.8
percent and for families headed by black women, 45.6 percent.
The concerted effort to remove families from the rolls has meant
that many poor parents are unable to support their own children,
leading to an enormous expansion in the foster care system.[87]

In *Just Mercy*, Bryan Stevenson describes the impact of banning
people with drug convictions, even simple possession of marijuana, from
safety net programs.

The collateral consequences of mass incarceration have been
equally profound. We ban poor women and, inevitably, their
children, from receiving food stamps and public housing if they

have prior drug convictions. We have created a new caste system that forces thousands of people into homelessness, bans them from living with their families and in their communities, and renders them virtually unemployable.[88]

According to the Sentencing Project, the prison population increased sevenfold from 1973 until its peak in 2009.[89] The forty-year period of mass incarceration known as the "prison boom," which lasted from 1970 through 2010, resulted in nearly half of Americans today with an immediate family member in prison or jail, "including more than 2 million children who currently have an incarcerated parent and 10 million children who have had a parent imprisoned at some point in their lives." In study after study, case after case, as this chapter shows, African Americans were disproportionately impacted. Some scholars estimate that one in four Black children have experienced parental incarceration by their teenage years, compared to one in ten Latino children and one in twenty-five white children.[90]

Though African American males were the most likely to be incarcerated during the prison boom and today, African American women, children, and Black marriages and traditional families have all been severely impacted by the overincarceration of Black men. Incarceration as the federal and state governments' response to manage, oppress, and contain poor Black men who overwhelmingly didn't graduate high school or have gainful employment had the opposite effect of strengthening Black families that Moynihan's report advocated for. People who decades later want to cite Moynihan's report as prescient to the decline of Black families ignore how the war on drugs and war on crime directly contributed to the breakdown of Black families. According to Sara Wakefield and Christopher Uggen in "Incarceration and Stratification,"

In addition to the health risks facing inmates' families, incarceration is linked to shifts in family structure, household disadvantage, and childhood mental health. Western & Wildeman have drawn explicit connections between mass incarceration and largescale structural shifts in the family, particularly for African Americans. Well-documented trends in the feminization and juvenilization of poverty since the 1970s closely mirror the upsurge in incarceration.[91]

As the rate of Black young men who were incarcerated began a staggering climb, the percentage of Black men and women who have ever been married took a steep decline. At the start of the prison boom era in 1970, 97.2 percent of Black women had ever been married. By 2012, that number had dropped to 65.2 percent.[92] Similarly, the rate of unmarried women giving birth began a historic climb starting in 1980 when it was 18.4 percent, and increasing every year until it reached 40.7 percent in 2012, with Black women having the largest rate of births outside of marriage.[93] According to the U.S. Census, in 2021 only 39 percent of Black people lived in U.S. households that were headed by married couples, compared to 31 percent in female-headed household families, and 5 percent in male-headed households.[94]

Under the tenure of President Barack Obama, the nation's first African American president, from January 2009 through his departure in January 2017, the incarceration rates for Black men and women fell each year of his presidency. By the time Obama's presidency ended, Black incarceration rates were at their "lowest points since the early 1990s and late 1980s."[95] These reductions were due in part to legislation passed during his presidency. In August 2010, Obama signed into law the Fair Sentencing Act of 2010, which reduced the one-hundred-to-one sentencing disparity between crack and powder cocaine offenses to eighteen to one, reduced the statutory penalties for crack cocaine trafficking, and eliminated the mandatory minimum sentence for simple possession of crack cocaine. As a result, "In 2014, approximately half as many crack cocaine offenders were sentenced in the federal system as had been sentenced in 2010."[96]

Even after Obama's presidency, in all fifty states, the rate of Black male incarceration continued to decrease, and by 2019 the lifetime risk of incarceration for Black men declined by nearly half. These positive changes have led today to more Black men earning a bachelor's degree by age twenty-five (17.7 percent) than serving time in prison (12 percent).[97] Though the decrease in incarceration rates is welcome news, it can be reversed if increases in crime during the pandemic result in policy changes that increase incarceration.

While one can appreciate the reduced rate of Black male incarceration (while acknowledging it is still disproportionately high compared to white and Hispanic men), society cannot overlook the millions of people still in prison or still suffering the impact of a felony conviction and history of imprisonment. In April 2022, a White House proclamation painted the dire picture faced by victims of the war on crime and the war on drugs.

More than 70 million Americans have a criminal record that creates significant barriers to employment, economic stability, and successful reentry into society. Thousands of legal and regulatory restrictions prevent these individuals from accessing employment, housing, voting, education, business licensing, and other basic opportunities. Because of these barriers, nearly 75 percent of people who were formerly incarcerated are still unemployed a year after being released.[98]

What is not specifically stated in the proclamation is that a disproportionate number of the seventy million Americans are Black. Though in 2020 African Americans made up 14 percent of the population, they were 43 percent of those incarcerated. Latinos made up 17 percent of the incarcerated population, so together Black and Brown people made up 60 percent of those locked in cages.

Since the abandonment of the Johnson administration's War on Poverty, no administration has invested adequate federal funds into remedying the root causes of racial inequality, systemic racism, and inner-city and rural unemployment that still plague predominantly Black and low-income communities. Instead, too many Black people are removed from their communities and incarcerated, only to be released at a later time with permanent social stigma and even greater barriers to equal access to employment, education, housing, and ability to take care of their families and loved ones.

In California alone, 70 percent of people experiencing homelessness in the state have been incarcerated. Though the U.S. Census shows about 6.5 percent of Californians identify as Black or African American, they account for nearly 40 percent of the state's homeless, according to a

Department of Housing and Urban Development report to Congress. This is also the trend nationally. Though people who identify as Black or mixed-race Black total 14 percent of the country's population, Black people make up 39.8 percent of the homeless population[99] and 50 percent of homeless families with children.[100]

Summing up the regression of civil rights and social progress for Black Americans caused by incarceration, Michelle Alexander wrote that the "old forms of discrimination—employment discrimination, housing discrimination, denial of food stamps and other public benefits, and exclusion from jury service—are suddenly legal" after a person has a felony conviction. "As a criminal, you are afforded scarcely more rights, and arguably less respect, than a black man living in Alabama at the height of Jim Crow. We have not ended racial caste in America; we have merely redesigned it."[101]

American laws, policies, politicians, and even overwhelmingly the public diminish people who have been convicted of a crime and incarcerated and perpetually condemn them to second-class citizenship, years of surveillance, high unemployment, and reduced lifetime earnings. As a civil rights attorney, Stevenson relays how those incarcerated or formerly incarcerated are permanently stigmatized:

> We've institutionalized policies that reduce people to their worst acts and permanently label them "criminal," "murderer," "rapist," "thief," "drug dealer," "sex-offender," "felon"—identities they cannot change regardless of the circumstances of their crimes or any improvements they might make in their lives.[102]

United States history portrays the civil rights movement as a success that eliminated racism from American society. Often, the ills still facing predominantly Black and poor communities are painted as "moral failings" that would be eliminated if Black people ceased having babies out of wedlock and stopped "committing crime." Yet, the Kerner Report directly contradicted the narrative that racism ended after the civil rights movement, and this chapter explained how over the next fifty years, a new form of social control emerged that ensnared millions of the lowest-income, uneducated, and unemployed African American men, and their families, into mass incarceration. Two truths can exist at the same time: that many African Americans have benefitted from the civil rights movement and attained a level of success and integration not possible before 1965, and that too many African American people and neighborhoods are grossly underfunded, segregated, overpoliced, incarcerated, and exiled from society postincarceration. There has never been one "Black community." Black Americans are diverse and have unique experiences depending on where they live, family history, opportunities, and disadvantages. Unfortunately, many of the Black Americans who have benefitted from the civil rights movement, moved out of impoverished neighborhoods, and achieved a level of success now join the white majority in condemning the African Americans not as fortunate as themselves without acknowledging the systemic inequality too many Black people still face. For example, research in the *American Sociological Review* by Bryan Levy, Nolan Philips, and Robert Levy found "Black neighborhoods are 77 times as likely as white neighborhoods to be *both* socioeconomically poor *and* socially isolated from better-resourced neighborhoods."[103] But African Americans who do not live in Black neighborhoods may have little exposure to such inequality or interactions with the residents in them.

As this chapter explained, "war on crime" and "war on drugs" weren't just slogans; they were federal government policies that were carried out in all fifty states and the District of Columbia and resulted in the explosion of the prison industrial complex. The next chapter will demonstrate that, to wage the war on crime and war on drugs, literal tools of war—from military-grade weapons to armored vehicles and SWAT teams—were unleashed against American citizens who were mainly Black, poor, and marginalized.

Chapter 4

Waging War

For to survive in the mouth of this dragon we call america, we have had to learn this first and most vital lesson—that we were never meant to survive. Not as human beings.

Audre Lorde, *The Cancer Journals*

On August 9, 2014, Michael Brown, an eighteen-year-old African American, was shot and killed by Darren Wilson, a white police officer who suspected Brown had committed a robbery. Dorian Johnson, who witnessed Brown's murder, stated in court that Brown had his hands up at the time Wilson opened fire, though the Department of Justice made different assertions. While a Black teenager being killed by a police officer in America is sadly not uncommon, news coverage of the police response to the protest in the aftermath of Michael Brown's killing that erupted in Ferguson, Missouri, shocked the nation and world.

As throngs of African Americans organized by Black Lives Matter marched for justice and against police brutality, they were met in the streets by heavily armed police officers wearing camouflage uniforms and carrying assault rifles, often pointed directly at the protesters. Armored vehicles roamed the city streets while police shot tear gas and dropped smoke bombs into the crowds.

The videos, social media posts, and photojournalism coming out of Ferguson evoked scenes of war zones in Afghanistan. As American citizens exercised their First Amendment right to free speech and protest, they were met with a military response. In an interview, Radley Balko, author of the book *Rise of the Warrior Cop* and a former longtime reporter for the *Washington Post*, reflected on the scenes:

When you arm police like soldiers and outfit them with military weapons and train them on military tactics and tell them they're fighting a war, whether it's a war on crime or drugs or looters and rioters, they're going to start seeing themselves as soldiers, and seeing the people they serve less as citizens with rights and more as potential threats, and that's what we're seeing.[1]

Throughout the history of the United States, from the period of the enslavement of people of African descent until the present, the state and federal government have considered Black people seeking liberation, free speech, and justice to be dangerous. Over and over again, all efforts to destroy liberation movements and either kill or permanently incapacitate their leaders were made by the government.

Though Martin Luther King Jr. is now remembered as an American hero, that wasn't always the case when he was alive. Like the civil rights movement that peaked in popularity during the passage of the Civil Rights Act, King's popularity also decreased the longer the movement for Black equality lasted. Over a series of years, Gallup polled the American public on their attitude toward King: from 1964 with a 43-percent positive rating to a 45-percent positive in 1965, his favorability plummeted in the last poll taken in 1966, to 32-percent positive.[2]

Beginning in 1964 and reaching a fever pitch after the assassination of King on April 4, 1968, the uprisings that occurred in Black communities caused tremendous fear among white people. The racial imagery of Black people vandalizing property, setting fires, and clashing with white police forces associated with the uprisings gave fuel to conservatives arguing that the civil rights movement had led to rampant crime, and that the northern and midwestern cities that had integrated were now victims of their kindness.

The war on crime that President Johnson called for in 1965 came eight months after the first major uprising in Harlem occurred. Elizabeth Hinton details that the Law Enforcement Assistance Act of 1965 "created a grant-making agency within the Department of Justice, which—with $30 million at its disposal . . .—purchased bulletproof vests, helicopters, tanks, rifles, gas masks, and other military-grade hardware for police departments." Much of the equipment provided to arm police forces came from the U.S. military arms used in Vietnam and Latin America.[3]

In *The New Jim Crow,* Michelle Alexander reports that when a new generation of Black activists in the late 1960s began to organize to protect their communities from police violence and provide services and social programs that the government would not, the government and white public became terrified.

> Growing numbers of black activists began organizing against police violence during this period, and some organizations, including the Black Panther Party (originally called the Black Panther Party for Self-Defense), boldly asserted the right of black people to arm themselves in order to defend their communities against police brutality. Media imagery of black men in leather jackets and berets, toting guns, proudly embracing their revolutionary politics, and preaching "Black Power" enhanced fears among many whites that violent insurrections were inevitable if law enforcement failed to gain control over black communities.[4]

In "Don't Believe the Hype: Debunking the Panther Mythology," Charles E. Jones and Judson L. Jeffries trace the rupture of the nonviolent integrationist-directed civil rights movement and the Black Power movement to the summer of 1966, when a leader of the Student Nonviolent Coordinating Committee (SNCC), Kwame Ture (then known as Stokely Carmichael), first coined the term "Black Power" during a march in Mississippi that same summer. "We been saying 'freedom' for six years," Ture declared in a speech. "What we are going to start saying now is 'Black Power.'" Though the civil rights movement had succeeded in legally overturning *de jure* segregation, a large segment of the Black population was still brutally policed and denied equal opportunities as well as full access to American society.

> Blatant acts of police brutality, inadequate housing, inferior social services, and rampant unemployment still plagued the African American community. By this stage it was clear that the traditional civil rights organizations were unable to alter the systemic forces that adversely impacted the lives of African American people, particularly in northern urban settings.[5]

In *From the War on Poverty to the War on Crime*, Hinton explains that White House officials and the Justice Department were increasingly concerned with the uprisings that occurred in Newark and Detroit during the summer of 1967. Policymakers responded by further militarizing the majority-white police forces without examining how their behavior along with the National Guardsmen and federal troops that responded further inflamed the uprisings.[6]

Johnson's administration focused on Kwame Ture, who had visited Cuba that summer and met with Fidel Castro, and watched with trepidation the burgeoning Black Power movement. They ignored the Black residents' frustration with being segregated in impoverished neighborhoods with rampant police brutality, lack of jobs and social programs, and dilapidated housing conditions, and instead blamed "black pathology" and Black "militant agitators."

Federal officials and policymakers feared that Black activists would organize residents into full-scale rebellion.

> The cabinet worried that black nationalists and revolutionaries were gaining ground and that the government's existing urban social programs had failed to address the community pathology they believed was behind the disorders, an "alienation" that seemed to be growing more receptive to the ideas of revolution. By linking urban uprisings to rising black militancy and demands for self-determination, Johnson and the cabinet could avoid fully coming to terms with the failure of the administration's urban policy to address the underlying causes of unrest and could focus instead on individual "pathological" behavior and a kind of black politics that, from the perspective of federal officials, must be opposed.[7]

To combat what they considered problems specific to African American communities, Johnson's administration developed strategies that encouraged the police to "seek out potential criminals in low-income urban neighborhoods" and initiate interaction with the residents. Unlike the police who ordinarily interacted with white communities when they were called on for assistance, police in low-income Black neighborhoods became "a ubiquitous part of the social and political landscape" with government justification that their presence would prevent rioting and crime. Soon police stations were installed inside public housing projects that had once been occupied by community action programs. Similarly, "Social welfare measures that provided education and training opportunities to poor people were increasingly replaced with police department programs that provided entertainment and recreation." Hinton describes one aspect of the Johnson administration's strategy for the war on crime as channeling Black youth who hadn't committed any crime into community-based crime control agencies because they were identified by policymakers as "in danger of becoming delinquent" and "potentially criminal."[8]

While the federal government was sending more police to African American neighborhoods, African Americans were organizing to support and protect their communities, often from those very police. According to Jones and Jeffries, the Black Panther Party for Self-Defense (BPP) emerged during this time of national tumult in Oakland, California, in October 1966. Founded by Huey P. Newton and Bobby Seale, the BPP represented the "institutionalization of Malcom X's notion of self-defense."

The BPP arguably became the most influential revolutionary nationalist organization in the United States and had four main components: "(1) The saliency of armed resistance, (2) a tradition of community service, (3) a commitment to the self-determination of *all* people, and (4) a model of political action for oppressed people."[9] The methods the BPP advocated to secure liberation for African Americans, including the call for an armed struggle to seize state power, were strikingly different from King's nonviolent strategy. Though King agreed with the basic political and social agenda of advocates in the Black Power movement, he condemned their endorsement of revolutionary violence and Black separatism.

The BPP grew into a national organization, and during its peak distribution period between 1968 and 1972, its newspaper, *The Black Panther*, sold an average of a hundred thousand copies per week. The Panthers created free breakfast programs for children, free clothes and shoes programs, liberation schools, armed security patrols, and other community projects. The Panthers also had solidarity with movements across the color line, including white leftist political organizations and the antiwar movement, the Chicano organization Brown Berets, and the Puerto Rican group Young Lords.[10] In a 1968 organizational directive titled "Black Panthers and Black Racism," activist and Black Panther leader Eldridge Cleaver stated, "Be strong enough not to yield, not to be Uncle Toms, not to bootlick, not to sell out—but we must also be able to realize that there are white people, brown people, red people, yellow people in this world who are totally dedicated to the destruction of this system of oppression, and we welcome that. We will always be open to working with that."[11]

As a response to the growing fear of the riots and Black Power activists in Black communities, President Johnson signed into law his last piece of major legislation, the Omnibus Crime Control Act and Safe Streets Act of 1968, which invested $400 million to fund the war on crime. In *The End of Policing*, Alex S. Vitale reports that Johnson's initial draft allocated resources for police improvement, better coordination between criminal justice agencies, and the commencement of innovative prevention and rehabilitation efforts. Before Congress passed the bill, however, the legislators stripped it of most of the prevention and rehabilitation provisions. Instead, the bill granted large bloc funds for states to use, which over the next decade led to a "massive expansion in police hardware, SWAT teams, and drug enforcement teams—and almost no money toward prevention and rehabilitation."[12] As Hinton sums up the irony, despite recommendations from the Kerner Commission and other committees, under Johnson a "federal employment drive to create jobs for black men never materialized, but the Johnson administration did, effectively, support a job creation program for police departments with nearly all-white forces."[13]

When Richard Nixon became president, he divested funding from the War on Poverty social programs and increased funds to fight the war on crime. Like Johnson, Nixon allocated resources for law enforcement to carry out the war—recruiting, training, and employing mostly white men from the suburbs—as well as funding private businesses to arm police and surveil Black neighborhoods reeling from high rates of unemployment and lack of resources. As Hinton wrote,

The emphasis on interagency planning and coordination in the Safe Streets Act also opened up possibilities for defense and intelligence agencies in the domestic law enforcement realm, and in Washington, DC; Montgomery, Alabama; and New York City, the Army and the Central Intelligence Agency (CIA) played a key role in offering seminars to local police on visual street surveillance, bomb disposal, and records filing. These training programs complemented the LEAA's ongoing effort to make law enforcement into an attractive, middle-class profession: the agency funded the tuition for some 50,000 officers enrolled in police science programs at more than 1,000 colleges and universities in mostly small suburban areas across the United States. Finally, the new federal crime control grants bolstered private businesses that had already contributed to improving the technological capabilities in the enforcement and criminal justice arena and gave rise to new ones. LEAA funding incentivized the private sector to manufacture cutting-edge equipment such as walkie-talkies and develop technologies such as computerized criminal justice databanks, tasks that the LEAA viewed as crucial to modernizing American law enforcement and making the crime fight successful but that were beyond its own abilities.[14]

While Congress vastly expanded the Office of Law Enforcement Assistance (OLEA) into the Law Enforcement Assistance Administration (LEAA), the Office of Economic Opportunity (OEO) was terminated. In 1968, the OEO director, Sargent Shriver, reflected on the riots that had occurred and pleaded for support in a memo to President Johnson: "For all their destructiveness, I can but read the riots as a terrible call. The Negroes want equal access to the fruits of participating citizenship—the opportunity both to earn and to control their destiny."[15] Neither the Johnson nor the Nixon administration heeded that call, and as LEAA grew exponentially, OLEO lost all support.[16]

In her 2021 *New York Times* Notable Book, *America on Fire*, Hinton provides an example of a "sensitivity training" film from 1968 that was shown to law enforcement officers across the United States into the 1970s titled, "Revolution Underway," which explicitly detailed the enemy the police were fighting.

Essentially anti-communist propaganda, it warned of a "revolutionary force" that aimed to "destroy" American cities and overthrow the government. It argued that the Kerner Commission, which found that the rebellions were not part of a larger conspiracy, had "suppressed" evidence about the role of "revolutionary Black Power" in stoking unrest. Featuring footage of "traitors" such as Malcolm X, Robert F. Williams, H. Rap Brown, and Stokely Carmichael, the film warned darkly of "outside agitators" who were primarily responsible for the "assault on American institutions from within. . . ." "Revolution Underway" depicted local police as the soldiers of the War on Crime—as the most important line of defense against the violent Black and Brown enemy.[17]

In addition to the war on crime, a long-term covert war was raging. An operation to surveil, infiltrate, and even kill Black American activists, undertaken by the FBI since the 1950s, was uncovered by a group of antiwar activists in 1971. They discovered the FBI had been spying on the NAACP and other Black people they believed were communists or radicals, as early as 1923. The government agency took unprecedented actions against African Americans in their program COINTELPRO. Though the full extent of the FBI program COINTELPRO took years to come to light, 1971 marked a turning point for the American public's understanding of the government's highest and most secretive agency under the leadership of J. Edgar Hoover.

In her book *The Burglary: The Discovery of J. Edgar Hoover's Secret FBI*, Betty Medsger details the plot and fallout of the burglary of an FBI office in Media, Pennsylvania. Medsger was drawn into the event as the journalist who broke the story at the *Washington Post*. A small group of people handpicked by William Davidon, a physics professor at Haverford College, broke into the Media office and removed suitcases full of FBI files. The activists purposely scheduled the burglary for Monday, March 8, 1971, the night more than 300 million people around the world watched the heavyweight championship boxing match between the former undisputed heavyweight champion, war-resister, and Muslim, Muhammad Ali, and the heavyweight champion and Vietnam War supporter, Joe Frazier. The largest number of spectators for any single sporting event tuned in that night for the "Fight of the Century."[18]

Davidon was part of the peace movement in Philadelphia, home to one of the largest and most diverse peace movements in the United States during the Vietnam War. After almost a decade of failing to stop the war, Davidon drew inspiration from the Catholic peace activists who had invented the concept of "burglary as a resistance method." Though U.S. leaders in the Catholic Church such as Francis Cardinal Spellman and John Cardinal Krol strongly supported the war, in 1963, Pope John XXIII emphasized the mandate to work for world peace in his encyclical *Pacem in Terris*. It "called on Catholics to work actively with one another and with non-Catholics to create world peace." The pope who followed, Pope Paul VI, called for the United States to end the war in Vietnam. During what was the first papal visit to the United States, Paul VI raised his fist and forcefully stated to an international gathering, "No more war, war never again! Peace, it is peace which must guide the destinies of people and of all mankind."[19]

Encouraged by the message from Rome, the teachings of Dorothy Day (founder of the Catholic Worker movement), and of Thomas Merton (a Trappist monk), the Catholic peace movement grew. What attracted Davidon to the movement in 1969 was the peace activists' more aggressive forms of nonviolent resistance. Brothers and Catholic priests, Daniel Berrigan and Philip Berrigan, burned draft files in a draft board parking lot before being arrested for the action. A loosely structured Catholic group of more than five hundred used burglary to break into draft boards and steal Selective Service records in an effort to make the conscription of American men more difficult. Made up of priests, nuns, ex-priests and ex-nuns, and young working-class Catholics, they succeeded in removing thousands of records, with very few captured and arrested.[20]

Davidon was not Catholic; he was a secular Jewish humanist who (like those in the Catholic peace movement) worked together with people of goodwill for peace. After numerous rumors were circulating that there were FBI informants in the peace activist community, Davidon became convinced he needed to find out if the FBI was suppressing dissent through clandestine operations. He decided he would burglarize the Media FBI office, inviting other peace activists to join the burglary. Medsger describes the group:

They ranged in age from twenty to forty-four. They included three women and five men—a religion professor, a daycare center worker, a graduate student in a health profession, another professor, a social worker, and two people who had dropped out of college to work nearly full-time on building opposition to the war. Though all of them owed their awareness of burglary as an act of resistance to the Catholic peace movement, only one of them was a Catholic. Four were Jews and three were Protestants. . . . Four of them were parents of young children. None of them had ever thought of doing anything as extreme as burglarizing an FBI office.[21]

The documents the Media group found contained powerful evidence that the FBI not only suppressed dissent and aimed to create an atmosphere of suppression and paranoia, but that the political spying it engaged in was the antithesis of ethical behavior within a law enforcement agency in a democratic society. The documents also contained information that FBI director J. Edgar Hoover was intently focused on monitoring the activities of the Black population and especially Black student groups. According to Hoover's directives, all higher education institutions, including two-year colleges, were to be surveilled in order to determine if their activities warranted an active investigation. Hoover justified the investigations by claiming "campus disorders involving black students pose a definite threat to the Nation's stability and security and indicate need for increase in both quality and quantity of intelligence information on Black student Unions and similar groups which are targeted for influence and control by violence-prone Black Panther Party and other extremists." The stolen FBI files revealed that in order to conduct the investigation, a network of informers provided the FBI with reports about the professors and students on campus. The informants included "switchboard operators, letter carriers, the postmaster, campus security officers, the local police chief, and some college administrators."[22] The FBI had also infiltrated Black organizations such as the Congress of Racial Equality, the NAACP, and the Southern Christian Leadership Conference with Black informants.

Medsger summarized Hoover's attitude toward African Americans based on the information from the stolen FBI documents:

> The overall impression in the Media files of how the FBI regarded black people was that they were dangerous and must be watched continuously. To become targets of the FBI, it wasn't necessary for African Americans to engage in violent behavior. It wasn't necessary for them to be radical or subversive. Being black was enough. . . . The FBI thought of black Americans as falling into two categories—black people who should be spied on by the FBI and black people who should spy on other black people for the FBI. The latter group was to be recruited by the bureaus to become part of its vast network of untrained informers.[23]

The records revealed the FBI was more concerned about surveilling civil rights and antiwar activities than fighting organized crime or government corruption, which garnered little attention. Though the only mention of COINTELPRO was the acronym on a document in the Media files, it led to a search to discover its meaning, which, after lawsuits and a Senate select committee in 1975—the Church Committee—uncovered sordid details about the secret FBI program. Hinton states that COINTELPRO was "responsible for some of the most devastating incidents of government repression in the history of the United States."[24]

COINTELPRO revelations included that the FBI program surveilled, infiltrated, and targeted prominent Black activists and their organizations, including Malcom X and the Nation of Islam, and later the Organization of Afro-American Unity, as well as Martin Luther King Jr. and SNCC. In a January 25, 2011, deathbed letter written by Raymond Wood, a former police officer, Wood provided firsthand information about the conspiracy between the FBI and NYPD to assassinate Malcolm X, who was shot and killed on February 21, 1965.[25]

Medsger believes the COINTELPRO activities directed toward Martin Luther King Jr. were the "most egregious," and Hoover's attitude toward King was "savage hatred." Under Hoover's directives, a years-long, multifaceted operation was conducted to destroy the civil rights activist that included office break-ins, informants infiltrating King's networks, and the bugging of his office, home, and hotel rooms. After King's "I Have a Dream" speech, Hoover considered the Black pastor a "demagogue who should be toppled by the bureau." The FBI director began a plot to remove King and select a replacement to lead Black Americans. After FBI surveillance uncovered King's extramarital sexual relationships, the FBI sent an unsigned letter to King's home urging him to commit suicide or face public humiliation just weeks before he received the Nobel Peace Prize in 1964. The FBI enacted a smear campaign against King, also failing to inform him of threats made against his life.[26]

Shortly after the August 1967 rebellion in Detroit, Hoover established a "Black Nationalist Hate Groups" section, which solely focused on Black Power organizations. The agents assigned to the program used "wiretapping, stop-and-frisk methods, and other questionable tactics introduced to prevent the rise of a 'messiah' who could unify and electrify the black nationalist movement," seeking to incriminate or completely obliterate political leaders and organizations. A month later, Hoover declared the BPP the "greatest threat to the internal security of the country." The FBI worked with local law enforcement in San Diego, Chicago, Los Angeles, and other urban areas with a strong BPP presence.[27]

In *The New Jim Crow*, Alexander writes that between 1969 and 1971, "at least forty Panthers were killed—some directly by police forces and others as a result of internal conflicts 'fanned to deadly flames' by the police and FBI through undercover operations. Over one thousand Panthers were jailed, many on false charges, as a result of informants, perpetual surveillance, and other law enforcement tactics."[28]

One of the most famous Panthers who was murdered during a raid was Fred Hampton. Hampton was born in Summit, Illinois, a southwest suburb of Chicago. A prelaw student in junior college, he became active in the NAACP as a leader of the Youth Council, which he expanded to more than five hundred members. Hampton learned about the BPP, and in November 1968 moved to downtown Chicago to work with the Illinois chapter. With a charismatic personality and effective public speaking skills, he grew in the ranks of the chapter and was appointed deputy chairman. In April 1969, Hampton formed the Rainbow Coalition with the Latino group the Young Lords Organization and the working-class white group Young Patriots to confront issues like police brutality and substandard housing. Their mission not only to provide programs and services for the poor but also to work together to end capitalism provoked increased scrutiny of Hampton and the BPP by the FBI and Chicago Police Department.[29]

William O'Neal, an FBI informant who infiltrated the BPP, became Hampton's trusted "friend" and bodyguard. It is believed that on December 3, 1969, O'Neal drugged Hampton's drink, rendering him defenseless on the night an FBI raid killed him (at age twenty-one) along with fellow Panther Mark Clark, who was twenty-two. The FBI and Chicago police worked together to plan the raid, and O'Neal had provided a diagram of Hampton's apartment, including the location of his bed. Though heavily armed police fired at least ninety bullets into Hampton's apartment when they stormed in while Hampton and his nine-month-pregnant fiancée, Deborah Johnson, were sleeping, neither of them was injured. But the police dragged Johnson out of the room and executed Hampton with two bullets to the head. The criminal charges filed against the other seven Panthers who had been present that night were dropped as the FBI and police's illegal actions became clear.[30]

The highest number of assaults launched by the FBI against the BPP occurred in the Los Angeles chapter. Working with the county sheriff's office Intelligence Division and the LAPD's Intelligence and Criminal Conspiracy Division, COINTELPRO agents in Los Angeles tracked the daily activity of the Panthers. Hoover had identified the Panther's breakfast program in Watts as potentially the greatest threat because of the success of the program.

> The Panthers were providing much-needed services in segregated urban neighborhoods, from breakfast programs to free health clinics to food drives, and Hoover recognized these initiatives— very much in the spirit of earlier War on Poverty programs—as a critical source of Panther power. Hoover ordered agents to "eradicate [the Panthers'] serve the people programs," and thereafter, Panthers in Los Angeles were arrested on a daily basis, although the charges against most were ultimately dropped.[31]

The full force of the militarization of the police during the war on crime was displayed on December 8, 1969, when the nation's first special weapons and tactics (SWAT) team raided the Black Panther Party's 41st and Central Avenue headquarters in Los Angeles. Half a century later, a *Los Angeles Times* opinion piece was written titled, "50 Years Ago, LAPD Raided the Black Panthers. SWAT Teams Have Been Targeting Black Communities Ever Since." In the piece, Matthew Fleischer explains that the LAPD created the nation's first SWAT team "out of concern that officers couldn't handle sniper and hostage incidents, such as those they encountered during the Watts riots of 1965." However, during the Panther raid, "SWAT was transformed from a tool of surgical precision into a blunt-force battering ram, and that's ultimately how it would find its calling in police departments across the country—especially in African American communities."

More than 350 LAPD officers launched an attack on thirteen Panthers, including three women and five teenagers, with the justification of executing arrest warrants.[32] The SWAT force descended on the BPP base at 5:30 in the morning, "equipped with battering rams, helicopters, army tanks, and trucks"—an action the press would call a "mini-Vietnam."[33] The law enforcement officers and Panthers exchanged more than five thousand rounds of ammunition, during which time the police detonated explosives on the roof of the Panthers headquarters and called in a tank for reinforcements before the Panthers surrendered and were taken into custody. Six Panthers and four SWAT officers were injured.

On December 11, 1969, a crowd of people numbering up to three thousand protested outside the Los Angeles Hall of Justice. Chanting "Power to the People" with raised fists, they called out the police harassment of the Black Panthers. The raid resulted in thirteen arrests and a total of seventy-two criminal counts being filed against the Panthers, but the BPP defense attorneys successfully argued that the group had acted in self-defense against a SWAT team that barged into their building armed and unannounced. A jury agreed and found the defendants not guilty on "almost all charges, including the most serious ones of assault with a deadly weapon and conspiracy to murder policemen."[34]

By mid-1975, five hundred forces modeled on the first SWAT team operated across the country.[35] SWAT teams became a prominent use of military-like force for police departments and the FBI as the federal government's war on drugs roared to life under President Ronald Reagan. According to Michelle Alexander, in "1972, there were just a few hundred paramilitary drug raids per year in the United States. By the early 1980s, there were three thousand annual SWAT deployments, by 1996 there were thirty thousand, and by 2001 there were forty thousand."[36]

Fleischer details how SWAT deployments have only increased since then:

> Between 2000 and 2008, more than 9,000 of the nation's roughly 15,000 law enforcement agencies employed a SWAT unit. Thanks to the Pentagon's controversial "1033 program," even small-town police departments across the country have stocked up on military-grade hardware, including armored vehicles built to withstand roadside bombs and rocket-propelled grenades. SWAT deployments increased by more than 1,500% nationwide between 1980 and 2000.[37]

A 2014 ACLU report, "War Comes Home: The Excessive Militarization of American Policing," examined data gathered from their organization's public records requests to more than 260 law enforcement agencies in twenty-five states, including the District of Columbia, and a number of cities in a twenty-sixth state, requesting all incident reports (or other records) documenting each time a SWAT team was deployed between 2011 and 2012. The ACLU found that "the majority (79 percent) of SWAT deployments in the data were for the purpose of executing a search warrant, most commonly in drug investigations. Only a small handful of deployments (7 percent) were for hostage, barricade, or active shooter scenarios."[38]

Peter Kraska, professor of police studies at Eastern Kentucky University, who has studied the militarization of American policing, described SWAT teams as using Navy SEAL techniques to search for evidence of crimes. "They bust down the door, throw flash grenades, handcuff everyone inside, ransack the place and leave. And these techniques are predominately used on communities made up of racial minorities."[39]

The direct involvement of the military in the drug war began under President Ronald Reagan. In 1981, Reagan pushed through Congress the

1981 Military Cooperation with Law Enforcement Act, which amended the Posse Comitatus Act (PCA) and provided the military with a larger role in the drug war. The PCA was approved on June 18, 1878, and prohibited the use of federal troops to enforce civilian law except in instances authorized by the Constitution or Congress. Balko explains that the 1981 law greatly aided the White House's drug war.

> The amended law encouraged the Pentagon to go further and give local, state, and federal police access to military intelligence and research. It also encouraged the opening up of access to military bases and equipment, and explicitly authorized the military to train civilian police in the use of military equipment. The law essentially permitted the military to work with drug cops on all aspects of drug interdiction short of making arrests and conducting searches.[40]

Under Reagan, the U.S. military actively supported counter-narcotics efforts, and a massive influx of federal money flowed to local police departments solely for drug policing. Another new policy in the National Defense Appropriation Act for fiscal year 1987 instructed the National Guard to fully cooperate with local and federal enforcement agencies investigating drug crimes and provided a budget for it to do so. The same year, Congress ordered "the secretary of Defense and the US attorney general to notify local law enforcement agencies each year about the availability of surplus military equipment they could obtain for their department." An office in the Pentagon was created that facilitated transfers of war gear to civilian law enforcement. As a result, Congress authorized the transfer of vehicles, armor, and weapons "that had been designed for use on a battlefield against enemy combatants to be used on American streets, in American neighborhoods, against American citizens."[41]

In 1996, Congress passed the National Defense Authorization Act for fiscal year 1997, which made permanent the Pentagon's temporary authority to give weapons of war to local law enforcement agencies and expanded its purview to "counterterrorism" as well, creating the "1033 program." Section 1033 operates under the Counter-Drug Activities titled "Transfer of Excess Personal Property to Support Law Enforcement."

Alexander details the impact of the federal legislation on local law enforcement agencies:

Almost immediately after the federal dollars began to flow, law enforcement agencies across the country began to compete for funding, equipment, and training. By the late 1990s, the overwhelming majority of state and local police forces in the country had availed themselves of the newly available resources and added a significant military component to buttress their drug-war operations. According to the Cato Institute, in 1997 alone, the Pentagon handed over more than 1.2 million pieces of military equipment to local police departments. Similarly, the *National Journal* reported that between January 1997 and October 1999, the agency handled 3.4 million orders of Pentagon equipment from over eleven thousand domestic police agencies in all fifty states. Included in the bounty were "253 aircraft (including six- and seven-passenger airplanes, UH-60 Blackhawk and UH-1 Huey helicopters), 7,856 M-16 rifles, 181 grenade launchers, 8,131 bulletproof helmets, and 1,161 pairs of night-vision goggles."[42]

Along with the involvement of the military and tools of war in the drug war, new federal programs were also developed to train and send officers to proactively search for drug use and possession. In 1984, the Drug Enforcement Agency (DEA) launched the federal program Operation Pipeline, which Alexander describes as training "police to conduct unreasonable and discriminatory stops and searches throughout the United States."

The federal program, administered by over three hundred state and local law enforcement agencies, trains state and local law enforcement officers to use pretextual traffic stops and consent searches on a large scale for drug interdiction. Officers learn, among other things, how to use a minor traffic stop and leverage it into a search for drugs, how to obtain consent from a reluctant motorist, and how to use drug-sniffing dogs to obtain probable cause. By 2000, the DEA had directly trained more than 25,000 officers in forty-eight states in Pipeline tactics and helped to develop training programs for countless municipal and state law enforcement agencies.[43]

It became evident that Black people were disproportionately targeted by police to be stopped, searched, and arrested for drugs. Renée McDonald Hutchins explains in "Racial Profiling: The Law, the Policy, and the Practice" that the term "racial profiling" was first used by the *New York Times* in a February 19, 1990, article referring to traffic stops conducted by New Jersey State Police.[44]

Black drivers in the late 1980s and early 1990s were reporting that the New Jersey troopers were disproportionately stopping them on the New Jersey Turnpike. Empirical data and police records produced through litigation proved that racial profiling was indeed occurring by the New Jersey State Police in selected locations from 1988 through 1991:

> Blacks comprised 13.5 percent of the New Jersey Turnpike population and 15 percent of the drivers speeding. In contrast, Blacks represented 35 percent of those stopped and 73.2 percent of those arrested. In other words, in New Jersey, Black drivers were disproportionally more likely to be stopped and arrested than White drivers.[45]

The targeting of African American males, especially, throughout the drug war had a devastating impact. In 1991, the Sentencing Project reported that one in four African American men were under the control of the criminal justice system.[46]

Despite the early media attention to the claims of racial profiling, the police practice of excessively targeting Black drivers continued. The police department's own internal audits produced evidence that police were engaging in racial profiling as early as the fall of 1996. Senior police officials rejected the chief of internal affairs' recommendation based on the audit to formally monitor officers involved in the practice. The officers responded by withholding additional information from federal civil rights prosecutors. A report released by the attorney general of New Jersey in April 1999 confirmed that the New Jersey troopers had engaged in racial profiling between 1997 and 1998, and that although 77.2 percent of the individuals searched were people of color, the searches resulting in seizure of illegal items were almost identical for white motorists and Black motorists. This proved that the police had stopped hundreds of thousands of Black motorists simply because of their skin color—not because they were more likely to engage in criminal behavior.[47] In December 1999, the state of New Jersey and its Division of State Police entered into a consent decree with the U.S. Department of Justice (DOJ) that included the establishment of an independent monitor to ensure the state troopers stopped racially profiling drivers.

The practice of racially profiling Black drivers did not exist only in New Jersey at that time, Renée McDonald Hutchins wrote. Incidents of police stopping people for "driving while Black" had been documented in other states such as Florida, Illinois, Ohio, Pennsylvania, Massachusetts, and Maryland.[48] A study conducted by Ravi Shroff and the Stanford Open Policing Project published in the May 4, 2020, *Nature Journal* found that Black drivers are twenty times more likely to be stopped than white drivers relative to their share of the residential population, even though contraband was found less often in car searches (29.4 percent for Black drivers compared to 32 percent of white drivers). The massive study examined 94,778,505 stops from 21 state patrol agencies and 35 municipal police departments across the nation between 2011 and 2018. The researchers also examined the effects of drug policy on racial disparities in traffic-stop outcomes by comparing patterns of policing in Colorado and Washington—two states that legalized recreational marijuana at the end of 2012—to those in twelve states in which recreational marijuana remained illegal. They found that legalization reduced both search rates and misdemeanor rates for drug offenses for white, Black, and Hispanic drivers, though the police still stopped Black drivers at a higher rate.[49]

Police bodycam footage from a December 2020 traffic stop in Windsor, Virginia, of a Black army lieutenant, Caron Nazario, drew public outrage at the evidence of continued racial profiling still widely occurring. The two officers pointed their guns at Lt. Nazario, who was wearing his army fatigues and asking why he'd been stopped, then pepper-sprayed him. After the incident, the police alleged they stopped Nazario for not having a rear license plate on his new truck. The lawsuit filed on behalf of Nazario stated that he had his cardboard temporary plates taped inside the rear window of the vehicle. Within six months, twenty-year-old Daunte Wright was shot and killed during a traffic stop in Brooklyn Center, Minneapolis, on April 11, 2021. Wright was pulled over by police for having air fresheners hanging from his rearview mirror.

Soon after Wright was killed, the *New York Times* produced the series "Deadly Police Encounters," which won the 2022 Pulitzer Prize for National Reporting in its revelation that hundreds of unarmed motorists across the country have been murdered by police after vehicle stops for nonviolent offenses. An investigation spanning the previous five years found "police officers have killed more than 400 drivers or passengers who were not wielding a gun or a knife, or under pursuit for a violent crime—a rate of more than one a week." Of those officers, only five were convicted for the killings.

The investigation also found that while police, juries, and judges underscore the danger associated with the law enforcement profession and vehicle stops specifically, the actual data demonstrates that vehicle stops are not as dangerous as thought. Of the roughly 280 officers who have been killed on duty since late 2016, 170 died in accidents on the job compared to 60 people killed by motorists they had pulled over. Compared to the tens of millions of traffic stops made each year, 60 deaths represents a uniquely low percentage. The *Times* found "an officer's chances of being killed at any vehicle stop are less than 1 in 3.6 million, excluding accidents, two studies have shown. At stops for common traffic infractions, the odds are as low as 1 in 6.5 million, according to a 2019 study by Jordan Blair Woods, a law professor at the University of Arkansas."[50]

According to the organization Mapping Police Violence, in 2022 the police killed at least 1,197 people that year, with Black people three times more likely to be killed by police than white people, and although Black people are 1.3 times *less likely* to be armed than white people. The report found the majority of the police killings begin with "traffic stops, mental health checks, non-violent offenses and where no crime was alleged. 1 in 3 of killings began with an alleged violent crime." From 2013 through 2022, officers in 98.1 percent of cases involving police violence were never charged for killing someone. During that same time period, "Chicago police killed Black people at 25x higher rate than white people per population. Minneapolis and Boston police killed Black people at 28x higher rate."[51]

Not only do police racially profile Black people while driving, they profile and target Black pedestrians and entire Black-majority neighborhoods. In Los Angeles in 1988, the California attorney general provided guidance to law enforcement in a confidential handbook, *Crips & Bloods Street Gangs*, that, according to Hinton, identified virtually all African American men in California as potential gang members or drug dealers. In addition to stating that Black males between the ages of thirteen and forty years old were gang members, they more specifically identified certain fashion styles like "heavy gold chains, national sport team shirts, brand name jogging suits, British Knights tennis shoes, and pagers," as gang attire. The handbook then warned that gang members may also not dress in gang attire at all in order to "throw off law enforcement authorities," leading police to potentially suspect any young Black male in any style of dress as a potential gang member.[52]

A great amount of attention to racial profiling has been focused on the city of New York and its stop-and-frisk policy, which started in the late 1990s and a judge found unconstitutional in 2013. In December 1999, New York Attorney General Eliot Spitzer released the results of an investigation by his office that reviewed 175,000 incidents during the fifteen-month period that ended in March 1999. The attorney general found Black people were stopped six times more often than whites, while Latinos were stopped four times more often. Black people made up only 25 percent of the city population but 50 percent of the people stopped and 67 percent of the people stopped by the New York City Street Crimes Unit.[53]

In spite of the results of the investigation, the practice continued unabated, subjecting tens of thousands of Black and brown people to intrusive stops in their own neighborhoods.

In "The Endurance of Racial Disparity in the Criminal Justice System," Marc Mauer details the following:

From a figure of about 97,000 pedestrian stops in 2002, the police department ratcheted up the practice in subsequent years, reaching a level of 685,000 stops annually by 2011. Of the total, 87 percent of those stopped were African American or Latino, a rate that resulted in many teenage boys being able to recount multiple experiences with these practices. . . . Of the 191,000 stops in 2013, 92 percent did not result in an arrest and guns were found in less than 1 percent of all cases. Black and Latino New Yorkers were more likely than whites to be frisked following a stop, yet were only half as likely to be found in possession of an illegal weapon. Following the decision by federal judge Shira Scheindlin to reduce the number of stops dramatically, no significant increase in crime resulted in the following year.[54]

A DOJ investigation of the Ferguson Police Department after Michael Brown's murder uncovered a pattern of racially discriminatory practices by the police, primarily rooted in the city's dependence on the criminal justice system to raise revenue. The investigation found that between 2010 and 2014 the city of Ferguson issued ninety thousand citations and summonses, although only twenty-one thousand people lived in the city. From 2012 to 2014, 85 percent of people stopped, 90 percent of those cited, and 93 percent of those arrested were Black, though Black people made up 67 percent of the population. Black drivers were twice as likely to be searched as white drivers during a vehicle stop though they were found in possession of contraband 26 percent less often than white drivers. The DOJ found that Ferguson's law enforcement practices were "shaped by the City's focus on revenue rather than by public safety needs," where a single missed, partial, or late payment could result in incarceration.

The DOJ investigation also uncovered racist and discriminatory language in the communications of influential Ferguson decision makers, including several court and law enforcement personnel, who were never admonished or disciplined. In behavior reminiscent of the slavery era, Ferguson police used dogs "out of proportion to the threat posed by the people they encounter, leaving serious puncture wounds on nonviolent offenders, some of them children." In every recorded incident of a canine bite, the person bit was African American.[55]

The Department of Justice's investigation into the Ferguson Police Department in 2015 is just one of many that have occurred throughout the country. The first pattern-or-practice investigation was authorized by

Congress in 1994 after the police beating of Rodney King, which was caught on tape. These investigations are reminiscent of the Department of Justice's investigations of convict leasing in the early 1900s. In the majority of the modern-day pattern-or-practice investigations, regardless of guilt found, very few, if any, police officers or departments charged with committing offenses are sentenced to prison; very few substantive changes are made that deter the behavior from occurring again; and heavy penalties are not issued or enforced at all.

After the 2014 ACLU report "War Comes Home" documented the 1033 program and highlighted the ways that militarized police aggressively and violently targeted Black communities and the fallout of the militarized response to the Ferguson protests, President Barack Obama signed Executive Order 13688 in 2015, which implemented reforms to the 1033 program. When Donald Trump ran for office, however, he promised to rescind Obama's 1033 restrictions, doing so in 2017.[56]

In response to the mass movement of Black Lives Matter protests that occurred in 2020 after the police murder of George Floyd, again a militarized police response was activated across the country. One such incident epitomized the problem of militarization facing Americans. On June 1, 2020, the plaza between St. John's Church and Lafayette Park in Washington, DC, was full of nonviolent protesters when U.S. Park Police and National Guard troops dropped tear gas and forcefully pushed the protesters out of the plaza. Gini Gerbasi, who was protesting at the park, posted on Facebook, "We were literally DRIVEN OFF of the St. John's, Lafayette Square patio with tear gas and concussion grenades and police in full riot gear." After the protesters were cleared, President Trump walked from the White House through Lafayette Park then stopped outside St. John's Church. Holding up a Bible (upside down), the president posed for pictures and stated, "We have the greatest country in the world. Keep it nice and safe."[57]

On May 12, 2021, the ACLU released an analysis of the history of the 1033 program and any effect Obama's executive order had on the demilitarization of the police. It found the following:

Since the program was created in 1996, the U.S. military has given roughly 10,000 law enforcement agencies $7.4 billion worth of equipment including grenade launchers, batons, combat vehicles, and hundreds of thousands of rifles. From 2011 to 2014 alone, the military distributed more than 29,000 military-grade rifles to 18,000 law enforcement agencies; today, state and local law enforcement possess more than 60,000 military-grade rifles, 1,500 combat-ready trucks and tanks, 500 unmanned ground vehicles (functionally landed drones), and dozens of military aircraft, machine gun parts, bayonets, and even an inert rocket launcher. Law enforcement attached to K–12 schools, colleges, and universities have received millions of dollars of heavily militarized equipment; and the categories of banned equipment were narrowly tailored to comprise a small fraction of controlled equipment—less than half a percent of all controlled equipment in circulation a month before the ban went into effect. As a result, many dangerous items escaped the ban.

At the time of this writing, the ACLU is calling on Congress to end the Department of Defense's 1033 program, the COPS (Community Oriented Policing Services) grants, and to rein in Byrne JAG (Justice Assistance Grant) grants.[58]

Since a percentage of Americans from all ethnic backgrounds across the country use illegal drugs every year, Michelle Alexander argued in 2010 the police could have made the decision to wage the drug war in many different places, including white suburbs or college campuses. Instead, the federal government, states, and law enforcement continue to racially profile entire Black communities with concentrated poverty and wage war against them.

The enduring racial isolation of the ghetto poor has made them uniquely vulnerable in the War on Drugs. What happens to them does not directly affect—and is scarcely noticed—by the privileged beyond the ghetto's invisible walls. Thus it is here, in the poverty-stricken, racially segregated ghettos, where the War on Poverty has been abandoned and factories have disappeared, that the drug war has been waged with the greatest ferocity. SWAT teams are deployed here; buy-and-bust operations are concentrated here; drug raids of apartment buildings occur here; stop-and-frisk operations occur on the streets here. Black and brown youth are the primary targets. It is not uncommon for a young black teenager living in a ghetto community to be stopped, interrogated, and frisked numerous times in the course of a month, or even a single week, often by paramilitary units.[59]

In 2020, in addition to the mobilization after George Floyd's brutal murder, Americans mobilized for justice for Breonna Taylor, a twenty-six-year-old Black medical technician who was killed in a botched no-knock warrant raid on her apartment shortly after midnight on March 2020 in Louisville, Kentucky. The three officers executing the warrant shot twenty-two bullets into Taylor's apartment building, one of which killed Taylor, and another wounded her boyfriend. The fact that people across the country not only took notice of the drug raid—which has become a common occurrence for Black residents in low-income neighborhoods—but also demanded accountability was notable and possibly a sign that larger numbers of Americans will no longer turn a blind eye to racial violence and discrimination in America's poorest neighborhoods.

Though the three officers involved in Taylor's murder were not convicted on state charges, the DOJ began its own pattern-or-practice investigation of the Louisville Police Department in April 2021. As a result, U.S. Attorney General Merrick Garland announced in August 2022 the DOJ had filed charges against four former and current Louisville police officers, which included civil rights offenses, unlawful conspiracies, unconstitutional use of force, and obstruction offenses. Among the allegations were that former Louisville detective Kelly Goodlett and Sergeant Kyle Meany falsified the affidavit used to search Taylor's apartment looking for drugs and conspired to lie to cover up the truth.

Taylor's case and Floyd's murder are indicative of the larger scourge of police violence and corruption used to carry out the war on drugs. My hope is to shed light on the covert and overt actions the federal, state, and city governmental organizations have taken for decades in the name of public safety. Like the civil rights activists who put their bodies on the line to protest segregation, the peace activists who risked their freedom to oppose the Vietnam War, and the protesters during the summer of 2020 who risked their safety and freedom to protest racial injustice, everyday Americans must act to end the atrocities committed against, and racist policies that target, African Americans. It's time to end the drug war, demilitarize the police, and finally invest in poor communities, especially Black communities, across the country.

Chapter 5
The Opioid Crisis

> It is impossible to speak honestly about mass incarceration without also speaking of the war on drugs. And it's impossible to speak honestly about the war on drugs without addressing the opioid crisis.
>
> —Patrick Radden Keefe, *Empire of Pain*[1]

On July 20, 2007, Ed Bisch and a group made up of other grieving parents, spouses, and friends who had lost loved ones to opioids convened in a courthouse in Abingdon, a small town in southwestern Virginia. Bisch and the others gathered to witness the sentencing of the men believed to have played a role in their loved ones' drug overdose deaths. From a rally at a nearby park where the group congregated, Bisch led them to the courthouse carrying a sign that read, "OXY KILL$."[2]

Six years earlier, Bisch's life changed forever on President's Day in 2001, when, while at work, he got a frantic call from his daughter. That morning she had found her brother, Eddie, bluish and unresponsive. The night before, she'd seen him incoherent in the bathroom. But when she had questioned him, he blamed it on drinking too much. By the time Bisch arrived home after his daughter's call, the paramedics told him that his son had died. Only eighteen years old, Eddie was a high school senior who played soccer, had decent grades, and planned to attend culinary school after graduation.[3]

Bisch relayed how he frantically asked Eddie's high school friends who had gathered at his house what happened to Eddie, causing his death. When one of the friends replied, "An Oxy," Bisch shouted, "What the hell is an Oxy?"[4]

Patrick Radden Keefe traces the origin of "Oxy" and the opioid crisis to Purdue Pharma, a company owned by the Sackler family, in his book *Empire of Pain: The Secret History of the Sackler Dynasty*. "In 1996, Purdue had introduced a groundbreaking drug," wrote Keefe, "a powerful opioid painkiller called OxyContin, which was heralded as a revolutionary way to treat chronic pain. The drug became one of the biggest blockbusters in pharmaceutical history, generating some $35 billion in revenue."[5]

The American government spends so much money and manpower to fight the "drug war," yet this chapter will reveal the stark difference between the way the legal system treats wealthy white executives selling and distributing opioids and Black American drug dealers and users. The harm caused by the opioid crisis is in many ways even more far-reaching, deadly, and costly than the crack epidemic. Yet those responsible for the crisis have largely not faced any criminal repercussions. There are two legal systems in this country: one for the poor and another for the rich; one for wealthy white Americans and another for Black people. People are using drugs and dying of overdoses at the level of an epidemic. As we'll see in this chapter, for all the trillions of dollars the government has spent to wage the drug war, those efforts have failed.

Since 1999, more than 600,000 people have died from opioid overdoses in the United States and Canada; and without intervention, 1.2 million more are estimated to die due to overdose by 2029.[6] From 1999 to 2020, nearly the same number of Americans died due to the opioid crisis—263,000—as were killed during World War II.[7] In 2020, fatal opioid overdoses reached 70,029 deaths in the United States, a record high until it was surpassed in 2021 with 80,816 deaths.[8] Howard Koh, professor of the practice of public health leadership at Harvard University, stated, "The current opioid crisis ranks as one of the most devastating public health catastrophes of our time."[9]

According to the U.S. Centers for Disease Control and Prevention, in 2017 alone, "fatal opioid overdoses and opioid use disorder cost the United States $1.02 trillion."[10] Beth Macy, a journalist covering the opioid crisis for decades, explains that opioid use disorder "is a lifelong and typically relapse-filled disease." While 40 to 60 percent of people with the disorder "can achieve remission with medication-assisted treatment, according to 2017 statistics . . . sustained remission can take as long as ten or more years."[11]

For Bisch and the others gathered at the courthouse in 2007, justice was not served. The three Purdue Pharma executives—Michael Friedman, the company's former president; Howard R. Udell, who was its top lawyer; and Dr. Paul D. Goldenheim, its former medical director[12]— were each criminally charged with a single misdemeanor instead of the prosecution-recommended felonies. The men were given sentences of probation, community service, and fines.

Neither Purdue Pharma nor the Sackler family faced legal ramifications. Instead, the company continued its aggressive marketing of OxyContin (and the generic version of the drug an affiliated Sackler-owned company made), and earned billions of dollars more as an unprecedented number of Americans became mired in addiction and succumbed to overdoses. In April 2021, the House Committee on Oversight and Reform reported that the Sackler family had built an enormous fortune valued at $11.1 billion, "in large part through the sale of OxyContin."[13]

At rallies in 2022, former president Donald Trump repeatedly called for drug dealers to be put to death. On September 3 in Pennsylvania, Trump said, "'Under Democrat control the streets of our great cities are drenched in the blood of innocent victims,' . . . and . . . drug dealers were responsible for killing hundreds of people every year." He called for the death penalty for drug dealers, which "he claimed would 'reduce drug distribution in our country on day one by 75%' and 'save millions of lives.'" While the *Business Insider* article stated that Trump pardoned the sentences of some people who had been convicted of drug crimes during his tenure as president,[14] it failed to mention that his deputy attorney general, Jeffrey Rosen, declined to criminally prosecute Purdue Pharma or its owners in 2020, though its painkiller had directly or inadvertently caused hundreds of thousands of American opioid-related deaths.

Based on the derogatory comments Trump has made about communities of color, his attack on drug dealers is most likely directed at people who sell drugs who are not white and do not live in suburban and rural areas. Trump may be ignorant that the opioid crisis has changed the demographics of people who are using, selling, and dying from drugs; some of the communities hardest hit by the opioid crisis are home to his white supporters. Take, for example, Idaho, which according to the 2020 Census had a population that was 81.1 percent white (not Hispanic or Latino) and .9 percent Black.[15] It has the highest incarceration rate of women in the country. While the number of people serving time for violent offenses in Idaho's prisons was the lowest in the country (27 percent), the state had the highest percentage (33 percent) of people who were convicted of drug-related charges.[16] Nationally, while Black women are still imprisoned at a rate that is 1.7 times higher than white women, according to the Sentencing Project, between "2000 and 2020, the rate of imprisonment in state and federal prisons declined by 68% for Black women, while the rate of imprisonment for white women rose by 12%."[17] Similarly for all Americans, the rate of imprisonment fell the most for Black Americans (37 percent), followed by Hispanics and Asians, native Hawaiians, and other Pacific Islanders (32 percent), and least among whites (26 percent) and American Indians and Alaskan natives (25 percent) during the same period.[18]

According to a report by the Council on Criminal Justice,[19] during that same period, the gap narrowed between Black and white incarceration rates with the largest decrease in drug crimes:

> Black–White disparity in imprisonment rates fell in each of four major offense categories over the study period—violent, property, drug, and public order (a broad category that includes obstruction of justice, liquor law violations, bribery, disorderly conduct, DUI/DWI, and weapons possession). The largest decrease occurred for drug crimes. . . . Black–White disparity in drug imprisonment rates fell by 75%, from 15 in 2000 to 3.6 in 2019.

While the reduction in disparity between Black and white incarceration rates is welcome news for Black people, part of that narrowing was a result of the white incarceration rate increasing because of opioid-related drug crimes—not a positive development. Specifically, from 2000 to 2005, when the first wave of the opioid crisis began, the white imprisonment rate increased at an average rate of 2.6 percent per year and the Black rate declined by an average rate of 1.7 percent per year.

In *Dopesick: Dealers, Doctors, and the Drug Company That Addicted America*, on which the Hulu minseries *Dopesick* was based, author Beth Macy outlines how the opioid crisis started in Appalachian communities already reeling from the closure of coal mines and mills and later the shuttering of factories after the North American Free Trade Agreement resulted in American corporations closing shop in the United States and moving overseas for larger corporate gains. The Appalachian region, comprising 205,000 square miles, covers 420 counties in all of West Virginia and parts of Alabama, Georgia, Kentucky, Maryland, Mississippi, New York, North Carolina, Ohio, Pennsylvania, South Carolina, Tennessee, and Virginia.[20] This is reminiscent of the way the crack cocaine epidemic hit Black communities the hardest, as they reeled from deindustrialization and white flight in the 1980s and '90s.

When President Lyndon Johnson visited the Appalachian region on April 24, 1964, he aimed to generate support for his proposed War on Poverty. At that time, over a third of the population faced chronic unemployment, and the poverty rate was more than 60 percent. During the visit, Johnson made a stop at the home of Tom Fletcher in Martin County, Kentucky. Fletcher, an unemployed sawmill operator with a wife and eight children, had earned only $400 the previous year and hadn't been able to find gainful employment for at least two years. Johnson's War on Poverty led to the creation of Medicaid, Medicare, Head Start, food stamps, and increased federal dollars for education. Despite the changes, on the fiftieth anniversary of the launch of the War on Poverty in 2014, Martin County remained one of the poorest counties in the country, with a poverty rate of 35 percent, more than twice the national average; high unemployment; and low educational attainment, with only 9 percent of adults earning a college degree.[21] From 1980 to 2010, the difference in life expectancy between Americans from the poorest fifth by income and the richest fifth widened by thirteen years. A contributing factor is that overdose mortality rates in Appalachia were 65 percent higher than the rest of the country.[22]

As Macy explains, when the opioid crisis began in the late 1990s, the Appalachian region "held national records for obesity, disability rates, and drug diversion, the practice of using and/or selling prescriptions for non-medical purposes."[23] The epidemic that started with the introduction of OxyContin in 1996 morphed into a heroin crisis in the mid-2000s.[24] Yet unlike the fate of Black drug dealers, who were incarcerated for selling crack and marijuana in Black neighborhoods, the fate of the manufacturers, sellers, and distributors of OxyContin would be vastly different.

To understand the trajectory of prescription pills to the opioid epidemic, one must understand the history of OxyContin and the Sackler family, which Keefe meticulously documents in *Empire of Pain*. In 1952, Arthur Sackler purchased a small pharmaceutical company, Purdue Frederick, for $50,000, which he intended to be owned jointly with his two brothers, Mortimer and Raymond. All three brothers were doctors.[25] Arthur Sackler, who had earned most of his fortune in medical advertising, became wealthy in his position marketing the tranquilizers Librium and Valium for the drug company Roche. Keefe notes that by the time the addictive nature of the drugs was investigated by the Food and Drug Administration (FDA) in 1965 and Roche agreed to new controls on the drugs in 1972, millions of Americans had become addicted—a history that would repeat itself with OxyContin, which was created by Arthur's young relatives with Purdue Pharma decades later. Keefe notes the irony that "moral panics over drugs had tended to focus on street drugs and to play on fears about minority groups, immigrants, and illicit influences; the idea that you could get hooked on a pill that was prescribed to you by a physician in a white coat with a stethoscope around his neck and a diploma on the wall was somewhat new."[26]

In the late 1970s, Mortimer, a Sackler partner who worked at Napp Laboratories in the United Kingdom, acquired by the Sacklers in 1966, oversaw the release of MS Contin, a pill form of morphine that slowly released into the body. Purdue Frederick then released MS Contin in the U.S. marketplace in 1984,[27] which would generate $170 million a year in sales.[28]

By 1990, additional Sackler relatives joined the Purdue Frederick board, and in 1991 the Sackler children created the company Purdue Pharma. Between 1993 and 2002, Richard Sackler was the company's president, and the company was developing a new drug, OxyContin. Richard wanted to extend the reach of the new pain pill beyond (traditionally) cancer patients to people experiencing other types of pain, such as back pain, neck pain, arthritis, and fibromyalgia.[29]

To secure the needed FDA approval of OxyContin, Purdue Pharma needed the drug's approval by Curtis Wright, who oversaw pain medication at the FDA. Though it was a strong opioid that was two times stronger than MS Contin, OxyContin was not tested by Purdue to determine its addictive properties. Instead, Purdue argued the Contin coating on the pill would "obviate the risk of addiction" because the drug would be released slowly into the bloodstream over twelve hours instead of instantly released.

Though Curtis Wright cautioned against Purdue claiming its drug was safer than other painkillers and some of Wright's FDA colleagues strongly believed opioids should not be used for nonmalignant pain, Purdue prevailed in the language it drafted for the package insert, information that accompanied each bottle. Later when lawsuits revealed the widespread addictiveness and abuse of OxyContin, no Purdue employee would take responsibility for writing the company's line that made it onto the final product approved by the FDA on December 28, 1995: "Delayed absorption, as provided by OxyContin tablets, is believed to reduce the abuse liability of the drug." There was no scientific research to back that claim up. Less than a year and a half after he argued for the approval of OxyContin by the FDA, Wright started a new position at Purdue Pharma "with a first-year compensation package of nearly $400,000."[30]

Not only did the packet insert contain information without scientific backing, but Purdue Pharma trained its sales representatives to assuage doctor's concerns about potential addiction and reassure them that iatrogenic (or doctor-caused) addiction was extremely rare. In a medical research paper, Art Van Zee, M.D., who was one of the earliest medical voices to raise red flags about the negative effects of OxyContin in Appalachia, wrote:

> Purdue trained its sales representatives to carry the message that the risk of addiction was "less than one percent." The company cited studies by Porter and Jick, who found iatrogenic addiction in only 4 of 11,882 patients using opioids and by Perry and Heidrich, who found no addiction among 10,000 burn patients treated with opioids. Both of these studies, although shedding some light on the risk of addiction for acute pain, do not help establish the risk of iatrogenic addiction when opioids are used daily for a prolonged time in treating chronic pain. There are a

number of studies, however, that demonstrate that in the treatment of chronic non-cancer-related pain with opioids, there is a high incidence of prescription drug abuse. . . . A recent literature review showed that the prevalence of addiction in patients with long-term opioid treatment for chronic non-cancer-related pain varied from 0% to 50%, depending on the criteria used and the subpopulation studied.[31]

As early as 1997, only a month or two after pharmacies in the Appalachian region started selling the prescription drug, Lieutenant Richard Stallard in Wise County, Virginia, was told by an informant about the abuse of OxyContin. Some taking Oxy learned to melt the Contin coating in their mouths and access the pure oxycodone in the pill, which also could be crushed, snorted, or injected. Macy described the "euphoria was immediate and intense, with a purity similar to that of heroin."[32]

According to Keefe, years later, when Purdue Pharma was under investigation, it was uncovered that Purdue had been receiving notes from its own salespeople as early as 1997 informing the company that abuse was happening. The sales representatives' field reports from 1997 through 1999 "had hundreds of references to words like 'street value,' 'snort,' and 'crush.'"[33] However, Purdue Pharma's sales reps were coached to give doctors a carefully scripted presentation that OxyContin was the painkiller "to start with and to stay with."[34] It's important to note that a person is at risk of becoming addicted to opioids after only three to five days of taking a painkiller like OxyContin even when it is taken as prescribed.

Similar to the ways drug markets in Black neighborhoods targeted people suffering from poverty and high unemployment, Macy explains how well trained the Purdue sales representatives were at targeting doctors in areas like the former coal mines, which already had high rates of people on disability from work-related injuries.

From a sales perspective, OxyContin had its greatest early success in rural, small-town America—already full of shuttered factories and Dollar General stores, along with burgeoning disability claims. Purdue handpicked the physicians who were most susceptible to their marketing, using information it bought from a data-mining network, IMS Health, to determine which doctors in which towns prescribed the most competing painkillers. If a doctor was already prescribing lots of Percocet and Vicodin, a rep was sent out to deliver a pitch about OxyContin's potency and longer-lasting action.[35]

The sales push immediately proved successful. Purdue's OxyContin profits doubled year after year and by 2000 had grown to almost $1.1 billion. Primary care physicians were prescribing the pain medication to their patients, which resulted in a nearly tenfold increase in OxyContin prescriptions for non-cancer-related pain management.[36]

Purdue's aggressive sales tactics resulted in abuse of OxyContin in the Appalachian region. Keefe writes,

> The abuse spread, quickly, like some airborne virus, from one small community to the next. The regions where the problem began often had large numbers of people who were out of work, or who worked hard, manual-labor jobs, people who were disabled or chronically ill, people who were suffering from pain. As it happened, these were also precisely the kinds of regions that Steven May and other Purdue sales reps had targeted—regions that the IMS data told them would be fertile terrain for OxyContin. In some cases, these communities also happened to have long-standing problems with prescription drug abuse. In some parts of Appalachia, people would pair an OxyContin with a Valium— one of Richard Sackler's pills and one of his uncle Arthur's. They called this "the Cadillac high."[37]

Similar to how crack cocaine and marijuana sales spurred an illicit economy in Black neighborhoods, the Purdue drug quickly flooded Appalachian communities, where gainful employment was scarce.[38]

The first instances of protest against Purdue Pharma and its deadly new drug emerged in Pennington Gap, Virginia. There, Dr. Art Van Zee, who saw the addictiveness of patients prescribed the painkiller and teenagers abusing it; Sister Beth Davies, a Catholic religious who ran the Addiction Education Center in the community; and attorney Sue Ella

Kobak, who was married to Van Zee, warned of an impending crisis. According to journalist Barry Meier, who wrote about the three activists in the first book to expose the opioid crisis, *Pain Killer*, in 2003, and continues to cover the opioid crisis, "Both Sister Beth and Ms. Kobak had previously taken on fights" in the Appalachian community "to protect the rights of workers and the environment."[39] However, they would soon learn Purdue Pharma was even more powerful, wealthy, and politically connected than the mining companies.

After Dr. Van Zee's initial letter-writing campaign to Purdue Pharma executives urging the company to reduce its marketing of the drug went ignored, Macy explains that in early 2001, Van Zee teamed with the Lee County Coalition for Health to launch a petition drive urging the FDA to recall OxyContin.[40] The petition received more than ten thousand signatures, and finally got the attention of Purdue Pharma, who flew executives to Pennington Gap for a meeting with Van Zee, Davies, Kobak, and others. The executives tried to convince the locals to drop the recall petition and offered $100,000 toward addiction treatment for the community. However, Sr. Davies was the loudest opponent to denounce what she considered "blood money," and the offer was rejected.[41]

A month later, in a move that in hindsight was almost as egregious as the FDA approval of the packet insert, the Drug Enforcement Agency asked Purdue Pharma to reign itself in, which was a first in the agency's history. In response, the company announced a plan to combat abuse and stopped distributing its strongest pill, the 160-milligram pill.[42]

In July 2001, the FDA announced it had put a "black-box warning" on OxyContin; in truth, that action did little to stem the sale and abuse of the drug or the windfall profits both Purdue Pharma and its sales reps were bringing in. At that time, Purdue reps could make as much as $100,000 a quarter in bonus pay. For its part, Purdue Pharma officially pushed back on claims that its drug was the issue; instead, the company kept to the line that OxyContin was a perfectly safe drug that provided pain relief to suffering patients, and drug abuse was a separate issue of drug users behaving illegally that needed to be addressed by law enforcement.[43]

In August 28, 2000, Purdue Pharma executives were among others in law enforcement, the medical community, attorneys general, district attorneys, and pain sufferers who testified before Congress in a hearing "Oxycontin: Its Use and Abuse." At that time, according to the DEA, the number of Oxycodone-related deaths had increased 400 percent since 1996, and the annual number of prescriptions for OxyContin had risen from approximately three hundred thousand to almost six million. Law enforcement blamed Purdue Pharma for its aggressive marketing of the drug and the drug's unprecedented potency, which led to abuse. Terrence Woodworth, from the DEA, stated, "While OxyContin diversion and abuse appear to have begun more in rural areas, such as Appalachia, it now has spread to urban areas." Andrew Demarest, senior deputy attorney general, testified about how OxyContin contributed to rising street crime in Pennsylvania:

> The distribution scheme that is illegal in the State is seen in the following circumstances: A doctor who fraudulently prescribes OxyContin to abusers for money. A pharmacist who illegally fills an abuser's prescription, or who forges prescriptions for abusers. Abusers who steal prescription pads, and then write their own forged prescriptions. And a phenomenon we call doctor-shopping. That is individuals that go from doctor to doctor faking illness to obtain several prescriptions of the same drug. Dealers or abusers also who then burglarize pharmacies. And we have had several armed robberies across the States of individuals breaking into pharmacies and seizing OxyContin at gun point.[44]

With the Oyxcontin-related death toll, abuse, street crime, and legal troubles mounting, in 2002 Purdue Pharma hired Rudy Giuliani and his consulting firm, Giuliani Partners, to help convince public officials that the company was trustworthy. With his reputation as "America's Mayor" after his handling of the September 11 terrorist attacks, Giuliani was seen as "a highly credible and well-connected political figure," who had just been on *Time* magazine's cover as the Man of the Year in 2001. In his legal role for Purdue, he met with the Drug Enforcement Administration and monitored security improvements at facilities that made the drug,[45] which was a source of contention for several top DEA staffers who wanted to impose severe sanctions on Purdue and even possibly restrict OxyContin's production.[46]

The *New York Times* stated, "Giuliani helped the company win several public relations battles, playing a role in an effort by Purdue to persuade an influential Pennsylvania congressman, Curt Weldon, not to blame it for OxyContin abuse," and though neither Giuliani nor his firm would confirm how much Purdue paid them in compensation, "one consultant to the drugmaker estimated that Mr. Giuliani's firm had, in some years, earned several million dollars from the account."[47]

While Purdue's legal team was securing victories in the multitude of civil lawsuits against the company, prosecutors in western Virginia had been quietly investigating Purdue Pharma since 2002—not for another civil suit—but for criminal prosecution. When John L. Brownlee was sworn in as U.S. Attorney for the Western District of Virginia on August 30, 2001, "his state was awash in OxyContin." The investigation led by Brownlee uncovered damning evidence that Purdue knew that OxyContin did not work as it was advertised, that patients who stopped using the drug experienced withdrawal symptoms, that people could shoot the drug intravenously after dissolving the pills in liquid, and that company supervisors coached sales representatives to make claims that Purdue officials knew were false.[48]

In a secret prosecution memo dated September 28, 2006, Assistant U.S. Attorney Rick Mountcastle detailed all of the incriminating evidence the prosecutors had found on Purdue Pharma over the five-year investigation. Keefe describes the memo that was over a hundred pages long:

> The memo was an incendiary catalog of corporate malfeasance. It wasn't just that it spelled out a litany of prosecutable misdeeds: it substantiated, in forensic detail, the knowledge and direction of those misdeeds at the highest levels of Purdue. "The conspirators trained Purdue's sales force, and provided them with training and marketing materials" to make fraudulent claims, the memo asserted. The sworn testimony of Friedman, Goldenheim, and Udell was flatly contradicted by the company's own documents, the report noted. The prosecutors did not mince words: the Purdue executives had testified "falsely and fraudulently" to Congress.
> ... The prosecution memo told the story of an intricate, yearslong, extraordinarily profitable criminal conspiracy. The company's records indicated that Purdue had already sold more than $9

billion of OxyContin. So, in addition to felony charges against the business and its senior executives, the prosecutors would demand a fine. They debated what a reasonable number would be, and any demand would be subject to intense negotiation with the defendants. But it was decided that the number they would put on the table was $1.6 billion.[49]

Though Dr. Van Zee was unable to attend, Sr. Davies and Ms. Kobak joined Ed Bisch and grieving family members and activists at the criminal sentencing of the Purdue executives in 2007. Not one executive incurred felony charges, however, and Purdue was not fined the suggested billion dollars plus. Instead, the "company pleaded guilty to felony misbranding of OxyContin with the intent to defraud and mislead, while its president, chief legal officer and former chief medical officer pleaded guilty to a misdemeanor charge of misbranding."[50]

Ed Bisch and the other opponents of the plea agreement voiced their opposition to the company's "free pass." As part of the plea agreement, none of the executives was sentenced to jail, even as parents who had lost their children to OxyContin attributed the misdemeanor pleas to Giuliani's influence.[51] The company's fine of $634.5 million was a fraction of the $2.8 billion Purdue had earned from the drug by 2007.

To add insult to injury, at the hearing the Purdue attorneys argued that the three executives were outstanding citizens who had done no harm. Letters of support from the men's friends and colleagues attested to their stellar reputations. The message conveyed was: wealthy white executives did not belong in prison.[52] As scores of Black people were locked in cages for simply *possessing* marijuana, the white executives who had made millions of dollars from selling OxyContin did not face a single day behind bars.

To soften the prosecution of Purdue, the pharmaceutical company went past Giuliani and appealed directly to senior officials at the Department of Justice. Purdue's attorneys argued Brownlee's team was being overzealous, and it was inappropriate for the executives to be charged with felonies when it was actually "rogue sales reps" who were responsible for the fraudulent drug marketing. After the meeting, Brownlee was told felony charges would not be sought against the three executives. Though sending the executives to jail likely would have influenced the way all drugmakers conducted business, the outcome of the criminal prosecution demonstrated the influence of Purdue Pharma on Washington, the FDA, and the Department of Justice. Purdue paid more than $50 million for its legal defense.[53]

What was even more egregious about the backroom deal was that Purdue Pharma did not plead guilty to the felony charge of misbranding. If it had done so, the company would have been barred from conducting business with government-funded programs like Medicare. Instead, it was agreed that only the legacy company, Purdue Frederick, would enter the guilty plea.[54] The vast majority of Black people who have spent decades—or even life—in prison for selling drugs did not have the money or political capital to negotiate or selectively choose their penalty as Purdue Pharma did. Yet, not penalizing Purdue Pharma enabled the company to continue selling its drug and ensnaring hundreds of thousands more people in opioid addiction.

In a 2019 interview, Dr. Van Zee, Sr. Davies, and Ms. Kobak told Barry Meier they "believe that the Justice Department could have changed the behavior of other opioid makers if it had charged executives of Purdue Pharma in 2007 with felonies, as federal prosecutors had recommended." Dr. Van Zee stated, "I think the trajectory would have been completely different. . . . It would not have reached the magnitude that it did." Without setting a precedent in the 2007 criminal case, the years that followed saw the opioid crisis balloon into a national crisis as "executives of other opioid makers and distributors kept shipping millions of addictive pain pills . . . apparently without fear of serious penalties."[55]

A 2022 opioid settlement with four large U.S. corporations in the sum of $26 billion attests to the *de minimis* role the 2007 plea agreement had in stemming the tide of opioid abuse. Johnson & Johnson, a company that manufactured generic opioid medications, agreed to pay $5 billion and "get out of the prescription opioid business in the U.S. altogether."[56] J&J manufactured the opioid drug Nucynta as well as the fentanyl patch Duragesic, which had also received scrutiny from the FDA because of its misleading marketing claims. Beginning in 1994, the company also developed and grew in the Australian island state of Tasmania the "Norman Poppy," which "once accounted for as much as 80% of the global supply for oxycodone raw materials."[57]

In addition, AmerisourceBergen, Cardinal Health, and McKesson are three large drug wholesalers who agreed to pay $21 billion combined. The "settlement resolves thousands of civil lawsuits filed against the companies beginning in 2014 by local and state governments as well as Native American tribes nationwide" and "will provide thousands of communities across the United States with up to approximately $19.5 billion over 18 years" to help devastated communities in all fifty states start to rebuild and "deal with this epidemic."[58]

For all the billions of dollars to be paid by wealthy drug companies and wholesalers, none of those executives or owners faced jail or prison time or held a criminal record. Unlike the scores of Black Americans prosecuted during the war on drugs for use and sale of drugs who faced long sentences and life-long repercussions from criminal records, the wealthy, overwhelmingly white Americans who profited from the opioid crisis did not suffer the same fate. According to Pew Charitable Trust, there was a "1,216% increase in the state prison population for drug offenses, from 19,000 to 250,000 between 1980 and 2008."[59] Even as recently as 2020, there were 40,000 people incarcerated for marijuana offenses.[60]

The actions Purdue Pharma would take in 2010 to reformulate Oxy-Contin resulted in the second wave of the opioid crisis, which was the explosion of people addicted to heroin. According to a working paper published by the National Bureau of Economic Research by a team of economists from the University of Notre Dame and Boston College, in "early August 2010, the makers of OxyContin, Purdue Pharma, pulled the existing drug from the market and replaced it with an abuse-deterrent formulation (ADF) that made it difficult to abuse the drug in this fashion. This made the drug far less appealing to opioid abusers and led many to shift to a readily-available and cheaper substitute: heroin."

OxyContin contains the ingredient oxycodone, which is an opioid that has been in clinical use since 1917. The reformulated OxyContin pill could no longer be crushed and turned into a powder and instead would become "a gummy substance that was much more difficult to snort or inject." The same poppy plant that forms the base of oxycodone also is used to produce heroin. Because heroin was much cheaper and easier to obtain in 2010 than it had been over the previous thirty years, "many OxyContin abusers switched to heroin after the product reformulation" because they could no longer experience the same high from Purdue's drug.

Due to Purdue's aggressive marketing tactics, millions of people were addicted to the high that came with taking OxyContin at the time of the reformulation. The data in the National Bureau of Economic Research paper "indicates that outcomes such as deaths, poisonings, emergency room visits, and enrollments in treatment programs from heroin abuse have all increased since August of 2010." From the economists' findings, "80 percent of heroin users moved from pain medicine abuse to the illicit drug."[61]

Keefe explains how eerily smooth the transition from OxyContin to heroin was for many people, and how Purdue laid the groundwork for the coming heroin surge:

> For some users, the reformulation of OxyContin triggered a transition to other, more readily abusable prescription opioids. But many graduated to heroin instead. Chemically speaking, the two drugs were closely related. In some ways, heroin had always been the benchmark for OxyContin. The tremendous potency of Oxy led to its reputation as "heroin in a pill." When it first became popular as a recreational high in Appalachia, OxyContin acquired the nickname hillbilly heroin. So, it might have been only logical that when they could no longer count on OxyContin, people who already had an opioid use disorder would make the short segue to heroin itself.[62]

According to the CDC, "the third wave of the opioid crisis began in 2013, with significant increases in overdose deaths involving synthetic opioids, particularly those involving illicitly manufactured fentanyl. The market for illicitly manufactured fentanyl continues to change, and it can be found in combination with heroin, counterfeit pills, and cocaine."[63]

Early in the third wave of the opioid epidemic, illicit fentanyl was often ordered through the dark web and came from Chinese laboratories; now the majority of fentanyl comes to the United States from Mexico. "Traffickers, who relied for decades on plant-based drugs such as heroin, cocaine and marijuana, are now using chemicals in clandestine laboratories to manufacture fentanyl powder and pills to meet the ever-increasing demand in the United States." The manufactured opioid is fifty times more potent than heroin, "and its compactness makes it far easier to smuggle. The synthetic opioid is so powerful that a year's supply of pure fentanyl powder for the U.S. market would fit in the beds of two pickup trucks." Fentanyl can be manufactured in a lab in only a few days.[64]

As the toll of the opioid crisis mounted, a joint investigation by the Associated Press and the Center for Public Integrity published in installments in 2016 described the length to which drug companies went to sell their drugs and use their wealth to secure political immunity to do so. Purdue and other pharmaceutical companies that manufactured opioids had spent "more than $880 million nationwide on lobbying and campaign contributions from 2006 through 2015," eight times more than the gun lobby spent during that same period. As the addictive nature and danger of opioids became increasingly scrutinized and lawsuits against pharmaceutical companies swelled, "the drugmakers and allied advocacy groups employed an annual average of 1,350 lobbyists in legislative hubs" who exercised an undue influence on state legislatures, Congress, and regulators.[65]

According to Keefe, the drug companies' lobbying power touched every facet of government, from the DEA to the FDA, Congress to the Justice Department. "Between 1994 and 2015, the quota of oxycodone that the DEA permitted to be legally manufactured was raised thirty-six times. A subsequent report by the inspector general of the Justice Department criticized the DEA for being "slow to respond to the dramatic increase in opioid abuse."[66]

In a retrospective, cross-sectional analysis using the 2016 National Survey on Drug Abuse, it was found, "Individuals who reported any level of opioid use were significantly more likely than individuals who reported no opioid use to be white, have a low income, and report a chronic condition, disability, severe mental illness, or co-occurring drug use." As a result, while Black incarceration rates were declining, more white people became arrested, prosecuted, and incarcerated for committing drug crimes. The survey found, "any level of opioid use was associated with involvement in the criminal justice system in the past year compared with no opioid use." After accounting for "sociodemographic, health, and substance use differences," it was found that "more than half of individuals with a prescription opioid use disorder or heroin use in the past year reported contact with the criminal justice system. We found that, as the level of opioid use increased, involvement in the criminal justice system also increased after accounting for sociodemographic, health, and substance use differences."[67]

Another demographic shift fueled by the opioid crisis is the increase in women incarcerated for drug-related charges. National data and studies have shown that women from the United States and Canada are more likely to misuse or abuse prescription opioid medication than men, even though men have higher rates of death from opioid overdose. Contributing factors to the discrepancy include women having higher instances of chronic pain and more sensitivity to pain, women being more likely to visit a doctor, and women more likely to be prescribed opioids by their doctors. Other studies found a link between women's trauma, chronic pain, and opioid use.

Multiple studies provide evidence to support the link between trauma, chronic pain, and risk for prescription medication misuse. Women who have experienced abuse and violence are more likely to experience chronic pain. A study involving female survivors of IPV [intimate partner violence] revealed that women who experienced IPV were at greater risk for chronic pain, even in the absence of physical assault. In addition, women who had experienced lifetime abuse-related injury or childhood abuse were also more likely to experience chronic pain. Similarly, a study involving primarily Caucasian women in New England (US) found that women who reported domestic or child abuse were more likely to report chronic pain than women in the control group. A study involving female veterans in the US found that the majority of women reported chronic pain (78%) and that a history of sexual trauma was associated with greater severity of pain. In a descriptive study involving women who had separated from an abusive partner, over one-third reported high disability pain. Women reporting high disability pain were more likely to be using more than the prescribed dosages of opioids and nonsteroidal anti-inflammatory medications. High disability pain was also associated with sexual abuse, child abuse, depression, PTSD, suicide attempts, insomnia, unemployment, and medical visits.[68]

According to the Sentencing Project, "Between 1980 and 2020, the number of incarcerated women of all races increased by more than 475%, rising from a total of 26,326 in 1980 to 152,854 in 2020," a five-fold increase.[69] The Prison Policy Initiative states that of those women, 57 percent in prison and 80 percent in jails are also mothers.

> Most of these women are incarcerated for drug and property offenses, often stemming from poverty and/or substance use disorders. Most are also the primary caretakers of their children, meaning that punishing them with incarceration tears their children away from a vital source of support. And these numbers don't cover the many women preparing to become mothers while locked up this year: An estimated 58,000 people every year are pregnant when they enter local jails or prisons.[70]

Though the opioid crisis has swept tens of thousands of white people into the criminal justice system, the owners of Purdue Pharma, the Sackler family, who created OxyContin, have been spared from criminal prosecution that would lead to imprisonment. Keefe details that in 2018, Massachusetts Attorney General Maura Healey filed what was the first lawsuit by a state specifically naming as defendants the eight Sackler family members who had served on Purdue's board. Massachusetts had been severely affected by opioids, and Healey had started investigating Purdue Pharma in 2015. Healey had harsh words for Purdue's attorney, Mary Jo White, who had been representing them since 2007. "Not that there isn't room to represent corporations, that's worthy work. But this corporation? These people? It's no different from representing a drug cartel, in my mind."[71]

Healey's 274-page complaint detailed how the Sacklers instructed their sales representatives to continue calling doctors who they knew were under criminal investigation related to their prescribing. One such doctor was a physician who prescribed more than 347,000 OxyContin pills in five years—200,000 of which were the 80-milligram dose. The doctor had given one patient a prescription for twenty-four 80-milligram pills a day for two years. Purdue gave that physician a $50,000 contract to give speeches before he lost his medical license.[72]

Letitia James, the New York attorney general, filed a lawsuit in March 2019 that also named Purdue Pharma and the Sackler family as well as a number of manufacturers including Johnson & Johnson and a number of distributors. James placed the blame for the start of the opioid crisis on Purdue and the Sacklers, stating, "The taproot of the opioid epidemic is easy to identify: OxyContin." In addition to alleging that Purdue launched a marketing campaign in 1996 "that relied on deception and insider payoff," James's complaint was the first to highlight that the Sacklers had fraudulently transferred billions of dollars from Purdue to offshore accounts after federal prosecutors began investigating them. At the time of filing the lawsuit, nine people were dying in New York State every day from opioid-related causes. The complaint stated, "These people are not—and cannot become—just statistics. They are our family, our friends, our neighbors. They are our fathers and our sons, our mothers and our daughters. They have real names and their deaths have left real, jagged holes in the fabric of the communities where they used to live."[73]

In September 2019, facing almost three thousand civil lawsuits, including from forty-eight states,[74] Purdue Pharma filed for bankruptcy. According to Keefe, Purdue Pharma effectively chose the bankruptcy judge who would oversee the case, Robert Drain, in White Plains, New York. Drain froze all the lawsuits against Purdue, which halted the trials that were set to begin in Ohio in a multistate case. Though the Sackler family had billions of dollars in personal wealth, they were able to file bankruptcy for their company, which James and Healey and other attorneys general protested, to no avail.[75]

Judge Drain set a deadline of July 30, 2020, for any additional claimants who wanted to join the bankruptcy proceedings as creditors. "More than a hundred thousand people filed individual claims, arguing that Purdue's opioids had upended their lives and that they should be entitled to some compensation." Insurance companies filed claims as well, including United Health, which claimed "hundreds of thousands" of its policyholders had been diagnosed with opioid-use disorder after being prescribed OxyContin. Even the Department of Justice filed a claim, stating that "civil and criminal investigations had revealed that between 2010 and 2018, Purdue sent sales reps to call on prescribers the company knew 'were facilitating medically unnecessary prescriptions'" and engaging in other criminal behavior like kickbacks to prescribers.[76]

Given that Purdue Pharma had repeated the criminal behavior it had pled to in 2007, the question became: would the federal government criminally charge Purdue Pharma executives with felonies? The answer came two weeks before the November 2020 election, when Jeffrey Rosen, President Trump's deputy attorney general, announced in a press conference there had been a global resolution of the federal investigation into Purdue Pharma and the Sackler family. The company would plead guilty to "conspiracy to defraud the United States and to violate the Food, Drug, and Cosmetic Acts, as well as to two counts of conspiracy to violate the federal Anti-kickback Statute."

Once again, no individual executives were charged criminally, let alone even mentioned. The federal penalties against the company totaled more than $8 billion, while the Sacklers agreed to pay $225 million to "resolve a separate civil charge that they had violated the False Claims Act." No criminal charges were filed against the Sackler family either. At the press conference, a reporter stated that the $225 million was only slightly over 2 percent of the $10 billion the family had taken out of the company, and another reporter asked Rosen if he tried to pursue that money. In reply Rosen stated, "There is no law that says if you've done something wrong we should just simply strip somebody of their assets.... That's not how it works."[77]

But for the millions of African Americans arrested and prosecuted for drug possession or for selling drugs that is exactly how it worked from the beginning of the war on drugs up to today. Black people disproportionately targeted by the drug war and incarcerated were literally stripped of everything down to the clothes on their backs and thrown into cages. And beyond incarceration, the repercussions of a drug conviction last long after a person is released from jail and prison, as they meet bans from public housing, welfare benefits, student loans, and many job opportunities. For Rosen to callously state that there are no laws that would punish the Sacklers, who made billions of dollars from a drug that started the opioid crisis, flies in the face of true justice.

After the initial bankruptcy deal was blocked, a $4.5 billion settlement was reached in 2022 that also resulted in the dissolution of Purdue

Pharma. The Sacklers will pay the $4.5 billion in installments over roughly nine years. According to the *New York Times*, the settlement will end the thousands of lawsuits against the company and family, "but the agreement includes a much-disputed condition: It largely absolves the Sacklers of Purdue's opioid-related liability. And as such, they will remain among the richest families in the country."

Though some of the Sackler money will come from their investments, a large amount will come from the sale of their international pharmaceutical companies—and will not touch their personal income. The money will go mainly to states for addiction treatment and prevention programs across the country, Native American tribes, and compensation to the "130,485 individuals and families of those who suffered from addiction or died from an overdose, in amounts ranging from $3,500 to $48,000. Guardians of about 6,550 children with a history of neonatal abstinence syndrome may each receive about $7,000." Dr. Joshua Sharfstein, a professor at the Johns Hopkins Bloomberg School of Public Health, stated, "I don't think anybody would say that justice has been done because there's just so much harm that was caused, and so much money that has been retained by the company and by the family."[78]

The opioid crisis is a rude awakening that the war on drugs completely failed either to stop the sale of drugs or to stem the number of Americans using drugs. According to the CDC, since 1999 more than 932,000 Americans have died from a drug overdose.[79] An investigative report by the *Washington Post* found that two-thirds of the 107,622 overdose deaths in 2021 in the United States were caused by fentanyl. That is a 94 percent increase from only 2019. Fentanyl kills more people than automobile accidents, gunshots, or suicides.[80] As of December 2022, fentanyl is the leading cause of death for Americans of ages eighteen to forty-nine. "More people have died of synthetic-opioid overdoses than the number of U.S. military personnel killed during the Vietnam, Iraq and Afghanistan wars combined."[81]

Similar to the transition from OxyContin to heroin after its reformulation, fentanyl, which was originally created in 1960 by the Belgian physician Paul Jannsen in a lab to be used to treat extreme pain and administered through an IV, became abused for its potent high.

The drug is cheaper than ever because supplies are so abundant. On the streets of U.S. cities in the early 2000s, the most popular prescription pain pill was made by Mallinckrodt Pharmaceuticals, one of the nation's oldest drug manufacturers. The company's 30-milligram oxycodone tablets, known as "blues" or "M-30s," sold for roughly $30 apiece on the black market. Today, fake M-30s made by Mexican cartels using fentanyl look identical but sell for $4 or $5 apiece on the streets of San Diego, and can be especially lethal to first-time users.[82]

In 2017, a ten-month-old became San Diego's youngest opioid fatality after he swallowed a bright blue pill he found on the bed where he sat between his two sleeping parents.

The *Washington Post*'s investigative series[83] highlights that the opioid crisis has spanned four presidential administrations now, with each president contributing to the problem.

The roots of the epidemic reach back to the Bush administration, which did little as countless Americans became addicted to oxycodone and other prescription opioids while U.S. drug manufacturers, distributors and chain pharmacies made billions in profits.

During the Obama administration, amid a wider questioning of the U.S. criminal justice system, the government defunded and dismantled key drug-monitoring programs in the years before fentanyl hit. President Barack Obama demoted the White House drug czar position, removing the role from the Cabinet. And when heroin use rose after the government crackdown on prescription opioids, authorities treated fentanyl as an additive, rather than a distinct threat requiring its own specific strategy.

For all of Trump's talk about executing drug dealers, the *Washington Post* outlines Trump's preoccupation with building a wall between Mexico and the United States that would have had no impact on the illegal drugs being transported via checkpoints at the border and further contributed to the explosion of the fentanyl crisis.

The Department of Homeland Security, whose agencies are responsible for detecting illegal drugs at the nation's borders, failed to ramp up scanning and inspection technology at official crossings, instead channeling $11 billion toward the construction of a border wall that does little to stop fentanyl traffickers.

Not only did Trump's administration continue to focus on China's exports of fentanyl instead of the emerging Mexican drug cartels beginning in 2017, which supplanted China as the main manufacturer and distributor of the synthetic opioid, but Trump also neglected the drug czar position, which would be tasked with responding to the growing crisis.

Soon after Trump became president, his administration proposed eliminating the drug czar's office entirely. It became a backwater for political appointees, many of them with scant or no drug policy expertise. A 23-year-old Trump campaign worker was named deputy chief of staff, but no one had been nominated to head the office. Nearly nine months into his presidency, Trump selected Rep. Tom Marino (R-Pa.)—a former federal prosecutor and one of Trump's first and most strident supporters in Congress—to be drug czar. But Marino soon withdrew his nomination after it was revealed in a joint *Washington Post*–"*60 Minutes*" investigation that he had co-sponsored legislation that made it more difficult for the DEA to hold drug manufacturers, distributors and pharmacies accountable when they violated federal law.

As the Trump administration was preparing to leave the White House in 2021, the drug czar's office issued its annual National Drug Control Strategy to Congress. The document is supposed to detail the government's plan to reduce drug demand and disrupt supply chains. But the 2021 strategy document was nearly identical to the one issued in 2020. Many of its sections had simply been copied from the previous year.

As the demographics of drug users in the country have changed to include more white Americans, so too has the country begun to shift the conversation and approach to the opioid crisis from a punitive position to one more focused on treatment and health. Beginning in 2014, 911 Good Samaritan and Naloxone Access laws were passed throughout the country, and now 47 states and Washington, DC, have enacted both to try and curb overdose deaths without criminal prosecution of the users. A HuffPost article discussed the motives behind the change:

> There are some who argue that the shift has to do with the danger and prevalence of prescription drugs, which are often abused by people of power and affluence. With the crack cocaine epidemic focused mostly in inner cities, or methamphetamine use most popular in poor rural areas, it was easy for people who make and enforce laws to crack down hard on drug users. But now, with drugs and overdose creeping into their own medicine cabinets, their own homes, with the suburban and middle class children of powerful people at risk, the laws are starting to change.[84]

In addition to the laws changing to protect people who use drugs from criminal punishment when they are seeking medical support, there has also been a sea change in the way the opioid crisis is portrayed by federal officials. Anne Milgram, who is the first Senate-confirmed DEA administrator since 2015, was sworn in on June 28, 2021. Milgram has taken a stance distancing the administration from the war on drugs.

> "This is not a war on drugs, this is a war to save lives," she said in a recent interview at DEA headquarters in Northern Virginia, where the lobby walls are covered with more than 4,000 portraits of fentanyl overdose victims sent in by their families. They are almost entirely young faces, many of them in their teens and 20s. "When you look at the faces, you have a sense of the enormity of what we're losing," Milgram said.[85]

Of course, there was no wall in the DEA headquarters filled with Black faces who used crack cocaine when it flooded inner-city neighbor-hoods. There was no sympathy for people who were called "crackheads," "crack whores," and "crack babies." There were no investigative reports tracing where exactly this new and potent drug was coming from. There was only stringent punishment, incarceration, shame, and derision for both African American drug users and those who sold drugs.

Systemic racism in the medical field actually spared African Americans from the first wave of the opioid epidemic. Doctors were less likely to prescribe opioid pain medication to Black people. Since the second wave in 2010, however, "opioid and stimulant deaths have increased 575 percent among Black Americans." Since 2019, the rate of Black people dying from overall drug overdoses exceeded that of white people for the first time (36.8 versus 31.6 per 100,000). The third wave has brought even more death with Black men aged fifty-five and older who had lived with heroin addiction for years now overdosing from fentanyl at rates "four times greater than people of other races in that age group." Research shows the discrepancy is due to racial inequities that result in Black people having more difficulty entering treatment programs and who are less likely to receive medications that treat substance use disorders.[86]

It's time to end the war on drugs, examine the commutation of long sentences for drug-related offenses, and redirect funds from policing and incarceration toward substance use disorder treatment and drug-prevention programs. In 2019, more than 1.56 million people were arrested for a drug-related crime than for any other offense. Out of that number, a vast majority (1.35 million) were arrested for possession. Yet, there were still arrests for property crime (1.07 million), simple assault (1.03 million), DUI (1.02 million), and violent crime (500,000), all adding to jail and prison populations.[87] Federal, state, and local policies, both past and present, have disproportionately targeted and incarcerated in this prison pipeline Black, poor, and unwell people, and this I unpack in the next chapter.

Chapter 6

Prison Pipelines

Plenty of room for dives and dens,
Glitter and glare and sin;
Plenty of room for prison pens,
Gather the criminals in;
Plenty of room for jails and courts
Willing enough to pay;
But never a place for lads to race,
No never a place to play.
Plenty of room for shops and stores,
Mammon must have the best;
Plenty of room for the running sores
That rot in the city's breast;
Plenty of room for the lures that lead
The hearts of our youth astray;
But never a cent on a playground spent,
No never a place to play.

S. Waters McGill (1916)[1]

In the early 1900s, Willa and Charles Bruce moved with their son, Harvey, to California from New Mexico. They heard about the vibrant, growing Black communities in Southern California. Charles found work as a chef on the Union Pacific train route between Los Angeles and Salt Lake City. By 1912 they had the funds and found a beachfront property to purchase in Manhattan Beach, for which they paid $1,225. Later, they bought a second parcel of beachfront property. By 1920, the Bruces' Beach resort was a large structure with changing rooms, rooms for overnight guests, as well as a dining and a dance area.

During that time period in California, civil laws allowed Black people to move around freely, though the laws intended to protect Black individuals weren't always enforced. After the Bruces established their resort, white landowners and the city's founder, George Peck, hired police officers to rope off the area near the Bruces' resort, preventing Black people visiting the Bruces' resort from being able to access the water.

The success of Bruce's Beach spawned a Black community, and other Black people bought cottages nearby looking to escape the anti-Black racism they experienced in the South and other parts of the country. By the 1920s, however, the white population in Manhattan Beach wanted to remove the Black people from town. A proposal was written in 1922 to take the beachfront property owned by the Bruces and other properties owned by Black families through eminent domain. The city and the Ku Klux Klan started harassing the African Americans on those properties through various means, including burning crosses. Then in 1924, the city seized the Bruces' and other Black owners' beachfront land through eminent domain.[2]

Though in 1929 each of the displaced families received funds for their land, the Bruces, because of the racism they experienced, chose not to buy another parcel in Manhattan Beach. After the land was taken from the Bruces it lay unused until 1948 when it was transferred to the state. By 2022, and as the result of racism in what was once a thriving Black community, the demographics of the community had significantly changed, with now less than .5 percent of Manhattan Beach's population of thirty thousand being Black and 84 percent white.[3]

In the early 2020s, a Black Manhattan Beach resident, Kavon Ward, started Justice for Bruce's Beach. This, coupled with the decades-long activism by Bruce family descendants, turned the nation's attention toward the racist past of Manhattan Beach. Though there was opposition to restitution from white residents, and the Manhattan Beach city council voted against a formal apology to the Bruce family, in October 2021, Governor Gavin Newsom signed a law that allowed ownership of the Bruce property to be transferred back to the family.

In June 2022, the Los Angeles Board of Supervisors unanimously approved the transfer of the parcels in the area once known as Bruce's Beach back to the Bruce family.[4] Once back in the ownership of the

Bruce family, the property was sold to LA County for $20 million in early 2023. The Los Angeles County Board of Supervisors chair, Janice Hahn, stated that the proceeds of the sale would help the descendants of the original Bruce owners in "finally rebuilding the generational wealth they were denied for nearly a century."[5]

In order for us to understand why such a large percentage of low-income African Americans live in segregated neighborhoods, attend underperforming public schools, have fewer resources and wealth, and are excessively policed and incarcerated, we need to revisit the forgotten history of the anti-Black racism in housing and land ownership. In *Color of Law: A Forgotten History of How Our Government Segregated America,* Richard Rothstein provides evidence showing how "until the last quarter of the twentieth century, racially explicit policies of federal, state, and local governments defined where whites and African Americans should live."

> Today's residential segregation in the North, South, Midwest, and West is not the unintended consequence of individual choices and of otherwise well-meaning law or regulation but of unhidden public policy that explicitly segregated every metro-politan area in the United States. . . . Without our government's purposeful imposition of racial segregation, the other causes— private prejudice, white flight, real estate steering, bank redlin-ing, income differences, and self-segregations—still would have existed but with far less opportunity for expression. Segregation by intentional government action is not *de facto*. Rather, it is what courts call *de jure*: segregation by law and public policy.[6]

During the Great Depression in the 1930s and into the early 1950s, there was a serious shortage of housing for both white and African American working- and middle-class families. In response, President Frank-lin D. Roosevelt's New Deal created public housing for civilians that either segregated them by race or that completely excluded Black people. One such federal housing project effort was created by the Public Works Administration (PWA) with the goal of alleviating the national housing shortage by creating construction jobs. Of the forty-seven housing projects, seventeen were assigned to Black people, six had segregated buildings for Blacks and whites, and the remaining twenty-four were whites only.

Though the PWA established a "neighborhood composition rule that stated federal housing projects should reflect the racial composition of the neighborhoods, the agency often segregated projects in neighborhoods that were integrated before." Across the Northeast and Midwest, the PWA purposefully segregated formerly integrated communities, and the newly created Black communities lacked the many resources white ones had, including community centers, playgrounds, and green space. In cities like Detroit, Indianapolis, Toledo, and New York, the PWA concentrated African Americans into low-income neighborhoods through these housing projects.

Rothstein describes one such PWA project:

> The first PWA project, the Techwood Homes in Atlanta, opened in 1935. It was built on land cleared by demolishing the Flats, a low-income integrated neighborhood adjacent to downtown that had included 1600 families, nearly one-third of whom were African American. The PWA remade the neighborhood with 604 units for white families only. The Techwood project not only created a segregated white community, it also intensified the segregation of African American families, who, evicted from their homes, could find new housing only by crowding into other neighborhoods where African Americans were already living.[7]

Though Congress ended the PWA program in 1937, the newly created U.S. Housing Authority (USHA) continued the government's practice of segregating neighborhoods. After Congress adopted the Lanham Act in 1940 to finance housing for workers in defense industries, the government provided war housing only for white people, or segregated Black people in housing. According to Rothstein, by the time World War II ended, the Lanham Act, PWA, and USHA programs had resulted in residential segregation throughout the country. Housing authorities across the nation constructed housing developments that were whites- or Blacks-only.[8]

After the Second World War, with millions of Americans returning home from fighting abroad, the lack of housing reached crisis level. In 1949, when President Harry Truman proposed new public housing legislation, the Senate and House rejected amendments that would have prohibited segregation and racial discrimination and passed the Housing Act, which permitted local authorities to continue segregating housing projects by race.[9]

Though African Americans desperately needed housing, the government segregated them in high-rise projects that left them with little access to jobs and social services in white communities. Massive housing projects in Chicago, Philadelphia, New York City, and St. Louis were undertaken. In other states such as California, Iowa, Minnesota, Virginia, and Wisconsin, constitutional amendments were adopted in the 1950s that allowed middle-class white communities to systematically veto low-income public housing proposals.[10] In the previous chapter I explained how, in the absence of available living-wage jobs, African Americans concentrated in impoverished neighborhoods were more susceptible to engage in illicit trades in order to survive, which could lead to incarceration.

An investigative report of federally funded developments in forty-seven metropolitan areas in the *Dallas Morning News* in 1984 described just how effective and long-lasting the government policies of segregating housing projects were:

> The reporters found that the nation's nearly ten million public housing tenants were almost always segregated by race and that every predominantly white-occupied project had facilities, amenities, services, and maintenance that were superior to what was found in predominantly black-occupied projects.[11]

To accelerate the move of white Americans from public housing projects to buying and owning their own homes, the federal government made changes. The majority of working- and middle-class families could not afford to put 50 percent down nor repay the mortgage in five to seven years, as was standard at that time. To remedy this, in 1933, Roosevelt's administration created the Home Owners' Loan Corporation (HOLC).

In addition to purchasing existing mortgages that were at risk of default and foreclosure and issuing new mortgages with a new repayment schedule of fifteen to twenty-five years, the HOLC loans were amortized, so the monthly payments went toward the principal balance. This allowed working- and middle-class homeowners to gain equity and profit from homeownership.

Yet these federal loans were not available to all Americans. The HOLC assessed the risk of potential homeowners and their potential neighborhoods, using local real estate agents to make the appraisals. Rothstein explains how mostly white realtors were tasked with gauging risk, something negatively impacting African Americans' ability to become homeowners.

> The HOLC created color-coded maps of every metropolitan area in the nation, with the safest neighborhoods colored green and the riskiest colored red. A neighborhood earned a red color if African Americans lived in it, even if it was a solid middle-class neighborhood of single-family homes.
>
> For example, in St. Louis, the white middle-class suburb of Ladue was colored green because, according to an HOLC appraiser in 1940, it had "not a single foreigner or negro." The similarly middle-class suburban area of Lincoln Terrace was colored red because it had "little or no value today . . . due to the colored element now controlling the district." Although the HOLC did not always decline to rescue homeowners in neighborhoods colored red on its maps (i.e., redlined neighborhoods), the maps had a huge impact and put the federal government on record as judging that African Americans, simply because of their race, were poor risks.[12]

A year later, in 1934, Congress and Roosevelt's administration created the Federal Housing Administration (FHA), which "insured bank mortgages and covered 80 percent of purchase prices, had terms of twenty years, and were fully amortized." The FHA conducted its own appraisals to determine eligibility for potential buyers of the property. "Because the FHA's appraisal standards included a whites-only requirement, racial segregation now became an official requirement of the federal mortgage insurance program." Properties in racially integrated neighborhoods or even all-white neighborhoods in close proximity to Black ones that could possibly integrate were considered too risky for an FHA loan. To further cement the growth of all-white suburbs, the FHA "discouraged banks from making any loans at all in urban neighborhoods rather than newly built suburbs."[13] Throughout the country, the FHA policy refused to guarantee mortgages for African Americans regardless of their income or creditworthiness.

The newly established Veteran's Administration also began to guarantee mortgages for returning servicemen and adopted the FHA housing policies. "By 1950, the FHA and VA together were insuring half of all new mortgages nationwide." Thousands of suburban subdivisions in every metropolitan area across the country were mass-produced "with the FHA- or VA-imposed condition that these suburbs be all white."[14] Similarly, a commonplace commitment in deed clauses was the promise to never sell or rent to a person who was African American. It wasn't until President John F. Kennedy issued an executive order in 1962 "prohibiting the use of federal funds to support racial discrimination in housing" that the FHA stopped financing subdivision developments whose builders would not sell to Black buyers.[15]

Many middle-class African Americans shut out of receiving FHA loans turned to contract buying in order to achieve the American dream of homeownership:

> In this model, buyers shut out from conventional lending are offered an alternative: They can make monthly payments on a home directly to the seller, instead of a bank, with the promise of receiving the deed only once the property is entirely paid off, 20 or 30 years down the road. In the meantime, they have few of the legal protections of a typical home buyer but all of the responsibilities of one. They don't build equity with time. They can be easily evicted. And if that happens, they lose all of their investment. . . .
>
> In the earlier era when this was common, between the 1930s and 1960s, contract lending was in some cities the primary

means middle-class blacks had to buy homes. Real estate agents and speculators jacked up the price of properties two- or three-fold. Then when families fell behind on a month's payment or on repairs, they were swiftly evicted. The sellers kept their deposits and found the next family.[16]

Because African Americans bought homes on contract, frequently at inflated prices, they had little money left to upkeep their houses, support their families, or invest in the stock market or businesses. Contract buyers were unable to build equity while they made monthly payments on their house and were kept from actually "owning" their homes until they made the last payment.

Another government program that led to the destruction of Black neighborhoods, the dislocation of Black families and businesses, and an increase in racial segregation was the construction of the national interstate highway system after 1956, "a 42,500-mile network of high-speed, limited-access highways that linked cities across the country." A research paper by Raymond A. Mohl, "The Interstates and the Cities: Highways, Housing, and the Freeway Revolt," explains how the routing of highways through Black communities in cities across the nation was not accidental. It was, instead, a public policy initiative to rid cities of "slums" and "blighted neighborhoods" that housed primarily African Americans.

Working within federal traffic engineering guidelines, but with few other constraints, highway builders at the state and local levels routed the new urban expressways in directions of their own choosing. Local agendas often dictated such decisions. In most cities, the result was to drive the interstates through black and poor neighborhoods. Urban blacks were heavily concentrated in areas with the oldest and most dilapidated housing, where land acquisition costs were relatively low, and where organized political opposition was weakest. Displaying a "two-birds-with-one-stone" mentality, cities and states sought to route interstate expressways through slum neighborhoods, using federal highway money to reclaim downtown urban real estate. Inner-city slums could be cleared, blacks removed to more distant second-ghetto areas, central business districts redeveloped, and transportation woes solved all at the same time—and mostly at federal expense.

Thus, urban expressways were conceived of by many as more than just traffic arteries. To be sure, the highway engineers in the BPR and at the state level were interested in building highways that would move traffic efficiently, although most of them also shared the two-birds theory. But business interests and government officials in the cities conceived of expressways as part of a larger redevelopment plan for the city centers. This rebuilding of the central city in many cases came at the expense of African American communities in the inner cities, whose neighborhoods—not just housing but churches, business districts, even entire urban renewal areas—were destroyed in the process of expressway construction. In other instances, the highway builders routed urban interstates through white working-class ethnic neighborhoods, historic districts, and parks, but building an expressway through a black community was the most common choice, the ubiquitous experience of urban America in the expressway era of 1956 to the early 1970s.[17]

According to Mohl, "From the late 1950s and well into the 1960s, urban expressway construction meant massive family dislocation and housing destruction." In Miami, Florida, an expressway completed in the mid-1960s tore through Overtown, leading to the destruction of housing for about 10,000 people and the main business district that was the "the commercial and cultural heart of Black Miami." Another interstate destroyed hundreds of homes and businesses in north Nashville's Black community, dividing what was left of it.

Interstate-10 devastated a Black community in New Orleans that had been "an old and stable Black Creole community, boasting a long stretch of magnificent old oak trees." Interstate-85 ripped through a Black community in Montgomery, Alabama, despite George W. Curry, a Black minister, garnering a petition with 1,150 signatures to reroute the freeway to a nearby alternative route that would have cost $30,000 less. Mohl's report listed city after city with Black communities torn apart by highways: Birmingham, Alabama; Columbia, South Carolina; Camden,

New Jersey; Tampa, St. Petersburg, Jacksonville, Orlando, and Pensacola, Florida; Columbus and Cleveland, Ohio; Milwaukee; Chicago; Atlanta.

Interstate highway construction, Mohl stated, resulted in the restructuring of cities and further segregation of African Americans into low-income neighborhoods.

> Thus, postwar urban expressway building brought massive housing destruction and a subsequent racial restructuring of the central cities, as those displaced sought relocation housing. Some large-scale, high-rise public housing projects of the 1950s, such as the Robert Taylor Homes in Chicago or the Pruitt-Igoe Project in St. Louis, absorbed some dislocated families, but highways and urban renewal were destroying a great deal more housing than was being built. In some places, public housing construction slowed or ground to a halt in the politically reactionary 1950s, when such projects were considered by some a dangerous form of socialism. The new, lily-white suburbs that sprouted in the postwar automobile era were unwelcoming to blacks. Essentially, most uprooted African American families found new housing in nearby low- and middle-income white residential areas, which themselves were experiencing the transition from white to black. The forced relocation of blacks from central city areas triggered a massive spatial reorganization of urban residential space. The expressway building of the 1950s and 1960s, then, ultimately helped produce the much larger, more spatially isolated, and more intensely segregated second ghettos characteristic of the late twentieth century.[18]

The government's policies and programs in the twentieth century to destroy Black communities, segregate neighborhoods, and deny loans to Black Americans resulted in fewer Black Americans being able to own homes, accumulate wealth from homeownership, and pass that wealth down. As I discussed in chapter 3, the high-poverty neighborhoods, regardless of ethnic background of residents, have the highest rates of crime, instability, and policing. So, the fact that a large segment of African Americans were purposefully segregated into neighborhoods without opportunities to own their homes and pass down generational wealth, and were in turn more susceptible to illegal activity and crime, directly contributes to higher numbers of impoverished African Americans incarcerated. To this day, African Americans still have the lowest home ownership rates, at 43.3 percent, compared to 72.1 percent of white Americans, 61.7 percent of Asian Americans, and 51.1 percent of Hispanic Americans. According to a study by Lending Tree, "Black Americans are 15 percent of the combined population of the 50 largest metro areas, but they own 10 percent of the owner-occupied homes in those cities. White Americans account for 64 percent of the population in those cities but own 76 percent of the owner-occupied houses."[19]

Now there is a 30 percentage-point gap between white and Black homeownership—a disparity greater than before the Fair Housing Act was passed (27 percent). Much of that disparity comes from the racially predatory housing policies that spurred the subprime mortgage crisis during the Great Recession. A U.S. Department of Housing and Urban Development study examined one million mortgages reported throughout the country in 1998. It found that subprime loans were five times more likely in Black neighborhoods (51 percent of home loans) than white neighborhoods (9 percent of home loans). This disparity was shown across income levels as well. Homeowners in upper-income white neighborhoods had only 6 percent of subprime loans, compared to 39 percent of homeowners in upper-income Black neighborhoods.[20]

As a result of the increase in subprime loans targeting Black and Latino neighborhoods, not only were Black and Latino homeowners paying higher costs and fees to own their homes, but they also lost their homes and wealth at disproportionate rates. According to CNBC,

> Between 2004 and 2007, Hispanic Americans and Black Americans were 78% and 105% more likely than White Americans to have a high-cost mortgage, respectively, according to data from the National Bureau of Economic Research. This led to a disproportionate number of Black and Brown families being negatively impacted by the 2007–2010 housing crisis. During this time, nearly 8% of Black American and Latino families lost their homes due to foreclosure, compared to 4.5% of White families.

In 2005, before the housing crisis, the median net worth of Black households was $12,124, compared to White households who have a median net worth of $134,992, according to the Pew Research Center. By 2009, the net worth of Black households had fallen to $5,677, and the median net worth of White families had dropped to $113,149.[21]

In *The Color of Law,* Richard Rothstein also demonstrated that in major cities throughout the United States, like Atlanta, Raleigh, Houston, and Chicago, to name a few, city officials purposefully segregated schools for children in the first half of the twentieth century.

> In southern and border states and in some northern cities where explicit school segregation was practiced before the Supreme Court's 1954 Brown decision, authorities developed another tactic to impose residential segregation where it would not otherwise exist: placing the only schools that served African American children in designated African American neighborhoods and providing no transportation for black students who lived elsewhere. African American families who wanted their children to be educated had no choice but to find new housing in the newly segregated areas.[22]

As a result of ongoing government-enforced segregation in housing and schools, alongside a lack of wealth, African American children and youth living in impoverished neighborhoods often attend underfunded, underresourced schools, making Black students more likely to be preparing for incarceration than success in the formal labor market.

This modern school-to-prison pipeline is often traced back to the 1990s when white lawmakers feared a rise in youth violence and wanted to stem juvenile crime. Similar to mandatory minimum sentences implemented in criminal courts, "zero-tolerance" policies were passed in schools that removed discretion from school administrators and imposed often draconian rules on both serious as well as minor school-related offenses.

> This is the climate in which zero tolerance policies proliferated and also expanded to encompass a wide range of misconduct

much less harmful than bringing a weapon to school. As early as the 1996–97 school year, 79 percent of schools had adopted zero tolerance policies for violence, going beyond federal mandates. To put some muscle behind these policies, the federal government and states began to increase funding for security guards and other school-based law enforcement officers and later to install metal detectors. Between the 1996–97 and 2007–08 school years, the number of public high schools with full-time law enforcement and security guards tripled. This shift in school disciplinary policy and practice mirrored changes in the juvenile justice system to make it more closely resemble the adult system.[23]

As a result, the number of students being disciplined by out-of-school suspensions and expulsions increased by 40 percent from 1972–73 to 2009. The policy brief also found that, though zero-tolerance policies were initially created to deter and punish students for bringing a weapon to school, "43 percent of expulsions and out-of-school suspensions lasting a week or longer were for insubordination" or other nonviolent offenses, including dress-code violations.

Not just inconvenient or overly punitive, school suspensions are directly linked to weakened student academic performance or students dropping out of school altogether.

For similar students attending similar schools, a single suspension or expulsion doubles the risk that a student will repeat a grade. Being retained a grade, especially while in middle or high school, is one of the strongest predictors of dropping out. In one national longitudinal study, youth with a prior suspension were 68 percent more likely to drop out of school.[24]

In 2016, a groundbreaking report from the UCLA Center for Civil Rights Remedies at UCLA's Civil Rights Project was the first to quantify the economic cost of suspending students from school. "Using national longitudinal data that tracked a cohort of 10th graders, the researchers estimated that 10th grade school suspensions result in more than 67,000 additional high school dropouts nationally." Over the course of a lifetime, "each additional dropout is responsible for $163,000 in lost tax revenue and $364,000 in other social costs, such as health care and criminal justice expenses. Cumulatively, the total cost of the 67,000 additional dropouts caused by school suspensions nationally exceeds $35 billion."[25]

Abundant evidence has shown that these punitive disciplinary policies are disproportionately used against Black students, including the youngest students. A U.S. Department of Education Office for Civil Rights Data Collection (CRDC) released in 2014 found that Black *preschoolers* represented "18% of preschool enrollment, but 42% of preschool students suspended once, and 48% of students suspended more than once."[26] The more recent 2021 CRDC found "Black preschoolers received one or more suspensions 2.5 times greater than their share." Black preschoolers accounted for 38.2 percent of expulsions though they made up only 18.2 percent of the preschool population.[27]

For students attending public high schools, African Americans made up 7.7 percent of the school population but were three times more likely to be disciplined by in-school suspensions (21.1 percent), out-of-school suspensions (24.9 percent), and expulsion (25.9 percent).[28]

The exponential rise in suspensions and expulsions coincided with the increase of police in schools. "Between 1975 and 2017, the number of public schools in the U.S. with police stationed on-site or regularly patrolling the campus increased from 10 percent to more than 60 percent."[29] Kristin Henning, the Blume Professor of Law and the director of the Juvenile Justice Clinic and Initiative at Georgetown Law School, explains that the increase in school resource officers (SROs) who are police officers permanently assigned to work in local schools is attributable to federal funding for the 1999 grant program initiated by the Office of Community Oriented Policing Services (COPS) to facilitate the hiring of SROs in primary and secondary schools. Funding for the program was renewed by the Obama administration after the Sandy Hook school shooting in Connecticut in 2012. While most recent mass school shootings have occurred in predominantly white, middle-class schools, SROs are most often stationed in urban public schools in poor, segregated neighborhoods.[30]

Though they are school officers, many SROs patrol the schools in uniform with guns or pepper spray and have minimal, if any, training relating to working with youth. In *The End of Policing*, Alex S. Vitale explains the impact of the police presence on the criminalization of youth.

> The US Department of Education found in a 2011–2012 survey of 72,000 schools that black, Latino, and special-needs students were all disproportionately subjected to criminal justice actions. While black students represent 16 percent of students enrolled, they represent 27 percent of students referred to law enforcement and 31 percent of students subjected to a school-related arrest. In comparison, white students represent 51 percent of enrollment, 41 percent of students referred to law enforcement, and 39 percent of those arrested. Some individual districts have even starker numbers. In Chicago, in 2013–2014 black students were twenty-seven times more likely to be arrested than white students leading to 8,000 arrests in a two-year period. Over 50 percent of those arrested were under fifteen.[31]

The violent and inappropriate behavior of SROs toward youth has been highlighted in news stories and lawsuits. One such lawsuit was filed in 2010 by the Southern Poverty Law Center on behalf of eight high school students in Birmingham, Alabama, who had been pepper-sprayed by SROs. The litigation revealed that between 2006 and 2014, SROs had sprayed 199 students who attended Birmingham City public schools with Freeze +P in 110 incidents. Except for one instance, none of the incidents involved a student who possessed a weapon. Freeze +P is a chemical agent used by the military that may cause "burning of the eyes, skin, mouth, and airway, tearing, reflexive closing of the eyes, coughing, gagging, and difficulty breathing," and what one trial expert called "severe pain."[32]

One of the pepper-spray incidents in the lawsuit happened to K.B., when she was a fifteen-year-old student at Woodlawn High School. K.B. and another boy named L.M. got into a verbal altercation after K.B.'s family told L.M. he could no longer live with them after K.B. caught him stealing from the family. L.M. cursed at K.B., called her derogatory names, and insulted her family members. K.B. cursed back and walked away, however L.M. followed her and continued to call her names. K.B.

became upset and began to cry loudly and went inside the girls' gymnasium. The judge's ruling outlined the SROs involvement at that point:

> Without explanation, Officer Silburn Smith approached K.B., grasped her arm, handcuffed her, and told her to calm down. K.B. insisted that she was calm, even though, by her own account, she was still upset and continued to cry hysterically. K.B. did not struggle with Officer Smith, try to pull away from Officer Smith, or call him any names. When Officer Smith asked K.B. about the dispute with L.M., K.B. started to tell him, and added that she did not understand why she was the only person in handcuffs. Officer Smith told her to calm down twice more, and when she failed to do so, with no warning, he sprayed her with Freeze +P. The spray made K.B.'s eyes burn and her face felt like someone had cut it and poured hot sauce on it. While K.B. waited for the paramedics to arrive, she vomited.
>
> Birmingham Fire and Rescue responded and talked to K.B., but did not provide any treatment. Instead, they asked her a few questions and told her to keep her eyes open and not to put water on her face. At the time of this incident, K.B. was five months pregnant. After Birmingham Fire and Rescue left, Officer Smith drove K.B. to Cooper Green Hospital. The car windows were up. At the hospital, K.B. signed a form declining treatment because Officer Smith told her there was nothing the medical personnel could do to help her and that they would sit at the hospital all day if K.B. requested treatment. After leaving Cooper Green, Officer Smith transported K.B. to the Family Court, where the staff strip searched her.

The court ruled in favor of two students, B.J. and K.B., on their excessive force allegations, and they were each awarded $5,000 in damages.[33] The court was "especially taken aback that a police officer charged with protecting the community's children considered it appropriate and necessary to spray a girl with Freeze +P simply because she was crying about her mistreatment at the hands of one of her male peers."

The court also found that the SROs violated all of the students Fourth Amendment rights by "failing to properly decontaminate them" after spraying them with Freeze +P. It stated:

> Having concluded that, absent extenuating circumstances, failing to adequately decontaminate an individual whom officers have exposed to chemical spray is excessive force and violates the Fourth Amendment, the court now turns to the question of whether the defendants adequately decontaminated the plaintiffs. The court's task here is eased, somewhat, by the fact that, with regard to most of the plaintiffs, the defendants did absolutely nothing other than call Birmingham Fire Rescue, whose paramedics, in turn, did nothing to ease the plaintiffs' pain.[34]

The lawsuit victory was short lived. In 2018, the Eleventh Circuit Court of Appeals overturned the federal court's ruling regarding the failure to properly decontaminate the students and cleared the six Birmingham school resource officers of constitutional rights violations and excessive force claims. The appeals court ruled that the SROs have "qualified immunity" and can't be held "individually liable" for their actions.[35]

The lawsuit also brought to light serious issues that young students, and especially Black students in low-income communities, are facing that cannot be addressed by SROs. One student had a history of sexual abuse and mental health issues; another student's boyfriend had died after being tazed by the police; another student was being kicked out of the house where they were staying; another student was pregnant at age fifteen; and another student with a history of mental illness had subsequently been criminally charged in an off-campus incident and incarcerated.[36] What is called for is not for cops to criminalize normal adolescent behavior, but for these students, and millions like them across the country, to be provided with emotional, therapeutic, and social support.

A 2019 ACLU report, "Cops and No Counselors: How the Lack of School Mental Health Staff Is Harming Students," examined CRDC data from the 2015–2016 school year and found the following:

- 1.7 million students are in schools with police but no counselors.
- 3 million students are in schools with police but no nurses.

- 6 million students are in schools with police but no school psychologists.
- 10 million students are in schools with police but no social workers.
- 14 million students are in schools with police but no counselor, nurse, psychologist, or social worker.[37]

Arming schools with police in urban neighborhoods characterized by low income and high violence at the expense of adequately staffing counselors, nurses, psychologists, and social workers sets up students for incarceration but not success. Students who are not receiving the social, emotional, and mental support they need, and instead are surveilled and policed at school, are at a greater risk of failing or dropping out of school. For Black men who in their teens dropped out of high school, their lifetime chances of imprisonment approach 70 percent.[38]

The likelihood of either attending a well-funded public school or high-achieving private or charter school with access to counselors, nurses, psychologists, and social workers significantly correlates to the neighborhood where young people live. In *Color of Law*, Rothstein states that "young African Americans (from thirteen to twenty-eight years old) are now ten times as likely to live in poor neighborhoods as young whites—66 percent of African Americans, compared to 6 percent of whites." For poor African Americans who are unable to climb the socioeconomic ladder, the American Dream is more of a myth than reality. "67 percent of African American families hailing from the poorest quarter of neighborhoods a generation ago continue to live in such neighborhoods today."[39] Rothstein lays out the consequences of young people exposed to neighborhood poverty, and how it impacts educational and employment prospects for youth.

The consequences of being exposed to neighborhood poverty are greater than the consequences of being poor itself. Children who grow up in poor neighborhoods have few adult role models who have been educationally and occupationally successful. Their ability to do well in school is compromised from stress that can result from exposure to violence. They have few, if any, summer job opportunities. Libraries and bookstores are less accessible.

There are fewer primary care physicians. Fresh food is harder to get. Airborne pollutants are more present, leading to greater school absence from respiratory illness. The concentration of many disadvantaged children in the same classroom deprives each child of the special attention needed to be successful. All these challenges are added to those from which poor children suffer in any neighborhood—instability and stress resulting from parental unemployment, fewer literary experiences when parents are poorly educated, more overcrowded living arrangements that offer few quiet corners to study, and less adequate health care, all of which contribute to worse average school performance and, as a result, less occupational success as adults.[40]

The link between poor and high-poverty neighborhoods and crime was explored earlier; it's also important to explore the link between abuse, mental illness, violence, and incarceration, and how living in poor neighborhoods without access to proper mental health treatment and a safe environment can exacerbate those conditions.

"The Sexual Abuse to Prison Pipeline: A Girl's Story" report found that "sexual abuse is one of the primary predictors of girls' entry into the juvenile justice system." Black, Indigenous, and Latina girls are disproportionately represented in the population of girls in the juvenile justice system. Though virtually no national data exist tracking histories of abuse for incarcerated girls, some local and regional studies indicate the link.[41]

One study in Oregon's juvenile justice system found that 93 percent of girls had experienced sexual or physical abuse; 76 percent had experienced at least one incident of sexual abuse by the age of thirteen; and 63 percent had experienced both physical and sexual abuse. A 2009 study of delinquent girls in South Carolina found that 81 percent reported a history of sexual violence, and 42 percent reported dating violence. Another study from California in 1998 of juvenile-justice-involved girls found that 81 percent of girls had experienced one or more incidents of physical or sexual abuse; 56 percent reported one or more forms of sexual abuse; and 45 percent reported being beaten or burned at least once.[42]

For a majority of the girls in these studies, abuse begins at extremely early ages, resulting in trauma that often has a lasting negative effect. According to the report,

> The California study found that the age at which girls were "most likely" to be fondled or molested was five years old; and the Oregon study found that the average age at which at least one instance of sexual abuse occurred was just under seven and a half years old. These findings are particularly significant in light of a recent study that found that traumatic exposure before high school is an even stronger predictor of girls' delinquency than such exposure during high school.[43]

A National Child Traumatic Stress Network report found that unaddressed trauma in girls that is not resolved may result in alcohol and drug use, involvement in violent activity, and the development of mental health problems such as PTSD. Too often, girls with a history of abuse are in turn criminalized for their behavioral reactions to trauma and abuse. Arrests of girls are most commonly for "running away, substance abuse, and truancy," which are the "most common symptoms of abuse." Once incarcerated, youth often are not provided competent treatment for the trauma and abuse they experienced. A census conducted by the U.S. Department of Justice's Office of Juvenile Justice and Delinquency Prevention found the following:

> Only approximately half the youth in the juvenile justice system are placed in a facility that provides mental health evaluations of all residents. Follow-up care is often insufficient even for youth who do receive evaluations. And a significant majority of juvenile justice youth (88 percent) resides in facilities in which mental health counselors are not licensed professionals.[44]

Black and Indigenous girls are disproportionately incarcerated in juvenile facilities. As the Sentencing Project data shows, when residential placement of girls in juvenile detention is viewed per capita, Native American girls have the highest rate of detention at 112 per 100,000, followed by African Americans at a rate of 77 per 100,000, compared to Latinas at a rate of 27 per 100,000 and white girls that are placed at 24 per 100,000.[45] Girls suffering abuse who were incarcerated as juveniles and who failed to receive appropriate treatment are those with the greatest likelihood of reoffending and being reincarcerated as adults.

Danielle Sered founded and directs the organization Common Justice, which works "to build transformative solutions to violence that can displace incarceration." In her book *Until We Reckon*, she writes, it "is estimated that roughly half of incarcerated women experienced serious physical or sexual abuse as children, 86 percent experienced sexual violence in their lifetime, more than two-thirds experienced intimate partner violence, and nearly all experienced some form of violence prior to their incarceration."[46]

Both women's and men's experiences of childhood trauma, commonly referred to as adverse childhood experiences or ACEs, directly correlate to adult mental health disorders and substance abuse. As Dr. Brandy F. Henry, assistant professor at Pennsylvania State University's College of Education, Rehabilitation, and Home Services, relates,

> Decades of research have documented the causal link between adverse childhood experiences and mental health/substance use disorders. A meta-analysis of the effect of adverse childhood experiences on health describes the findings of 37 studies and presents the pooled risk of various health conditions. For people with four or more adverse childhood experiences, the risk of anxiety, depression and schizophrenia was found to be about four times higher, as compared to people who experienced less than four adverse childhood experiences. . . . People with four or more adverse experiences were also at higher risk of alcohol and drug use with problematic alcohol use nearly six times higher (OR 5.84) and problematic drug use over 10 times as high (OR 10.22).[47]

Using data from a 2004 Survey of Inmates in State and Federal Correctional Facilities (SI-SFCF), Henry studied the link between adverse childhood and adult experiences, mental health and substance disorders, and incarceration. She found that 38.1 percent of people incarcerated identified as having a mental health disorder (12.6 percent had a Serious Mental Illness, defined as either bipolar disorder or schizophrenia, and 25.5 percent had Other Mental Health Disorder, which included any depressive disorder, post-traumatic stress disorder, anxiety disorder, or personality disorder). In the year before their incarceration, 32.6 percent had alcohol use disorder and 43.6 percent had a substance use disorder.[48]

In the 2019 *Prison News Legal* article "Imprisoning America's Mentally Ill," Edward Lyon discusses how the rise in the incarceration of people with mental health or substance use disorders directly correlated with the decrease in mental health treatment institutions.

> From the 1960s to the present the U.S. incarceration rate more than tripled, and around 2.2 million people are currently incarcerated nationwide. During that same period of time, the population of institutionalized mental patients shrank by 90 percent to under 60,000. Alisa Roth, author of *Insane: America's Criminal Treatment of Mental Illness*, estimates that half of U.S. prisoners suffer from a mental illness, since the lack of other treatment options means they are more likely to end up behind bars.[49]

National legislation addressing mental health in the twentieth century was not passed until the Community Mental Health Act, which was championed by President John F. Kennedy and signed into law in 1964. In 1955, the number of patients inside public mental hospitals nationwide peaked at 560,000, and the Community Mental Health Act redirected the responsibility of patients with a mental health diagnosis from the state to the federal government.

Kennedy, whose younger sister Rosemary had been mentally disabled and received a lobotomy, had wanted to create a network of community mental health centers where people suffering from mental health issues could live in the community while receiving care instead of living in large institutions plagued with histories of abuse and inhumane conditions. Less than a month after signing the new legislation, Kennedy was assassinated, and community mental health centers never received stable funding. Less than fifteen years after the legislation was enacted into law, fewer than half the promised centers were built.[50]

In 1965, Congress created Medicaid and Medicare, which allowed federal dollars to pay for patients in community mental health centers but did not support patients in psychiatric institutions. This encouraged states to reduce the number of psychiatric patients from state hospitals in order to pay for their care through the federal government. The Mental Health Systems Act of 1980, signed into law by President Jimmy Carter, provided additional federal money to community mental health centers to further and improve on legislation started by Kennedy's dream.[51] Ronald Reagan, the next president to take office, repealed the law and "slashed mental health spending by 33 percent." Lyon surmises that the "deinstitutionalization of the mentally ill, who were moved from in-patient facilities to poorly-funded community-based programs, resulted in more people with mental health problems ending up in jails and prisons."[52]

As we saw in an earlier chapter, the decades after Reagan officially launched the war on drugs resulted in the exponential growth in prisons across the nation. The same, however, did not happen for mental health and substance use disorder treatment facilities. The National Alliance for Mental Illness (NAMI) states that "jails and prisons have become America's de-facto mental health facilities."

> People with mental illness are overrepresented in our nation's jails and prisons. About 2 million times each year, people with serious mental illness are booked into jails. Nearly 2 in 5 people who are incarcerated have a history of mental illness (37% in state and federal prisons and 44% held in local jails). Many people with mental illness who are incarcerated are held for committing non-violent, minor offenses related to the symptoms of untreated illness (disorderly conduct, loitering, trespassing, disturbing the peace) or for offenses like shoplifting and petty theft.[53]

For youth, the number of people suffering from mental health issues is even higher. A NAMI infographic "Mental Illness and the Justice System" states that "70% of youth in the juvenile justice system have a diagnosable mental health condition," and youth in detention are ten times more likely to suffer from psychosis than youth in the community.[54]

People suffering from mental health disorders while incarcerated have very low rates of adequate treatment. Sixty-three percent of people incarcerated in state and federal prisons with a history of mental illness do not receive mental health treatment while incarcerated. Similarly, fewer than "half of people with a history of mental illness receive mental health treatment while held in local jails." Instead of treatment, people suffering from mental health disorders are often targeted for abuse by prison and jail guards and staff as well as other incarcerated people. They are also often punished for the symptoms of their illness by measures such as solitary confinement. NAMI estimates four thousand people with serious mental illness are held in solitary confinement inside U.S. prisons.[55] The United Nations has classified periods of solitary confinement that exceed fifteen days as torture. Short- and long-term periods of solitary confinement can create debilitating mental health consequences that can last long after the person is removed from solitary.[56] Given the lack of treatment and likelihood of punishment for their illness, it is understandable why suicide is the leading cause of death for people in jails.

A Department of Justice investigation into the Santa Rita jail in Dublin, California, which is run by the Alameda County Sheriff's Office, offers a glimpse into the issues plaguing jails and prisons across the nation. Santa Rita jail representatives have estimated approximately 40 percent of its population is on the mental health caseload, approximately 20 to 25 percent of the population likely has a serious mental illness, and approximately 50 percent of the incarcerated people in the most restrictive "safety cells" have a serious mental illness.[57]

The one primary unit for men with mental health needs, Unit 9, isolates and stigmatizes those suffering from mental health disorders:

> While Jail officials refer to Unit 9 as a mental health unit, it largely functions not as a therapeutic setting but rather, in all but name, as a restrictive housing unit, because these prisoners are confined to their cells for the vast majority of the day, alone or with another prisoner. Within Unit 9 are different pods, based on security classification. Most prisoners in these pods are placed in two-person cells and are locked in those cells for the vast majority of their waking hours. Jail records show that, depend-

ing on their pod, prisoners were limited to less than 1.5 to three hours out of their cells each day. And prisoners on most pods received yard time outdoors for as little as one hour per week, with many receiving no yard time. Instead of going to the clinic for mental health care, or to a classroom for educational or other programming, prisoners in Unit 9 remain on the Unit. They have access to few group programs on the Unit, and are prohibited from attending the many other programs available to general population prisoners. Mental health staff meet with the prisoners on the Unit, at large tables in the day-room-type area. Prisoners on Unit 9 must wear different color uniforms from the rest of the population, which not only discloses sensitive health information, because staff and other prisoners know that the uniform signifies a mental health diagnosis, but also serves to stigmatize them and marginalize them.[58]

While California law states that incarcerated people with mental health disorders need to be treated, when a jail like Santa Rita fails to address their mental health needs, it places the incarcerated people at significant risk of harm. As observed at Santa Rita, lack of treatment often results in the deterioration of people's mental health, engagement in self-harm, including suicide, and transfer to the nearby acute mental health center, John George Psychiatric Hospital. The DOJ stated, "of 21 prisoners known to have died in the Jail or from injuries or other causes sustained in the Jail between January 12, 2017, when we opened our investigation, and 2020, at least 13 either had apparent indicators of serious mental illness or died due to suicide." Importantly, the courts also found that jails providing psychotropic medications alone, without accompanying mental health treatments like psychotherapy, are insufficient. "Without therapy and programs that might, for example, help them learn cognitive or emotional skills, plan for recovery from substance use disorder, and make healthy life choices, prisoners with serious mental health needs are at risk of deterioration and eventual reinstitutionalization upon their release from incarceration."[59]

The DOJ also found that proper mental health screens and safety measures were not sufficiently used in Santa Rita. The report describes a twenty-year-old man brought in by police who was experiencing a mental health crisis. Though the man's parents repeatedly told the police their son was not a danger and needed mental health treatment, the deputies ignored the parent's request for a mental health evaluation. Instead, a lieutenant ordered the twenty-year-old still experiencing symptoms of a mental health crisis to be chained to a cell door, a violation of the sheriff office's restraint policy. Left unattended, the man attempted to strangle himself with the chains, later dying from his injuries.[60] This is the reality for the majority of jails and prisons across the nation.

Another pipeline to prison is violence. In the tenth-anniversary edition of *The New Jim Crow*, Michelle Alexander addressed the issue of people serving time for violent crimes.

> We will never close prisons on a large scale in this country, or drastically reduce the prison population, if we do not change the way we view and respond to violent crime. As many advocates have pointed out, the distinction between survivors and perpetrators of violence is largely illusory, as virtually no one commits violence without first surviving it. Reflexively locking people in cages and subjecting them to degradation and humiliation—inflicting violence and suffering upon people in order to teach them that violence is wrong—is a doomed strategy, especially considering that most people who commit violent crimes are victims as well. If we want to reduce violence in our communities, we need to hold people accountable in ways that aim to repair and prevent harm rather than simply inflicting more harm and trauma and calling it justice.[61]

A 2019 Vera Institute of Justice report found that in the United States, law enforcement made an arrest every three seconds. Yet, contrary to the popular belief that police are taking "dangerous criminals" off the street in order to protect communities, the data actually revealed that "non-serious, low-level offenses such as 'drug abuse violations' and 'disorderly conduct' make up over 80 percent of arrests," with fewer than 5 percent of arrests being for serious violent offenses.[62]

Nonetheless, as Alexander explains, over half (52 percent) of people in state prisons have been convicted of a violent offense. This is due to the fact that people "who are convicted of violent crimes tend to get longer prison sentences than those who commit nonviolent offenses. As a result, people who are classified as violent offenders comprise a much larger share of the prison population than they would if they had shorter sentences."[63]

The United States has proven it cannot police and incarcerate its way out of violence—or it would have done so by now. Currently the nation spends the largest amount of money on policing and incarcerating the largest number of people in the history of the world.

It's important to note that though African Americans account for a disproportionate number of people incarcerated, they statistically do not commit the most crimes. One FBI report including crime statistics for the year 2020 listed the breakdown of arrestees by race (different from ethnicity), with the highest being 67.7 percent white; 27.1 percent Black; 2.9 percent of other races; and 2.2 percent of unknown race. Of known offenders, more than half (50.8 percent) were white; 29.6 percent were Black; 2.2 percent other races; and the race was unknown for 17.4 percent.[64]

Another misconception is that Black Americans are killed the most often by guns in the form of gun homicides. The truth is more Americans die by gun suicide than gun homicide. According to the Centers for Disease Control and Prevention (CDC), in 2020, 54 percent of all gun-related deaths in the United States were suicides, compared to 43 percent that were murders.[65] The racial/ethnic group with the highest suicide rates in 2020 was American Indian (23.9 per 100,000), followed by white (16.9 per 100,000), Native Hawaiian/Pacific Islander (12.5 per 100,000), multiracial (9.6 per 100,000), Black (7.8 per 100,000), Hispanic (7.5 per 100,000), and Asian (6.4 per 100,000).[66]

In 1975, James Cone wrote:

> White people have a distorted conception of the meaning of violence. They like to think of violence as breaking the laws of their society, but that is a narrow and racist understanding of reality. There is a more deadly form of violence, and it is camouflaged in such slogans as "law and order," "freedom and democracy," and "the American way of life." I am speaking of white-collar violence, the violence of Christian murderers and patriot citizens

who define right in terms of whiteness and wrong as blackness. These are the people who hire assassins to do their dirty work while they piously congratulate themselves for being "good" and nonviolent." The assassins are the police who patrol our streets, killing our men, women, and children.

I contend, therefore, that the problem of violence is not the problem of a few black revolutionaries but the problem of a whole social structure which outwardly appears to be ordered and respectable but inwardly is "ridden by psychopathic obsessions and delusions"—racism and hatred. Violence is embedded in American law, and it is blessed by the keepers of moral sanctity.[67]

Even the method the FBI uses to report crime, the Uniform Crime Report, is biased against Black people.

The FBI's Uniform Crime Report, which is considered the official measure of the national crime rate, has always emphasized street crime to the exclusion of organized and white-collar crime. As such, the figures that inform law enforcement strategies and priorities tend to reflect the crimes committed by low-income and unemployed Americans who, in part because of structural inequalities, are disproportionately black.[68]

White-collar crime, whose offenders are majority white, is not listed prominently alongside the other reported crimes in the Uniform Crime Report, though white-collar crime encompasses a type of theft and fraud that can result in enormous sums of money being stolen, harming organizations, the government, and individuals. For example, corporate fraud, securities and commodities fraud, and money laundering are not listed in the Uniform Crime Report.

The Uniform Crime Report also does not list crimes committed by police officers, including murder, rape, and assault; nor does it list crimes committed by prison and jail guards and staff, including murder, rape, and assault. Nor does the FBI report the millions of deaths caused by corporate and government action, inaction, or coverup, such as environmental pollution and climate-change-related natural disasters.

As mentioned earlier, over half of people incarcerated in prisons are serving time for violent offenses. To understand why violence is so prevalent in neighborhoods with concentrated poverty that are predominately composed of Black residents, one must reexamine everything that encompasses the reality of violence and why Black people living in neighborhoods of concentrated poverty suffer a disproportionate share of firearm homicide deaths committed by other Black people and the police.

> Modern research on gun homicide has honed in on a number of societal factors—specifically, income inequality and residential segregation—that drive gun homicide and other types of violent crime. Researchers have found that inequality and segregation disrupt social cohesion and trust, foreclose opportunities for social mobility, and limit access to high-quality education and housing, all of which contribute to higher rates of violence. Access to guns, at both the individual and societal levels, is also associated with higher rates of homicide.[69]

In the report "Invisible Wounds: Gun Violence and Community Trauma among Black Americans," by Everytown for Gun Safety Support Fund, the question is asked: "What if police sirens, gunshots in the distance, and sidewalk memorials to those gunned down are a feature of daily life? How do we understand the experiences of people who have never directly experienced a terrible, unexpected event but nonetheless suffer from severe trauma symptoms?" The report examines three types of violence facing low-income Black communities with high rates of gun violence: interpersonal violence, which includes gun victimization, witnessing gun violence, and hearing gunshots; structural violence, which includes concentrated poverty, residential segregation, differential sentencing, and inadequate funding for schools, housing, health care, and public transportation; and historical and intergenerational violence, which includes the legacy of America's painful colonial history, predatory housing lending, police violence, and broken intergenerational relationships.[70]

These forms of violence, compounded and persisting for generations, enact a heavy toll on predominantly Black and low-income neighborhoods and underscore the fact that violence begets violence.

Every three hours, a young Black male dies by gun homicide in the United States. This reality can have a devastating impact. It can leave these young men feeling fatalistic about the present and hopeless about the future. Couple these curtailed dreams with other forms of violence—such as employment discrimination, police violence, mass incarceration, and inadequate funding for mental health services—and the challenges to overcome become high barriers. The symptoms of this trauma pervade every aspect of teen and young adult lives. The trauma too often inflicts a toll on self-image and worsens their physical and mental wellbeing. It impedes their ability to concentrate and learn. And it makes it difficult to maintain healthy interpersonal and intimate relationships.[71]

According to Annette Bailey of Ryerson University, growing up and remaining in an environment of constant exposure to violence, both on an individual and a community level, combined with systemic racism, can result in a "trauma-altered identity" that leaves people "feeling trapped in the assumptions and biases of others" that "hamper their ability to chart a healthy course for themselves." Violence can be seen as the norm, and one must be ready to commit violence to protect oneself when they do not feel anyone else is able to guarantee safety.[72]

In response to trauma born out of persistent violence, coupled with distrust that police will protect them, young people too often resort to arming themselves. A Chicago survey revealed that 93 percent of the young men surveyed carried guns to protect themselves. Only 6 percent carried guns to commit crimes. A New York City study of young people who were at risk for being victimized by gun violence showed that 81 percent of these youth, mostly Black men, had been shot or shot at. And 88 percent had a loved one or friend who had been shot. The majority surveyed said they wished guns were not in their communities, but three-fourths reported that guns made them feel safe. The result is a cycle of violence fueled by firearms.[73]

In addition to interpersonal violence, young Black men have to navigate the reality that they are on average twenty-one times more likely to be shot and killed by police than their white counterparts.[74] Police violence damages community trust, which results in people seeking redress for violence committed against them instead of turning to police intervention (due to that lack of trust). In 2020, according to the FBI, the percentage of murders that were solved—known as the "clearance rate"—declined from 61 percent in 2019 to 54 percent in 2020.[75] FBI data from 2019 shows that, in spite of how much money is spent on law enforcement, clearance rates are low, and only "45.5 percent of violent crimes and 17.2 percent of property crimes were cleared by arrest or exceptional means." This breaks down to the clearance of 61.4 percent for murder offenses, 52.3 percent of aggravated-assault offenses, 32.9 percent of rape offenses, and 30.5 percent of robbery offenses. Property crimes are even lower, with clearance rates of 18.4 percent of larceny-theft offenses, 14.1 percent of burglary offenses, and 13.8 percent of motor-vehicle theft offenses.[76]

When Black people do report crime to the police, overall the police do not investigate the crime as aggressively as they do when reports are made by white people. In New York, for instance, the clearance rate for murders "has been significantly higher for white murder victims over the last decade—most recently, at 84% for white victims, compared to 61% for Hispanic victims and 53% for Black victims during that same year."[77] In 2018, the *Washington Post* published its research examining 54,868 homicides that occurred in 55 American cities over the previous decade. Fifty percent of homicides did not result in an arrest. Of the nearly 26,000 murders that have gone without an arrest, more than 18,600 of the victims—almost three-quarters—were Black.[78]

A tragic case that highlights this racial discrepancy occurred in Memphis, Tennessee. A white woman named Eliza Fletcher, who was a school teacher and mother of two young children, disappeared in the early morning of September 2, 2022, after jogging near the University of Memphis. Fletcher was from a wealthy family, and her disappearance gained national news coverage. On September 4, a Black man named Cleotha Abston-Henderson was charged with Fletcher's kidnapping. The next day, September 5, the Memphis Police Department, the Tennessee Bureau of Investigation, the Federal Bureau of Investigation, ATF, Homeland Security, and the Shelby County Sheriff's Office Search and

Rescue searched for Fletcher and found her deceased with a gunshot wound to the back of her head.[79]

What came to light after Abston-Henderson's arrest is that Alicia Franklin, a young Black woman (who revealed her identity to tell her story), had reported to the police in September 2021 that Abston-Henderson had raped her at gunpoint. Franklin gave the police detectives Abston-Henderson's phone number, home address, social-media handle, and a description of his car. In spite of the evidence provided by Franklin, the police did not investigate or arrest Abston-Henderson. Although the police did submit Franklin's rape kit after her exam, it was never tested until after Fletcher's disappearance. Though the Memphis Police Department receives 40 percent of the city's operating budget, the department's clearance rates are only 18.3 percent for rape cases, 10.3 percent for forcible sodomy cases, and 13.9 percent for cases of rape with an object. Only 23.2 percent of all crimes against a person result in arrest in Memphis.[80] Had Franklin's report of rape been acted upon by police, Abston-Henderson would have had a much lower chance of killing Fletcher.

In *America on Fire*, Elizabeth Hinton details how Black people in the early 1990s successfully worked to stem the tide of violence in Los Angeles. The Crips and Bloods gangs, who were based out of Watts and had been fighting with each other and the police for three decades, comprised mostly young men locked out of society.

> With few opportunities for formal employment, even within the lowest levels of the service sector, young Black men began to form groups commonly referred to as gangs to claim territory, protect themselves, and keep neighborhoods safe from outsiders. Gang members defaced businesses, schools, parks, churches, and public walls with graffiti. By force or theft, they acquired sneakers, leather jackets, and cash, establishing protection rackets to extort money from local businesses. And they clashed with one another, throwing Molotov Cocktails, attacking rivals with fists and switchblades, and firing cheap, "Saturday Night Special" handguns.[81]

From the 1970s until the 1990s, gang membership expanded and handguns were traded for "Uzis, MAC-10 submachine guns, and semiautomatic rifles to enforce contracts in the underground economy," which would be used in drive-by shootings. In 1992, however, the two rival gangs decided to work together to end their internal warfare and instead focus their efforts on uniting against systemic racism and the police. They began formal truce talks on April 26, 1992, which was three days before Watts would erupt in riots after the acquittal of the four police officers who had beaten Rodney King. Mediated by the organization Amer-I-Can, which was run by the former NFL star Jim Brown, the gangs declared a truce.[82]

After National Guard troops withdrew from Los Angeles, the Crips and Bloods sponsored a unity picnic that drew more than five thousand people. Organizers of the truce had a larger goal of cleaning up the community and equipping gang members with tools to succeed in the formal economy. They viewed the riots that had occurred as "an opportunity to push the city for a massive investment in health care, education, and employment, and they called for residents themselves to have a say in how it was apportioned."

> In mid-May 1992 . . . members of the Crips and the Bloods drafted a comprehensive proposal for a $3.728 billion investment into the community that would accompany the end of the internal warfare. The ten-page document became known for its memorable closing line, "Give us the hammer and the nails, we will rebuild the city." The majority of the funds, or about two billion dollars, would be spent on "LA's Face Lift": building new community centers and recreation facilities to replace burned and abandoned structures, erecting more street lights ("we want a well-lit neighborhood"), properly maintaining the landscape ("new trees will be planted to increase the beauty of our neighborhoods"), and improving trash removal and pest control. The proposal also called for universal health care and the construction of new hospitals, health care centers, and dental clinics; for an end to welfare through new jobs for able-bodied workers; and for free daycare for single parents. There was another request, too: $700 million for the complete transformation of the Los Angeles Unified School District.[83]

The effects of the truce were immediate, with only four killings, down from twenty-two, in the first two months. Drive-by shootings fell by nearly 50 percent, and gang-related homicides declined by 62 percent. A year later, homicides in Los Angeles dropped by 10 percent.[84]

Because local authorities would not in good faith negotiate with the gang leaders and organizers of the truce, they announced their own plan to rebuild Los Angeles. They formed Rebuild LA, which ultimately failed to deliver on its promise of creating jobs and providing assistance for businesses trying to rebuild after the riots. "It invested less than $400 million in the revitalization effort, falling far short of its lofty goals and the sums—in the $4–$6 billion range—that would have been required to set South Los Angeles on a meaningful road not just to recovery but to transformation."

Without the city or government's financial support to change the material, social, and employment conditions of residents, the truce would only last for a decade. Even as the money requested in the gang proposal to uplift the community during the truce did not materialize, what did find funding was a newly built $30 million police station that opened in 1997.[85]

Federal inaction to stop gun violence in Black communities has continued since the 1990s, and only resulted in more Black people dying and going to prison. According to a ProPublica article, "How the Gun Control Debate Ignores Black Lives," by Lois Beckett, when Black leaders and clergy met with the Obama administration in 2013 after the Sandy Hook Elementary School shooting the year before, their request for financial support for community programs proven to reduce gun violence in inner-city neighborhoods fell on deaf ears. The program, Operation Ceasefire, which aggressively targeted both Black men at risk for committing gun violence as well as stopping illegal drug trafficking to Black neighborhoods, was statistically a success. Gun violence was reduced by 31 percent in Boston, where the program was first piloted; 42 percent in Stockton, California; 34 percent in Indianapolis; and 44 percent in Lowell, Massachusetts. Rev. Charles Harrison, a pastor from Indianapolis, stated the Black leaders were told by Obama officials that there was no political will in the state capital to fund violence prevention that affected Black Americans. "What was said to us by the White House was, there's really no support nationally to address the issue of urban violence.... The support was to address the issue of gun violence that affected suburban areas—schools where white kids were killed."[86]

Though in his 2014 budget President Obama had "recommended tripling the funding for a Justice Department grant that helped cities adopt Ceasefire from $8 million to $25 million" and overall "requested $79 million for grants to support similar initiatives," Congress "rejected his proposed increases for Ceasefire and similar programs" and "took many of the small grants and made them even smaller. . . . In all, Congress spent $31 million on five urban-violence-related grants—less than half of what it approved for research on how to make schools safer."[87]

Danielle Sered explains how the drivers of violence are only amplified when we incarcerate people in toxic prison environments.

> Decades of research about the individual-level causes of violence (as opposed to community conditions like poverty and disenfranchisement) has demonstrated four key drivers: shame, isolation, exposure to violence, and a diminished ability to meet one's economic needs. At the same time, prison is characterized by four key features: shame, isolation, exposure to violence, and a diminished ability to meet one's economic needs. As a nation, we have developed a response to violence that is characterized by precisely what we know to be the main drivers of violence.[88]

Sered argues that the United States supports policies and institutions that drive violence like "poverty, instability, substandard education, and insufficient housing." Instead of spending money to remedy these factors, money flows to law enforcement and prisons to incarcerate people in prisons, which intensifies violence by "interrupting people's education, rendering many homeless upon return from prison, limiting their prospects for employment and a living wage, and disrupting the social fabric that is the strongest protection against harm, even in the face of poverty."

> Mass incarceration also fails to solve the problem of violence because it is a response that treats violence as a matter of "good vs. evil." The reality is far more complicated. Nearly everyone who commits violence has also survived it, and few have gotten

formal support to heal. Although people's history of victimization in no way excuses the harm they cause, it does implicate our society for not having addressed their pain earlier. And just as people who commit violence are not exempt from victimization, many survivors of violence have complex lives, imperfect histories, and even criminal convictions. But just as it would be wrong to excuse people's actions simply because they were previously victimized, it is also wrong to ignore someone's victimization because the person previously broke a law or committed harm in the past. Such a response to violence reinforces the notion that some people deserve to be hurt—the exact thinking about violence that should be uprooted.[89]

To examine the realities of people experiencing shame, isolation, violence, and the inability to meet their economic needs requires us to humanize people who commit violence or are incarcerated instead of demonizing them. Each of the issues I detail in this chapter—segregation of African Americans in neighborhoods of concentrated poverty, underfunded and overpoliced schools, mental health issues that are untreated and criminalized, and violence—are not solved by incarcerating people in toxic and abusive prisons and jails. Removing African Americans from their communities and locking them in cages where they are often treated worse than animals does nothing but temporarily move people from an unhealthy situation and place them into an even worse one. Once returned to their communities, the same cycle often repeats.

As we've seen through the centuries and up to today, African Americans have been dehumanized by slavery, redlining, segregated schooling, the taking of their wealth, policing, the withholding of resources for Black communities, and targeted incarceration methods. Until Black people are treated as fully human and American society rectifies their social contributors to mass incarceration, we won't see change. Chapter 7 fleshes out the history of stereotypes of Black people, men especially, as less than human and criminal, and calls to discard them.

Chapter 7
From Subhuman to Superpredator

> Neither the motivation for nor the impact of the war on drugs had much to do with drugs. Nor did the narrative that secured the rise of mass incarceration. That narrative was largely about violence. . . . At the heart of that narrative is the story of an imagined monstrous other—a monster who is not quite human like the rest of us, who is capable of extraordinary harm and incapable of empathy, who inflicts great pain but does not feel it as we do, a monster we and our children have to be protected from at any price. This is not a new story. It is as old as our nation. And it is not a race-neutral story. To the contrary: it has long been a story white people have told about black people.
>
> Danielle Sered, *Until We Reckon*[1]

B efore the transatlantic slave trade, slavery had been practiced for tens of thousands of years. Howard French states in *Born in Blackness*, "White-Arab and white-on-white slavery (mostly involving Slavs, a name that shares an obvious common root with the word 'slave') had survived in Italy, southern France, and Iberia into the sixteenth century."

Though in sharp decline by the late fifteenth and early sixteenth centuries, enslavement remained "at least a minor aspect of economic life throughout the Mediterranean world until the eighteenth century."[2] But race-based chattel slavery did not emerge until Portugal began the practice in the African island colony of São Tomé, which it colonized in 1485. French explains that the word chattel "shares a common root with 'cattle,' and it means dehumanized beasts of burden."[3] In order to justify and legitimate race-based slavery, both the ideas of white supremacy and Black inferiority became ingrained in the consciousness of Europeans and their colonies in the Americas and throughout the world, including what would become the United States. In America, this belief in the inferiority of Black people and superiority of white people still persists both on an individual and systemic level to this day.

While there is no biological basis for race, the concept emerged in colonial America in the mid-1600s, enshrined by laws and theories that justified the perpetual enslavement of people of African descent and their children.

As M. Shawn Copeland, an influential Black Catholic theologian, underscores in *Enfleshing Freedom,* "scholarly efforts to define and theorize race coalesce in the consensus that race, as commonly understood, is a social construct with no basis in biology. Thus, there is only one race— the human race."[4] Copeland details how major Enlightenment thinkers shaped European notions of national, cultural, and racial superiority of Europeans, and especially superiority over people with African blood. "From the eighteenth century until well into the twentieth, their ideas about race served to reinforce proslavery attitudes, to sustain racial segregation and discrimination, and to exert subtle, perhaps devastating, influence on metaphysics and ethics."[5]

According to Katherine Bankole-Medina, professor of history and author of *Slavery and Medicine,* after slavery had taken firm root in America, Black people's very humanity was called into question by whites. "Racial ideology of the 1800s rejected the notion that the condition of slavery was a dominant factor in the intellectual and physical condition of African people. They accepted, more often vigorously and sometimes passively, the notion that Africans were simply not human beings." Statesmen and even founding fathers such as Thomas Jefferson questioned the humanity of Africans.

The issue of Africans as subhuman operated in two categories: psychological and physical. White people considered Black people intellectually inferior and "possibly incapable of intellectual improvement." Africans were also considered physically inferior to whites and better suited to the intensive agricultural labor slavery demanded because some enslavers argued enslaved Black people were not human but closer to animals. Those who did believe Africans were human often believed they were a different human "species" from white people.[6]

Danielle Sered argues that the white supremacist view that people of African descent were subhuman was a necessary tool for whites to allow and inflict inhumane violence on the people they enslaved.

> It is hard for anyone to inflict extreme pain on people we see as fully human and whose experience we see as reflective of our own. Our capacity for empathy is powerful, and when it is present, it interferes with our ability to hurt others. The act of empathizing is one of linkage—we draw on our own experience to imagine the experience of another person. So to imagine how extreme punishment would feel (lashings, beatings, burnings, and more), we would have to imagine how it would feel to survive it ourselves. But if we can persuade ourselves that there is something about the person we seek to punish that is fundamentally different from us, less than us, we become more capable of disabling our empathy, of telling ourselves that the pain they feel will not be like ours because they are not like us. In that way, racism is a profound enabler of cruelty by white people, because it provides a way to bypass the otherwise natural and often overpowering capacity for empathy. In so doing, it augments white people's capacity to engage in punishment that exceeds what a person would otherwise regard as appropriate or allowable within shared human community.[7]

The white American belief that people of African descent were not fully human was not only ignorant and egregious; it was sacrilegious. Copeland emphasizes its effect on Christianity:

> No Christian teaching has been more desecrated by slavery than the doctrine of the human person or theological anthropology.... Three convictions central to theological anthropology derive from Christian interpretation of this narrative: (1) that human beings, created in the image and likeness of God (*imago Dei*), have a distinct capacity for communion with God;

(2) that human beings have a unique place in the cosmos God created; and (3) that human beings are made for communion with other living beings. Slavery deformed these convictions. It aimed to deface the *imago Dei* in black human beings, constrain black human potential, and debase black *being-in-communion* with creation. Slavery sought to displace God and, thus, it blasphemed. Its sacrilegious extension in white racist supremacy has had consequences for *all* people—black people, especially, and black women, in particular.[8]

Cyprian Davis explains that the belief that Black people were subhuman was held by even well-meaning Americans, including clergy. William Henry Elder, who would become the archbishop of Cincinnati and a supporter to Black Catholics after the Civil War, wrote about the enslaved people in the southern diocese of Natchez, Mississippi, in a newsletter for the Society for the Propagation of the Faith located in Lyons, France, to garner donations for his work in the United States.

> The poor negroes very often have at first a fear of a Catholic Priest, or imagine they can never understand him; but they are not ill disposed towards religion. Indeed they often have a craving for its ministrations. Having few comforts and no expectations in this world, their thoughts and desires are the more easily drawn to the good things of the world to come. I say often because often again they are so entirely animal in their inclinations, so engrossed with the senses, that they have no regard for any thing above the gratification of the body.[9]

While Elder did genuinely care for the spiritual well-being of the enslaved people, that care did not include working for their liberation from the chains of slavery, which Pope Gregory XVI condemned in his 1839 apostolic letter *In Supremo Apostolus Fastigio*. Davis explains that not only did two prominent American bishops, John England and August Marie Martin, not condemn slavery, but they were apologists for slavery and felt "obligated to defend it on the basis of Catholic tradition and Scripture."[10]

August Marie Martin, who urged all able-bodied males to take up arms and fight to defend the Confederacy during the Civil War, believed people of African descent were from the "race of Canaan," and were therefore saved from their inhumanity through slavery.

> In the admirable dispositions of His Providence, God, the Father of us all, who loves the souls for whom He has given His only begotten and well-beloved Son, and who uses even purely human motives for the profit of eternal interests, for centuries God snatches from the barbarism of savage morals some thousands of the children of the race of Canaan on whom there continues to weigh nearly everywhere the curse of an outraged father.

Martin argued that the brutal enslavement and violence used to maintain the slavocracy were "an eminently Christian work, the redemption of millions of human beings, passing from the night of the intellect of the blackest type to the sweet and life-giving brightness of Gospel light." Davis points out that, ironically, Martin admits most enslavers did not live up to that ideal.

> Let us say that blinded by materialistic teachings, and without any respect for God, in the image of whom their immortal souls as well as ours have been created; in those very persons that we should have, in regenerating them, raised them up from their original degradation, most of us saw only the means for our own profit and exploitation, too often making them the docile instruments of brutal passions.[11]

Those "brutal passions" included the rape and impregnation of Black women who were enslaved, and children born out of such circumstances were further contradictory proof of the humanity of Black people.

The code of silence surrounding white men impregnating Black women permeated all aspects of society. Copeland describes such silence:

> Whether dissuaded by the conventions of Victorian society or the indifference of arrogance, few white people associated with

the slave trade spoke publicly about sex between slaveholding white men and the black women whom they had enslaved. Mary Boylin Chestnus, whose husband was a slaveholder, confided the following to her diary: "Like the patriarchs of old, our men live all in one house with their wives and their concubines; and the mulattoes one sees in every family partly resembles the white children. Any lady is ready to tell you who is the father of all the mulatto children in everybody's household but her own. Those she seems to think, drop from the clouds."[12]

Black children born into slavery, regardless of whether their father was white or Black, "were severed from their sacred humanity and deprived of person-identity, their bodies and spirits endangered and traumatized."[13]

While the white fathers' sexual exploitation of Black women and refusal to parent their children was excused in silence, Black women were degraded, and sexual stereotypes that persist to this day were reinforced about them. "Sexual purity was the definitive quality of true—that is, white—womanhood; smeared as promiscuous, black women were deemed incapable of chastity and, consequently, of true womanhood. Black women not only were dehumanized, but degendered and desexed."[14]

The notion of Black inferiority did not subside after slavery was abolished; instead, it was used as a justification for the strict segregation of Black people from mainstream white society that emerged after Reconstruction. Cyprian Davis gives an example of the nineteenth-century white American mindset when describing a Catholic convert named Orestes Brownson, whom Davis described as "perhaps the best example of an authentic intellectual and an original thinker that the American Catholic Church possessed in the mid-nineteenth century." Though Brownson had opposed slavery and believed it was wrong morally, socially, and politically, Brownson, according to Davis, also had a very racist view of people of African descent that he espoused in his writings.[15]

The vast majority of African Americans lived and worked in the South under oppressive sharecropping arrangements, white terror, and neoslavery, as discussed in chapter 2. The 10 percent of African Americans who lived in the northern cities also faced racism, discrimination, segregation, and high rates of unemployment, which led to participation in the informal economy. In the 2019 preface to his book *The Condemnation of Blackness*, Khalil Gibran Muhammad summarizes how immediately after the end of slavery the nation used crime statistics to criminalize the freed Black population and perpetuate the belief in their inferiority.

> Crime statistics became an innovative and scientific way of communicating the inferiority and pathologies of black people after slavery. . . . Despite the oppression of those early years of freedom, arrest rates and prison data were considered objective, nonpartisan, race-neutral, and even post-racial. . . . It is hard to truly appreciate how soon after slavery many northern white elites, and some black ones, used crime statistics to emphasize that personal responsibility—bad behavior and broken homes—and not systemic discrimination in the age of "separate but equal" accounted for racial disparities. Crime statistics fueled gendered notions of black male pathology, and when linked to illegitimacy rates, doubly burdened black women by defining them as sexually deviant and underserving of the protections of womanhood.[16]

Muhammad describes how social scientists analyzed newly available data from the 1870, 1880, and 1890 U.S. Census reports to create new justifications for why the Black population should be denied equal rights and opportunities in the country, which paved the way for Jim Crow laws.

> Racial knowledge that had been dominated by anecdotal, hereditarian, and pseudobiological theories of race would gradually be transformed by new social scientific theories of race and society and new tools of analysis, namely racial statistics and social surveys. Out of the new methods and data sources, black criminality would emerge, alongside disease and intelligence, as a fundamental measure of black inferiority. From the 1890s through the first four decades of the twentieth century, black criminality would become one of the most commonly cited and longest-lasting justifications for black inequality and mortality in the modern urban world.[17]

In May 1896, a German-born immigrant, Frederick L. Hoffman, published "Race Traits and Tendencies of the American Negro," a 330-page article in the prestigious *Publications of the American Economic Association*. Hoffman was a statistician at the Prudential Life Insurance Company, and the article was a "compilation of statistics, eugenic theory, observation, and speculation, solicited by the Prudential in response to a wave of state legislation banning discrimination against African Americans. "Race Traits" immediately became a key text in one of the central social preoccupations of the turn of the century: the supposed "Negro Problem."

> Hoffman peppered the text with demographic figures, morbidity and mortality tables, miscegenation rates, and incarceration trends. He used Gould's anthropological tables, the eleventh U.S. Census (1890), reports from the hospitals of the Freedmen's Bureau, and the measurements of soldiers collected during the Civil War. He created the largest compilation of data about the American Negro then available in print, and he presented it all to the reader both as interpretation and as raw data.[18]

Though Hoffman claimed he was an "outsider" immune to American bias, the reality was that he was a proponent of white supremacy who interpreted the data to prove the inferiority of Black people, a group he claimed was a barrier to American progress.[19] In 1892, Hoffman had begun to correspond with government officials such as Carroll D. Wright, who was a "highly esteemed economist, census official, and commissioner of the U.S. Bureau of Labor," and was able to gather data that showed, from Hoffman's perspective, that "every statistic or expert testimony was scientific proof of inferiority and degeneration" of Black people. This led Hoffman to argue, "we reach the conclusion that the colored race is showing every sign of an undermined constitution, a diseased manhood and womanhood; in short, all the indications of a race on the road to extinction."[20]

Contemporary social scientists like W. E. B. Du Bois contested the narrative Hoffman told and argued that African Americans could not be lumped together as a whole without taking into account the different classes and conditions of life Black people found themselves in. Du Bois also "pointed out that the health outcomes of African Americans were entirely comparable to those of immigrant groups with similar economic resources." For example, the mortality rate of Black Americans in the United States at that time (32.61) was slightly lower than whites in Munich, Germany (32.80).[21]

Another opponent of Hoffman's statistical interpretations was M. V. Ball, a prison doctor at Eastern State Penitentiary in Philadelphia. Ball argued that the high Black prisoner mortality rate from tuberculosis cited in Hoffman's data was accurate but misinterpreted. Ball argued that the causes "were related to childhood poverty, unsanitary living conditions, and poor hygiene," not race, and that social distinctions were not taken into account in statistics. To prove his point, Ball cited the New York Board of Health statistics that revealed comparable childhood mortality rates among Italian immigrants and Black people who were struggling financially. Both groups had rates that were higher compared to New York City's childhood mortality rate in general. Ball insisted that the conditions for Black children had to be as favorable as conditions for white children before it could be deduced that Black children were more disease prone. He argued the same when it came to Black versus white criminality.[22]

In contrast, Hoffman and white American thinkers like Carroll Wright viewed the problems facing white people, such as a high suicide rate, crime, and disease, not as proof of white inferiority but social problems that needed to be solved. The men believed that the government and society in general had a responsibility to protect "the health and welfare of the white citizenry" in order to prevent "crime, disease, and death."

> As Wright put it, "The health of the workers of a community is essential to their material prosperity, and the health of a community has much to do with the volume of crime." Within the general population, among Anglo-Americans and new European immigrants, the problems of disease, death, and self-destruction were rooted in industrialization and modern civilization.[23]

Hoffman, like white Americans in the North, refused to acknowledge the existence of racism against African Americans and that discrimination could affect outcomes such as unemployment and imprisonment for criminal offenses. Hoffman argued that the higher crime rates of African Americans in the North compared to the South proved that education had failed to cause Black progress. The hypocrisy when viewing and "interpreting" the data was glaring. In one example, though Black people in Massachusetts in 1890 were five times more likely than Black people in Mississippi to serve time for a crime, white men in Massachusetts were ten times more likely than white people in Mississippi to serve time.[24]

Contrary to the belief that Black people faced a level playing field in society and decided to turn to crime, the truth was that white racism proved to be a tremendous hindrance to Black people making gains in society. The prevailing white consensus held that African Americans were responsible for their own societal uplift despite the centuries of enslavement and oppression they'd endured. Muhammad quotes one Black northern reformer named Fannie B. Williams who corrected her white counterparts. African Americans could not pull themselves up by their proverbial bootstraps if they did not possess boots.

> "In every community the Negro is practically dependent, for nearly everything of importance, upon the dominant race." That black people are segregated in "the worst portions of the city," limited to the worst jobs despite "merit" and "education," and are even being replaced at the bottom of the job chain by new immigrants, she continued, were not conditions they alone could reverse. The Negro "is the victim of more injustice than is meted out to any other class of people." The real problem among blacks was their lack of "preparation" to deal with segregation and racism when those around them "among other nationalities" found "elevating and liberalizing influences." . . . . "My friends," the bottom line is "that society . . . is doing everything that heart and brain can devise to save white young men and white young women, while practically nothing is being done for the colored young men and women, except to prosecute and punish them for crimes for which society is largely responsible for."[25]

As Black and liberal white voices pushed back against Hoffman's interpretation of statistics, they were largely ignored or dismissed while Hoffman and his work received praise and accolades. According to Muhammad, Hoffman and other emerging social scientists greatly shaped the national understanding of the "Negro Problem." "The national white consensus emerging at the turn of the century . . . was that African Americans were inferior human beings whose predicament was three parts their own making and two parts the consequence of mis-guided philanthropy."[26]

A century later, in 1995, the predictions of Black youth criminality by another white political scientist, Princeton professor John DiIulio Jr., contributed to the mass incarceration that the nation is experiencing today. In an article titled "The Coming of the Super-Predators," DiIulio coined the term for his cover story in the *Weekly Standard*, a new conser-vative political opinion magazine. The use of the term "superpredator" had what Carroll Bogert and LynNell Hancock describe in the Marshall Project as "a game-changing potency, derived in part from the avalanche of media coverage that began almost immediately." In a review of forty mainstream news outlets' coverage for five years after that article, Bogert and Hancock found that the word "superpredator" was used in at least three hundred articles.[27]

In "The Coming of the Super-Predators," DiIulio quoted the district attorney of Philadelphia, Lynne Abraham, who described her fear of "boys whose voices have yet to change. We're talking about elementary school youngsters who pack guns instead of lunches. We're talking about kids who have absolutely no respect for human life and no sense of the future." DiIulio's predictions were not race-neutral, stating, "the trouble will be greatest in black inner-city neighborhoods," yet he also cautioned all of America that "other places are also certain to have burgeoning youth-crime problems that will spill over into upscale central-city dis-tricts, inner-ring suburbs, and even the rural heartland." Like Hoffman, DiIulio backed his prediction with questionable academic research on youth crime and violence, warning, "All of the research indicates that Americans are sitting atop a demographic crime bomb. And all of those who are closest to the problem hear the bomb ticking."[28]

DiIulio cited statistics that between 1985 and 1992 males ages four-teen to seventeen committed murder at a rate that was 50 percent higher for whites and 300 percent higher for Blacks. From this, he deduced that a staggering wave of new youth crime was inevitable:

> Nationally, there are now about 40 million children under the age of 10, the largest number in decades. By simple math, in a decade today's 4 to 7-year-olds will become 14 to 17-year-olds. By 2005, the number of males in this age group will have risen about 25 percent overall and 50 percent for blacks.
>
> To some extent, it's just that simple: more boys begets more bad boys. But to really grasp why this spike in the young male population means big trouble ahead, you need to appreciate both the statistical evidence from a generation of birth-cohort studies and related findings from recent street-level studies and surveys:
>
> James Q. Wilson and other leading crime doctors can predict with confidence that the additional 500,000 boys who will be 14 to 17 years old in the year 2000 will mean at least 30,000 more murderers, rapists, and muggers on the streets than we have today.[29]

DiIulio explained that "moral poverty" was to blame for this impend-ing societal threat. While the majority of American children grow up with loving and responsible adults in their lives who teach them right from wrong, there was a new subset of youngsters who were surrounded only by "deviant, delinquent, and criminal adults in abusive, violence-ridden, fatherless, Godless, and jobless settings." DiIulio laid out in no uncertain terms what the future held for these youth.

> On the horizon, therefore, are tens of thousands of severely morally impoverished juvenile super-predators. They are per-fectly capable of committing the most heinous acts of physical violence for the most trivial reasons (for example, a perception of slight disrespect or the accident of being in their path). They fear neither the stigma of arrest nor the pain of imprisonment.

They live by the meanest code of the meanest streets, a code that reinforces rather than restrains their violent, hair-trigger mentality. In prison or out, the things that super-predators get by their criminal behavior—sex, drugs, money—are their own immediate rewards. Nothing else matters to them. So for as long as their youthful energies hold out, they will do what comes "naturally": murder, rape, rob, assault, burglarize, deal deadly drugs, and get high.[30]

DiIulio, a practicing Catholic, suggested what he saw as the solution, which he borrowed from "three well-known child-development experts—Moses, Jesus Christ, and Mohammed. It's called religion. If we are to have a prayer of stopping any significant fraction of the superpredators short of the prison gates, then we had better say 'Amen,' and fast." DiIulio acknowledged that Black churches in low-income neighborhoods were struggling financially and even closing due to lack of funds, but he believed public funds should be provided to them in order for churches to be "havens for at-risk children." He imagined that churches would provide services like adoption placement, parenting classes, substance abuse treatment, daycare and preschool programs, and other supports to boost social and economic development.[31] In other words, DiIulio was advocating for investment in the same root cause solutions that African Americans had been advocating for since the 1890s—solutions never actualized under President Johnson's administration or any subsequent one.

The following year, DiIulio published an even more racially explicit and unapologetic warning about the threat of Black youth criminality titled "My Black Crime Problem, and Ours: Why are so many Blacks in prison? Is the criminal justice system racist? The answer is disquieting." Again, opening with "statistical predictions," DiIulio began the article as follows:

Violent crime is down in New York and many other cities, but there are two big reasons to keep the champagne corked. One is that murder, rape, robbery, and assault remain at historic highs: the streets of Manhattan, like those of Houston, Philadelphia,

Detroit, Chicago, and Los Angeles, remain much less safe today than in the 1950s and 1960s. Worse, though policing and prison policies matter, nothing affects crime rates more than the number of young males in the population—and by the year 2010, there will be about 4.5 million more males age 17 or under than there were in 1990: 8 percent more whites and 26 percent more blacks. Since around 6 percent of young males turn out to be career criminals, according to the historical data, this increase will put an estimated 270,000 more young predators on the streets than in 1990, coming at us in waves over the next two decades. [32]

DiIulio argued that a study conducted in 1993 found there are no racially disparate sentences for cocaine traffickers—an argument thoroughly debunked in the crack versus cocaine ten-to-one sentencing ratio discussed previously. He also misused statistics to argue the war on drugs and death penalty were both racially unbiased. Planting misleading and often-without-context statistic after statistic, DiIulio made the case that Black people were committing more crimes than whites, more likely to victimize a white person than a white person victimizing a Black person, and attacked the Sentencing Project and other organizations calling out racial disparities in incarceration.[33]

Like Hoffman, DiIulio was lauded as a truth teller, and his influence over the direction the country took regarding youths who committed crime cannot be overstated. In *Policing the Black Man*, Kristin Henning states, "DiIulio was not alone in promoting this demographic theory, which gained extraordinary traction in the media and among politicians seeking to earn a reputation as being tough on crime."[34] Bogert and Hancock remark that by "the end of the 1990s, virtually every state had toughened its laws on juveniles: sending them more readily into adult prisons; gutting and sidelining family courts; and imposing mandatory sentences, including life sentences without parole."[35]

Also, like Hoffman, who falsely predicted that the African American population would die out and become extinct after the turn of the twentieth century, DiIulio's predictions of a youth crime surge proved to be patently wrong. Instead of the youth crime soaring, by 2000 "the rate of juvenile crime dropped by more than half."[36] That steep decline continued, and according to the Justice Department, "by 2020, the number of violent crime arrests involving youth reached a new low, 78% below the 1994 peak, and half the number 10 years earlier."[37] A *San Francisco Chronicle* investigative report on the steep decline of youth violence since the mid-1990s states, "Systemically, there is no clear explanation for why the crime rate dropped, and continued to decline through the 2008 recession and to the present day." Some possible theories are that the decline of lead poisoning in children could have played a role. Similarly, the decline in demand for crack cocaine and the lengthy incarceration sentences for drug dealers may have resulted in less recruitment of young people in the violent drug trade.[38]

After pushback, accurate statistics, and responses, DiIulio would go on to abandon his theory, a change detailed in a 2001 *New York Times* article. Forty-two years old at the time, DiIulio was working in a new position as director of the White House Office of Faith-Based and Community Initiatives and conceded that "he wished he had never become the 1990s intellectual pillar for putting violent juveniles in prison and condemning them as 'superpredators.'" He traced his change of position to a Palm Sunday Mass in 1996 when he had a conversion of heart.[39] DiIulio told the reporter, "God had given me a Rolodex, good will and a passion that was sometimes misdirected, and I knew that for the rest of my life I would work on prevention, on helping bring caring, responsible adults to wrap their arms around these kids." DiIulio claimed he tried to "put the brakes on the superpredator theory, which had all but taken on a life of its own." He began publishing articles that emphasized "churches over prisons, or opposing Congress's welfare overhaul as legislation that undercut the most vulnerable families."[40] As we've seen throughout the book, however, the state and federal governments did not invest in churches; instead, they pumped billions of dollars into constructing juvenile and adult facilities for incarceration while slashing funding for welfare and other social programs. Franklin E. Zimring, who at the time of the *New York Times* article was a University of California–Berkeley professor of law and director of the university's Earl Warren Legal Institute, stated, "[DiIulio's] prediction wasn't just wrong, it was exactly the opposite.... His theories on superpredators were utter madness."[41]

Zimring told the Marshall Project, "As some criminologists explained at the time, what drove juvenile homicides in the 1990s wasn't a new breed of violent teens. It was probably the greater availability of guns, making fights and gang rivalries among kids more lethal than before.... But to paraphrase Mark Twain, the truth was still putting on its shoes while the 'superpredators' ran out the door."[42]

Henning states, in spite of DiIulio's conversion and change of heart, the "damage has been unyielding."

> Notwithstanding statistical evidence that by 2001 had firmly dis-proven the predictions of an imminent juvenile super-predator, children as young as thirteen and fourteen are still being tried as adults, and hundreds of juveniles have been sent to prison for life without parole in the wake of horrific legislation designed to stave off the impending black threat.
>
> More troubling is the lingering and pervasive influence of the super-predator myth on the psyche of the police and the public. Although it is impossible to trace any one event to the image police have of black youth, it is hard to believe that DiIulio's rhet-oric did not emblazon the image of violent black boys running amok on the minds of those who police our streets.[43]

The term "superpredator" was used by police, academics, legislators, judges, district attorneys, and even first lady Hillary Clinton, in a way that was reminiscent of the slavery days. Young Black boys and men were not fully human; they were animal-like predators with no conscience or abil-ity to tell right from wrong or feel human emotions like love and empathy. The only recourse to "manage" these superpredators was subjugation in the form of lengthy—if not lifetime—incarceration. While DiIulio coined the term "superpredator," the dehumanizing language used to stereotype and dehumanize African Americans was already widespread and often racially coded since the Nixon and Bush administrations.

Once such racially coded acronym came to light after the brutal beat-ing of Rodney King and the subsequent jury acquittal of the police offi-cers in a trial in Los Angeles in 1992. In an open letter to her colleagues in academia, Sylvia Wynter wrote about a news report she had heard on the radio that stated "public officials of the judicial system of Los Angeles routinely used the acronym N.H.I. to refer to any case involving a breach of the rights of young Black males who belong to the jobless category of the inner-city ghettoes. N.H.I. means 'no humans involved.'" Wynter asked her colleagues a question that all Americans still need to grapple with:

> If, as Ralph Ellison alerted us to in his *The Invisible Man*, we see each other only through the "inner eyes" with which we look with our physical eyes upon reality, the question we must confront in the wake of the Rodney King Event becomes: What is our responsibility for the making of those "inner eyes"? Ones in which humanness and North Americanness are always already defined, not only in optimally White terms, but also in optimally middle-class (i.e. both Simi Valley, and secondarily Cosby-Huxtable TV family) variants of these terms? What have we had to do, and still have to do, with the putting in place of the classifying logic of that shared mode of "subjective understanding" [Jaime Carbonell, 1987] in whose "inner eyes" young Black males can be perceived as being justly shut out from what Helen Fein calls the "universe of moral obligation" that bonds the interests of the Simi Valley jurors as Whites and non-Blacks (one Asian, one Hispanic), to the interests of the White policemen and the Los Angeles judicial office-holders who are our graduates?[44]

Wynter points to the similarities between how young, jobless African Americans are discarded in American society and narrative in the 2015 book by Helen Fein about the Armenian genocide by the Turkish pan-nationalists and the Nazi Holocaust of millions of Jewish people. Fein pointed out that "both Jews and Armenians had been decreed by the dominant group that was to perpetrate the crime to be outside the sanctified universe of obligation—that circle of people with reciprocal obligations to protect each other whose bonds arose from their relation to a deity or a sacred source of authority," and they were therefore "misrecognized as aliens, as strangers who were, as if it were, of a different species."[45] So, too, with very low income, and often unemployed, Black Americans who have not been able to climb the socio-economic ladder are treated as less than human—outside of society and deserving of any brutal punishment that may be inflicted on them by the dominant class. Wynter states, these Black people like Rodney King have, since the 1960s,

> come to occupy a doubled pariah status, no longer that of only being Black, but of also belonging to the rapidly accelerating Post-Industrial category of the poor and jobless. As the category which, defined by the sociologist Zygmunt Bauman as that of the New Poor, embodies a plight, which like that of the ongoing degradation of the planetary environment, is not even posable, not to say resolvable, within the conceptual framework of our present order of knowledge.[46]

Fania Davis argues the root issue is racial capitalism, which she states is "a socioeconomic order in which all social institutions are inextricably bound up with the slave trade and slavery, indigenous land seizure, genocide, and colonization." The same capitalist system that profited from enslaved Black people during the antebellum period and re-enslaved during convict-leasing neoslavery is now warehousing "surplus" African Americans.

> Today, racial capitalism uses prisons to manage marginalized populations, especially people of color. Neoliberal policies in the last decades have shifted massive amounts of wealth from working and middle-class families to the wealthiest 1 percent through tax cuts, deregulation, and cutting social programs. These policies shred social and safety nets and render millions of people unemployed, poor, unhealthy, and homeless, creating "surplus populations." Incarceration is then deployed to contain and manage these populations and the problems created by racial capitalism's failure to address social ills.[47]

It is no wonder, then, that in Los Angeles, where the police used the acronym N.H.I., the Marshall Project found the "L.A. Times used 'superpredator' more than any other major newspaper."[48]

The *San Francisco Chronicle* investigative report also found severe racial discrepancies in the prosecution of youth as adults. "In Los Angeles County, 96% of the 1,551 juveniles prosecuted as adults from 2007 to 2016 were black or Latino. In Kern County, the figure was 92%." In the state of California, while "black and Latino people represent 70% of inmates in prison, they made up 86% of all juveniles charged as adults in California over the past decade."

The numbers were not a mere record of Black and Latino youth committing more crimes but a record of the way prosecutors chose to file the cases. "A 2016 study by several juvenile justice organizations, including the W. Haywood Burns Institute in Oakland, found that black youths charged with crimes were 11 times more likely than white youths to have their cases directly filed to adult court." Altogether, "from 2003 to 2018, more than 11,500 youths ages 14 to 17 were moved into adult courts across California."[49]

Nationally, the Juvenile Justice Network states that an estimated "250,000 youth are tried, sentenced, or incarcerated as adults every year across the United States" and "on any given day, 10,000 youth are detained or incarcerated in adult jails and prisons." Youth who are incarcerated in facilities with adults are "36 times more likely to commit suicide and are at the greatest risk of sexual victimization."[50]

The American penal system strips people of their human dignity and often exposes them to environments that are brutally and unconscionably inhumane. The Brennan Justice Center sums up this reality:

> American prison life is built upon the dehumanizing rituals of induction, initiation, hierarchy, degradation and routine, all designed to assert authority and control over the bodies and lives of incarcerated people. Individuality is stripped away upon prison entry, replaced by an inmate number and a standardized, nondescript uniform.
>
> Life in a U.S. prison is filled with an endless parade of security measures (caging, handcuffing, shackling, strip and cell searches, and lockdowns) punctuating a daily routine marked by enforced idleness, the ever-present risk of violence, often adversarial relationships with prison staff, and only sporadic opportunities

for constructive activities offering rehabilitation, education, or treatment. Solitary confinement is often used as punishment for minor violations of prison rules, such as talking back, being out of place, or failure to obey an order. Incarcerated individuals in America live in a harsh, dystopian social world of values and rules, designed to control, isolate, disempower and erode one's sense of autonomous self.[51]

As a result of the Thirteenth Amendment, which allows slavery as a condition of punishment, hundreds of thousands of people incarcerated in America's prisons and jails are subjected to the same dehumanization, degradation, violence, sexual violence, and economic exploitation that enslaved people faced.

In September 2021, after the chief medical doctor at Rikers Island publicly raised the alarm that there was a "public health disaster unfolding before our eyes," two elected officials toured the prison complex on the New York island. Emily Gallagher, an assembly member, posted a tweet thread describing the conditions she witnessed at the Otis Bantum Correctional Center (OBCSS). Though people are supposed to be taken to OBCSS, processed, and out within twenty-four hours, Gallagher encountered people who had been there for three months. Most people were not being held for serious allegations and believed their charges would eventually be dismissed once they had a hearing date.

> There's garbage everywhere, rotting food with maggots, cockroaches, worms in the showers, human feces and piss. Most of the toilets are broken so men are given plastic bags to relieve themselves in. . . .
>
> There's a lot of serious mental illness and many hadn't been given their prescription medication for months. I met multiple men with broken hands and legs that were not being treated. . . . Because of the lack of security, everyone's scared they're going to be injured or killed. Most people have fashioned some kind of homemade weapon to defend themselves.
>
> While one man was begging me to hug him through bars and weeping, around the corner another man yelled to my colleague,

"Miss, look at me" and turned to see a man jump into a noose he had made out of a sheet.[52]

A *New York Times* investigation concluded that over a decade of mismanagement and neglect were responsible for creating the human rights crisis in the notorious jail.

The groundwork for the violence and disorder on Rikers was laid over the years by successive mayoral administrations, which allowed power to shift to lower-level wardens and the guards' union and then to incarcerated gang members themselves. As a result, guards have been posted throughout the system in wasteful and capricious ways, generous benefits like sick leave have been abused and detainees have had the run of entire housing areas.[53]

In 2018 when the top criminal justice adviser of then-mayor Bill de Blasio wrote a memo warning that high rates of guard absenteeism may have driven the rise in jail violence, de Blasio's administration took none of the "recommended steps to stabilize staffing and reduce violent incidents. . . . Not only did incidents where guards used force rise, but some gangs were positioned to take over housing areas when the pandemic swept through and caused staffing problems."[54]

Though policymakers in 2022 tried to say improvements had been made in Rikers since the elected officials' visit sounding an alarm in 2021, the Vera Institute for Justice denies substantive changes were made, but "judges and prosecutors continue to send people to these facilities to await trial. In September 2022, the Gothamist published images depicting people "caged in tiny showers, sleeping on excrement-smeared floors, and attempting chest compressions on the seriously ill because no medical care was available. They also showed people without access to functional toilets being left to suffer in their own feces for hours on end." Eighteen people died in the New York jails in 2022 alone.[55]

In San Francisco in 2019, several people in jail, all except one were pretrial detainees, who were held in a particular housing section, CJ4 and CJ5, were alleging that their constitutional rights were violated because they were denied outdoor recreation time and exposure to direct sunlight. In a lawsuit against the County of San Francisco, the plaintiffs requested that all inmates "in CJ4 and CJ5 be given three hours per week of 'outdoor recreation time' and one hour per day of out-of-cell time." The district court held that under the Fourteenth Amendment, "even if the evidence shows that access to direct sunlight is not medically necessary, forcing people to live without direct sunlight for many years is simply 'punishment,' unless the deprivation is 'for a short period of time.'" Therefore, the district court ordered the city to "provide one hour per week of direct sunlight (which it defined as light 'not filtered through a window') to inmates in CJ5 who had been incarcerated for more than four years."

Both the plaintiffs and defendants appealed the district court's decision. The plaintiffs believed the district court's ruling did not go far enough and that all people who were incarcerated for more than six weeks should receive three hours of exercise time outdoors per week. The appellate court did not agree with the plaintiffs. It ruled that the plaintiffs "have not identified authority that establishes a constitutional right to a particular quantum or quality of direct sunlight 'not filtered through a window.'" The court also ruled that the plaintiffs did not identify any risk of harm from having their exercise time take place indoors instead of outdoors.

While this is not as egregious an example as the Rikers Island case, most Americans literally treat their dogs who are walked outdoors daily better than the court and city of San Francisco believe that people who are incarcerated deserve to be treated under the law. Denying people the ability to have direct sunlight hit their skin for over four years speaks to the dehumanization of the people who for the most part had not even been found guilty of a crime and were awaiting their day in court.[56]

Prisons across the United States are places where the people incarcerated in them are subjected to conditions that are so inhumane they would not be tolerated in mainstream society but are ignored and even joked about by people on the outside. In *Until We Reckon*, Danielle Sered states, "Violence is not an exception in prison—it is the daily, defining norm. Aside from the physical pain and injury so many people experience, the constancy of violence results in peak levels of hypervigilance, fear, and the pained, interminable alertness that surviving prison requires."[57]

Investigations by the U.S. Department of Justice detailed extremely cruel and inhumane treatment of people incarcerated in prisons in Alabama. Since 1983, the population of people incarcerated in Alabama has increased 149 percent. Though African Americans make up 28 percent of state residents, they account for 43 percent of people in jail and 54 percent of people in prison. "Since 1978, the Black incarceration rate has increased 193 percent. In 2017, Black people were incarcerated at 2.8 times the rate of white people." Comparatively, white people make up 66 percent of state residents and 44 percent of people incarcerated.[58]

On April 2, 2019, the U.S. Justice Department Civil Rights Division and the three U.S. attorney's offices for the state of Alabama provided a written report that "revealed that an excessive amount of violence, sexual abuse, and prisoner deaths occur within Alabama's prisons on a regular basis." The report mentioned the decrepit conditions of one of Alabama's prisons, Draper, that was closed after inspectors viewed it:

> After the inspection, our experts informed ADOC [Alabama Department of Corrections] of their shock at the state of the facility. In fact, during our inspection of Draper, one of our experts had to leave the kitchen area before becoming sick from the toxic fumes of the cleaning chemicals. Approximately one month after our site visit, we learned through press reports that ADOC was closing Draper after engineering experts hired by ADOC concluded that the facility was "no longer suitable to house inmates, or to be used as a correctional facility."[59]

As of January 2020, Alabama's remaining thirteen ADOC prisons housed approximately 16,600 males with varying custody levels, which put them over their capacity by 6,000 men. Altogether, including the Julia Tutwiler Prison for Women and work release facilities, Alabama incarcerated approximately 21,000 individuals, though the DOJ investigation reviewed only the men's prisons.[60]

According to the Department of Justice's Bureau of Justice Statistics, "Alabama's prisons have the highest homicide rate in the country." In addition to violence committed by and against people who are incarcerated, correctional officers have also "been stabbed, punched, kicked, threatened with broken broomsticks or knives, and had their heads stomped on."[61]

Among other reasons, the report attributed the high prevalence of violence to the severe overcrowding at the prisons and staffing shortages. "Alabama has one of the most overcrowded prison systems in the nation" and the fourth highest imprisonment rate in the United States. According to ADOC's staffing report from June 2018, "Alabama's prisons employ only 1,072 out of 3,326 authorized correctional officers," resulting in a "system-wide occupancy rate of 165%."

To understand the impact of the staffing shortage, the report gave the example of the warden at the Holman prison who said she probably has eleven "security staff, both officers and supervisors, per shift for the entire complex," which housed approximately eight hundred men. Adding to the staffing issues is the illegal behavior of some correctional officers. At the time the report was written, dozens of correctional officers had been arrested in the prior two years for crimes related to drug trafficking and other misconduct within Alabama's prisons, and many of the staff still employed are "bringing illegal contraband into Alabama's prisons."[62]

As a result of the staffing shortages, the report detailed one unit of an Alabama prison run by incarcerated people, which left others in the unit vulnerable to physical and sexual assault.

The "Hot Bay" at Bibb was a housing unit populated exclusively with prisoners with disciplinary infractions. It had limited supervision and no programming. On a Friday in September 2017, three days before the Department of Justice arrived at Bibb for the first full facility tour of our investigation, two prisoners stood guard at the doors of the Hot Bay, an open dormitory housing men in bunkbeds multiple rows deep, watching for rarely-seen correctional officers. At the back of the dormitory and not visible from the front door, two other prisoners started stabbing their intended victim. The victim screamed for help. Another prisoner tried to intervene and he, too, was stabbed. The initial victim dragged himself to the front doors of the dormitory. Prisoners banged on the locked doors to get the attention of security staff. When an officer finally responded, he found the prisoner lying on the floor bleeding from his chest. The prisoner eventually bled to death. One Hot Bay resident told us that he could still hear the prisoner's screams in his sleep.[63]

Though the "Hot Bay" was closed after the visit, there were many such unsupervised units throughout Alabama's prison system. The DOJ investigation found that an "alarming number of prisoners are killed by other prisoners using homemade knives," and though ADOC often had knowledge that people had been previously stabbed and were told by the victims that their lives were at danger, the correctional officers "took no meaningful efforts to protect these prisoners from serious harm—harm that was eventually deadly."[64]

In addition to the extreme violence in Alabama's prisons, the report also found sexual abuse to be "severe and widespread" and "too often undetected or prevented by ADOC staff." From late 2016 through April 2018, the DOJ reviewed over six hundred incident reports of sexual abuse committed by and against men who were incarcerated. The majority of incidents described forced anal or oral sex, though the report also detailed painful instances of prisoners being assaulted by broomsticks forced into their rectums. The documented sexual abuse occurred in the "dormitories, cells, recreation areas, the infirmary, bathrooms, and showers at all hours of the day and night," and there was not "a single incident in which a correctional officer or other staff member observed or intervened to stop a sexual assault." This attests to how widespread and inadequate the supervision by correctional officers is, and how dangerous the conditions are. Additionally concerning is the likelihood of instances of sexual abuse being greatly undercounted because many of those sexually assaulted "do not report abuse out of fear of retaliation, shame, or because they do not believe that ADOC's system to address complaints of sexual abuse will result in any changes."[65]

The experts who conducted the investigation and interviewed prison captains and lieutenants came to the conclusion that many of the ADOC staff "appear to accept the high level of violence and sexual abuse in ADOC as a normal course of business, including acquiescence to the idea that prisoners will be subjected to sexual abuse as a way to pay debts accrued to other prisoners." Much of the sexual abuse is connected to "the drug trade and other contraband problems that result from inadequate supervision and corruption in Alabama's prisons." Many of the men reported that they were sexually assaulted because of debts they owed; or they and their outside family members were extorted for money at the risk of sexual abuse if not provided the money demanded; or men were drugged and then sexually abused when they were under the influence and unable to defend themselves. Two shift commanders of death row and segregation at Holman estimated that 50 to 60 percent of their prisoners were using drugs. One shift commander over general population at Holman estimated that 95 percent of that facility's prisoners were using drugs. The consensus is that most of the drugs enter the prison through staff smuggling it in.

On July 23, 2020, the U.S. Justice Department of Civil Rights Division and the three U.S. attorneys' offices for the state of Alabama provided another written report outlining the conditions of severe and frequent excessive force by prison guards and staff against the people incarcerated in Alabama's prisons.

In 2017 alone, the ADOC's "incident reporting system documented 1,800 uses of force" by correctional officers, which is also most likely vastly undercounted. The incidences of excessive force depicted brutality carried out by the guards on the men they were paid to supervise, cover-ups of that brutality, and indifference to the pain and suffering that was caused on people who were treated like dangerous, caged animals and not humans deserving of respect and dignity. Correctional officers beat people with their fists and batons, choked people, kicked, shoved, and sprayed people with mace regularly. Two such instances in 2019, which resulted in the death of two men who were incarcerated, are detailed below.[66]

As part of the autopsy, an ADOC investigator informed a coroner that, after an officer opened his cell, the prisoner rushed toward another prisoner carrying two prison-made weapons. A correctional officer ordered the prisoner to drop the weapons, but the prisoner failed to comply. As a result, the officer sprayed the prisoner with a chemical agent, but it had no effect. The officer then struck the prisoner on the arm, causing the prisoner to drop one weapon. A second correctional officer responded to the scene and administered palm-heel strikes to the prisoner's head as well as knee-to-head strikes as he tried to disarm the prisoner. . . . The prisoner was airlifted to a hospital due to the extent of his injuries. Photographs revealed extensive and severe bruising and swelling along the prisoner's face, left ear, eyes, and nose. The level of force used caused the prisoner to sustain multiple fractures to his skull, including near his nose, both eye sockets, left ear, left cheekbone, and the base of his skull, many of which caused extensive bleeding in multiple parts of his brain. The autopsy listed 16 separate and distinct injuries to the prisoner's head and neck, in addition to multiple fractured ribs and bleeding around a kidney.

Two months later, in December 2019, a prisoner at Ventress died after the use of force by staff. The autopsy revealed that the prisoner died from blunt force trauma to the head. He sustained multiple areas of intracranial bleeding, fractures of his nose and left eye socket, and had at least six teeth knocked out. ADOC personnel informed hospital medical personnel that the injuries occurred after the prisoner fell from a bunk bed. Two correctional officers were placed on mandatory leave while ADOC investigated the circumstances surrounding the death.[67]

The DOJ investigators surmised from interviews and incident reports that "uses of force happen so regularly in Alabama's prisons that some officers appear accustomed to that level of violence and consider it normal." Additionally, the report stated that the "overwhelming majority of uses of force do not receive scrutiny beyond an institution-level use of force investigation." The majority of correctional officers who brutalize the people who are incarcerated do not face any substantial discipline and very rarely face termination or criminal prosecution.[68]

ADOC tends to address uses of excessive force initially through "corrective action" as part of an institution's disciplinary process. ADOC rarely suspends or dismisses correctional officers for uses of excessive force where such action would be warranted. During the course of our investigation, we issued a subpoena for documentation related to discipline or investigations of correctional officers for excessive force as well as other improprieties such as extortion, bribery, sexual abuse, and smuggling of contraband. ADOC produced documentation identifying 97 disciplinary actions, mostly from 2016 and 2017. Nearly half of the disciplinary recommendations during that time related to correctional officers' late arrival to work or failure to show up for work. During those two years, ADOC considered suspending or dismissing only one employee for excessive force. In that incident, a lieutenant at Donaldson witnessed an officer stomping a prisoner on the back of the head as the prisoner was lying face down. As mentioned in this Notice, ADOC witnessed other instances of excessive force, and, based on the documentation provided, very few of those resulted in suspension or dismissal.[69]

On December 9, 2020, the DOJ filed a lawsuit against the Alabama Department of Corrections and said that "after multiple rounds of negotiations beginning in the spring of 2019, 'the state has failed or refused to correct the unconstitutional conditions in Alabama's prisons for men.'"[70] According to the Equal Justice Initiative, there have been at least 52 homicides in the state's prisons since the April 2019 Justice Department's report. In the first 11 months of the 2022 fiscal year, the ADOC report showed 204 deaths, "making it the deadliest in the department's history. Alabama's prison homicide rate over the same time period was 80 homicides per 100,000 people incarcerated. This is nearly seven times higher than the national average most recently reported by the federal Bureau of Justice Statistics."[71]

On September 26, 2022, men at the thirteen prisons in Alabama started a strike from their prison service jobs such as food service, laundry, maintenance, and janitorial jobs that they receive no pay to do.[72] Alabama is one of seven states—Arkansas, Florida, Georgia, Mississippi, South Carolina, and Texas—that do not pay incarcerated people for the work they perform. According to the ACLU, across the United States "incarcerated workers produce more than $2 billion a year in goods and over $9 billion a year in services for the maintenance of the prisons where they are warehoused, yet only 1 percent of state correctional budgets goes to their wages."[73]

The men striking in Alabama's prisons outlined their demands: "Eliminating life-without-parole sentences; Repealing Alabama's Habitual Felony Offender Act, which mandates longer sentences for those with prior convictions; Establishing parole criteria that mandate release if met; Reducing the 30-year minimum for juveniles to no more than 15 before parole eligibility; Creating a review board overseeing the Alabama Bureau of Pardons and Paroles." While Governor Kay Ivey "called the demands 'unreasonable,'" Clinique Chapman, associate director of Vera's Restoring Promise Initiative, responded, "The demands are not unreasonable. They are simply asking for standards of confinement that center dignity and a justice system that considers all of their humanity."[74]

Though prison conditions have been intolerable for years, it was the change made to the parole board that was the impetus for the prison strike. A Vera report explained how the changes only worsen the overcrowding in the Alabama prisons:

> Alabama's parole board is made up of three people who are appointed by the governor. The board currently includes one former prosecutor, one former probation officer, and one former state trooper. There is no representation from anyone with a criminal defense background.
>
> Since 2019, when former prosecutor Leigh Gwathney became board chair, the number of people granted parole in Alabama has fallen 83 percent. In 2018, 3,732 people were granted parole. But that number plummeted to 648 in 2021. Between 2016 and 2018, parole was regularly granted in roughly half of hearings. So far, in 2022, just 11 percent of people before the board have received parole. The parole board decisions show racial disparities, with Black people receiving parole just 7 percent of the time, compared to 16 percent for white people.
>
> Although the board sets parole guidelines—including taking classes, not getting into fights, and generally following ADOC

rules—that are meant to be the bases for its decisions, the board followed its own guidelines in just 39 percent of cases in fiscal year 2021.[75]

In spite of the horrendous prison conditions, Alabama plans to use $400 million of the $2.1 billion in the American Rescue Plan Act funds provided to the state along with an additional $900 million to construct two new megaprisons.[76]

It is the epitome of hypocrisy that the American legal system labels certain behavior like violence, rape, and drug use "illegal," yet tolerates taxpayer-funded institutions to allow all of those behaviors to flourish unabated. One eight-month-long Senate Judiciary Committee investigation found that "at least two-thirds of the federal prisons that have housed women over the past ten years have employees of the Federal Bureau of Prisons (BOP) that sexually abused female inmates."[77]

People who are incarcerated lack access to the most basic things human beings need to survive like healthy food and personal hygiene products. "According to a 2020 national survey conducted by the criminal justice reform nonprofit Impact Justice, most states spend less than $3 to feed prisoners a day, and 75 percent of formerly incarcerated people surveyed said they were 'served spoiled or rotten food while in prison.'" Gina Clayton-Johnson, founder and executive director of Essie Justice Group, told *Allure* magazine:

> When we talk about access to personal care products, we are talking about access to basic hygiene necessities that are crucial for people to feel human and maintain their dignity. . . . The fact that incarcerated women often struggle to access necessities such as soap, shampoo, hand sanitizer, tampons, pads, and toothpaste is part of this dehumanizing design. This is simply a human rights issue.[78]

The situation in these prisons is a call for action. American taxpayers must demand an end to the egregious human rights violations occurring in jails and prisons across the country in the name of public safety. The dehumanization of incarcerated people begins with the ways American society refers to them: convict, prisoner, inmate, felon, superpredator, or simply a number. Such language, similar to N.H.I., creates distance, which allows people on the outside to ignore the suffering incarcerated people face, and even provides justification for their suffering.

In contrast to dehumanizing and discarding people who are incarcerated, Pope Francis affirmed their humanity and place within society, writing, "No cell is so isolated as to exclude the Lord, none. He is there, he weeps with them, works with them, waits with them."[79] So too, this book is a wake-up call for Americans to understand the plight of the incarcerated in our country and to advocate for change. To advocate for change—to create change—we need a new lens through which to look at the American legal system, and in the next chapter I propose models for change, including how restorative justice seeks to bring dignity, repair, and healing.

Chapter 8

Restorative Justice, Reparations, and Repair

When the Hebrews were emancipated they were told to take spoil from the Egyptians. When the serfs of Russia were emancipated they were given three acres of ground upon which they could live and make a living. But not so when our slaves were emancipated. They were sent away empty handed, without money, without friends, and without a foot of land to stand upon. Old and young, sick and well were turned loose to the open sky, naked to their enemies.

Frederick Douglass's Speech at Elmira,
New York, August 3, 1880

On September 22, 1979, George Powell, a Black twenty-five-year-old, lay in bed in his apartment in South Side Chicago with his fiancée and baby just over a year old. Around six in the morning, his fiancée opened the front door after police knocked on it. Barging into the apartment and Powell's bedroom, Chicago Police Department commander Jon Burge and two or three police officers demanded Powell's identification card. Directed to a shirt on the radiator, they lifted it, and Powell's ID fell out. They examined the card, then one of the officers pushed Powell onto the bed and began questioning him about his uncle and an acquaintance. Handcuffing Powell, they marched him out of the apartment complex, and then forced him into a squad car.

The police did not take Powell to the police station nearest his house. Instead, they drove him to the Area 2 police station at 91st and Cottage

Grove, where they led Powell to an interrogation room and secured him to a handcuff ring on the wall. One of the police officers placed a plastic Sears bag over Powell's head.

About ten to fifteen minutes later, one of the police removed the plastic bag from Powell's head, and Burge entered the room with a long stick that had a metal grid-like object around its length that looked like a cattle prod. Burge began to question Powell and electric shock him with the stick.

Burge and the other officers asked what he knew about a woman named Catherine Tines, who had been murdered, insinuating that Powell knew about it. Though Powell didn't know anything about the murder, as the electric shock torture continued, he began to agree with whatever the police said in the hope that they would stop.

Powell tried to bite a hole through the plastic bag so he could breathe. One officer told him to stop, slapped him, and punched him in the mouth, busting his lip. The police then pulled the bag's drawstring, tightening it around his head, which caused Powell to feel like he was going to suffocate. He was unable to breathe. They would release the string and allow him to breathe before tightening it again. Police officers alternated between punching Powell in the chest and applying the shock treatment throughout his body: chest, leg, arms, groin, and genitals. He was shocked between forty and fifty times.

After a number of hours, Powell was transferred to another station at Harrison and Kedzie Avenue. In neither place was Powell given anything to eat; nor was he allowed to use the restroom. Around 4:30 in the afternoon, the police had Powell sign a twenty-nine-page statement confessing to the murder of Catherine Tines.

That evening around seven or eight, Powell was allowed to see his mother, fiancée, and other family. After seeing him, Powell's mother filed a written complaint depicting the torture her son had endured. Nothing was done in response. Instead, Powell was convicted of the murder and kidnapping of Catherine Tines. He served twenty years in prison, from 1979 to 1999, though to this day he adamantly denies any involvement in the murder.[1]

George Powell was not the only one tortured by Burge and falsely incarcerated. Between 1972 through 1991, Jon Burge and a unit of white detectives known as the "Midnight Crew" targeted, kidnapped, and tortured over 120 people, predominantly African American males, leading to confessions of crimes they did not commit. According to Chicago Torture Justice Center, "Burge was a Vietnam War Veteran and used war torture interrogation tactics from Operation Phoenix on the survivors, such as racial epithets, electric shock, suffocation, and brutal beatings." The survivors spent years and sometimes decades in prison. Ten of those people received death sentences. In spite of concrete evidence of the torture, Chicago public officials at the city, county, and federal level refused to take action to stop Burge. No criminal charges of torture were ever brought against him.[2]

Though Burge was not charged and punished for his torturous acts, he received a sentence to federal prison in 2011 for lying under oath in civil lawsuits brought against him related to the torture. But his four-and-a-half-year sentence was cut short when he was released early for good behavior, followed by a stay in a halfway house, then house confinement. In spite of his misconduct, Burge was allowed to keep his $3,039-a-month pension from his employment with the Chicago Police Department. In 2018 at the age of seventy he died.[3]

In spite of the initial apathy on the part of the Chicago public, police department, legislatures, media, and public officials, after decades of organizing by survivors and activists, in May 2015, the Chicago City Council passed legislation to provide reparations for torture survivors. Chicago became the first municipality in the United States to provide reparations for victims of police violence. That month in *Prison Culture,* organizer, educator, and prison-abolitionist Mariame Kaba wrote the following, describing the effort on the ground that resulted in the passage of the legislation:

> Over the past six months, a coalition of individuals and groups organized tirelessly to pass this legislation. We held rallies, sing-ins, marches, light actions, train takeovers, exhibition-ins, and more. The price of being immersed in this struggle is to be a witness to unspeakable acts of cruelty committed against other human beings. . . . The rooms where commander Jon Burge and his fellow officers tortured and forced confessions from suspects

were called the "House[s] of Screams." Those screams echoed in my head yesterday as I heard the Chicago City Council vote on the reparations legislation for survivors of Burge's torture. Slowly those screams became whispers: "Thank you for believing us and for refusing to forget," they seemed to say.[4]

The legislation instituted a $5.5 million reparations fund that included direct payments to fifty-seven victims of the police torture, free city college tuition for victims and relatives, counseling services, a memorial to victims, inclusion of Burge's actions in the school curriculum for eighth- and tenth-grade students, and a formal apology.

At the time the Chicago City Council unanimously approved the reparations package, George Powell was among the many survivors in attendance who was recognized by Chicago alderman Joe Moreno. The Chicago mayor at that time, Rahm Emanuel, apologized to the survivors and said, "This stain cannot be removed from our history of our city, but it can be used as a lesson of what not to do and the responsibility that all of us have."[5] Despite the money he will receive and the apology, Powell will never get back the twenty years of his life he spent wrongfully incarcerated, the wedding to his fiancée he never could have, or the chance to watch his son grow from a baby to an adult.

In spite of the police department's and individual police officers' culpability in torturing Black people, it's the taxpayers of Chicago who are still paying the pensions of those who committed the crimes. By the time of his death, Burge's pension payments totaled over $900,000. John Byrne and Peter Dignan, who worked closely with Burge and were found to be torturers by the Office of Professional Standards investigators and a federal civil jury, have received a combined $2.65 million. Adding in all the detectives and supervisors who have been found or repeatedly accused of torture and cover-up, and the commanders and police superintendents from Area 2 who played important roles in the scandal, the pensions amount to $48.37 million. The city of Chicago is responsible for funding 80 percent of that cost.[6]

"Our nation was born in the horrific traumas of genocide and slavery. Because we have neither fully acknowledged nor reckoned with these twin traumas, much less worked to heal them, they perpetually reenact themselves transgenerationally," Fania Davis wrote in *The Little Book of Race and Restorative Justice.*[7] Davis is a longtime social justice activist who was born into Jim Crow segregation in Birmingham, Alabama. Her sister, Angela Y. Davis, was a political prisoner falsely accused of murder during the Black Power movement who has become a social-justice icon as a decades-long prison abolitionist, activist, and professor. After a successful career as a civil rights attorney, Fania Davis earned a PhD in Indigenous studies and is now a "leading national voice on the intersection of racial and restorative justice."

A social movement growing in popularity in the United States, restorative justice seeks to transform the criminal legal system and stem the tide of mass incarceration. Fania Davis, who is also a founding director of Restorative Justice for Oakland Youth (RJOY), states that restorative justice is not only a reaction to harm but a "proactive relational strategy to create a culture of connectivity where all members of a community feel valued."[8]

While "the concept and philosophy of restorative justice emerged during the 1970s and '80s in the United States,"[9] its indigenous roots have become increasingly recognized and honored. When making connections between restorative justice and indigenous African traditions, Davis states that "African justice making, rather than an occasion to inflict punishment, is an opportunity to teach, learn, reemphasize social values, and reaffirm the bonds of our inherent interrelatedness." Even as it seeks to do so, indigenous justice does not ignore or dismiss the harm caused. Essential to restorative justice is that the person harmed is vindicated and that either the person who committed the harm or their family is "obligated to offer apology, recompense, and reparation to the harmed person or community." When damage is done to relationships within a community because of harm, restorative justice seeks the rebuilding of relationships and social harmony by righting the wrong done.

In keeping with the worldview and principles of African and other indigenous justice systems, restorative justice invites a paradigm shift in the way we think about and do justice—from a justice that harms to a justice that heals. Our prevailing adversarial system is based upon a Roman notion of justice as just deserts.

Causing someone to suffer creates an imbalance in the scales of justice, and the way to rebalance the scales and do justice is to cause the responsible person to suffer; we respond to the original harm with a second harm. Ours is a system that harms people who harm people, presumably to show that harming people is wrong. This sets into motion endless cycles of harm. Restorative justice seeks to interrupt these cycles by repairing the damage done to relationships in the wake of crime or other wrongdoing, and do so in a way that is consonant with indigenous wisdom— Africa's and that of other traditions. Justice is a healing ground, not a battleground.[10]

Howard Zehr, called both the pioneer and grandfather of restorative justice in the United States, was born in 1944. His father was a pastor in the Mennonite faith, a tradition known for a commitment to peacemaking and nonviolence. Though Zehr began his college studies at Goshen College, a Mennonite school in Indiana, he transferred and became the first white student to graduate from Morehouse College in Atlanta, the historically Black college for men. After earning a PhD from Rutgers, Zehr returned to Indiana and the Goshen College area in the late 1970s and "became the founding director of the first U.S. victim-offender reconciliation program, Elkhart County Prisoners and Community Together (PACT)."

Zehr was on a mission to provide better support and options for survivors of crime, increase accountability for offenders, and include the community in the legal process. He published *Changing Lenses: A New Focus for Crime and Justice* in 1990, followed by *Little Book of Restorative Justice* in 2002, which "popularized the term and concepts of restorative justice, helping to spark an explosion of interest from academics and practitioners worldwide."[11]

In defining the meaning of restorative justice, Zehr states that the term "restorative" does not imply returning to the past. People who commit harm often have a history of abuse or trauma and often do not have a "healthy personal or relational state to which to return." Instead of going backward, restorative justice is transformative, forward thinking, and healing. "Restorative justice often involves movement toward a new sense of identity and health or new, healthier relationships. Many advocates see it as a way to restore a sense of hope and community to our world."[12]

Restorative justice to Zehr is rooted in an understanding that "'crime,' or wrongdoing is a violation of people and interpersonal relations; violations create obligations; the central obligation is to put right the wrongs, i.e., to repair the harms caused by wrongdoing."

> Underlying this understanding of wrongdoing is an assumption about society: we are all interconnected. In the Hebrew scriptures, this is embedded in the concept of shalom, the vision of living in a sense of "all-rightness" with each other, with the creator, and with the environment. . . . Although the specific meanings of these words vary, they communicate a similar message: all things are connected to each other in a web of relationships.
>
> In this worldview, the problem of crime—and wrongdoing in general—is that it represents a wound in the community, a tear in the web of relationships. Crime represents damaged relationships. In fact, damaged relationships are both a cause and an effect of crime. Many traditions have a saying that a harm to one is a harm to all. A harm such as crime ripples out to disrupt the whole web. Moreover, wrongdoing is often a symptom of something that is out of balance in the web.

Therefore, restorative justice emphasizes making amends and is concerned with healing all those involved, including "those directly harmed, those who cause harm, and their communities."[13]

In contrast to restorative justice, Trudy D. Conway explains in *Redemption and Restoration: A Catholic Perspective on Restorative Justice* that the American penal system is based on *retributive* justice. The organization Catholic Mobilizing Network (CMN) works to "end the use of the death penalty, to transform the U.S. criminal justice system from punitive to restorative, and to build capacity in U.S. society to engage in restorative practices." CMN offers a definition of restorative justice through a Catholic social lens as

> an approach to justice that emphasizes living in right relationship and resonates deeply with Gospel values and Catholic social

teaching. In restorative justice, crime and harm are understood in terms of the people and relationships impacted, rather than solely the law or rule that was broken. Restorative practices seek to repair harm through transformative encounters that model Jesus' reconciling way.[14]

Instead of people and communities responding to wrongdoing, as Zehr and Davis advocate, the U.S. legal system has institutionalized a "retaliatory principle, requiring that the state mete out suffering to wrongdoers for their actions." Through prosecutors arguing the state's case against those charged with violating the law, the legal system is focused on "payback for wrongdoing."

> The present-day result is a legal system that often sidelines the needs and concerns of victims and other persons affected by crime. Justice herein requires the state to address the breaking of the law through a legal system directed to meting out just retribution through retaliatory suffering. Offenders must get what they deserve from the state, their punishment being seen as assurance that justice has been done. Personal and communal response has been replaced by a complex jurisprudence system directed by the state through a legal conduit of arrests, trials, and punishments governed by procedural rules. States have the responsibility to respond to wrongdoing codified as illegal and deserving of state-inflicted punishment. And states have the power and resources to ensure this is done.[15]

While Zehr believes the Western criminal justice system intends to promote good in society, it does so in a way that arguably negates the positive.

> The Western criminal justice system is intended to promote important positive values—a recognition of the rights of others, the importance of certain boundaries on behavior, the centrality of human rights. But it does so in a way that is largely negative; it says that if you harm others, we will harm you. As James Gilligan

has argued, it is a mirror image of the offending act. Consequently, to make it humane, we have to bring in other values to govern and mitigate it. It does not, in itself, offer us a vision of the good.

In contrast, restorative justice "provides an inherently positive value system" that emphasizes the interconnectedness of all people.[16] Conway believes that restorative justice requires a "paradigm" or "lens" change from "punitive to reparative responses to harm."

> Refusing to reduce offenders to their worst acts, such an approach opposes punitive measures that give up on offenders, defining them reductively and permanently as criminals and marginalizing them from society. It also focuses on harms that may have been done to offenders that played a role in their path toward wrongdoing, economic inequalities that influence crime, and the pervasive injustices of the system that result in disparate and wrongful convictions. . . . In shifting the lens through which we view crime and criminal justice, human harms and needs in all their complexity and range come into focus.[17]

A common restorative justice model practiced in the United States is victim–offender mediation (VOM, also called conferences or dialogue). Victim–offender mediations involve those directly harmed, those who committed the harm, including serious harm like rape or assault, and a trained facilitator who guides the process. They can either occur before formal charges are brought in court, during court proceedings, or after the offender is already charged and incarcerated or released on parole. The two parties work with the facilitators individually to prepare for the mediation, and once in agreement to proceed, they are brought together for the meeting or conference in a safe place.

One victim–offender reconciliation program (VORP) begun in the 1980s is the Community Justice Initiatives Association (CJI), a community-based, nonprofit society located in Langley, British Columbia, Canada. It is one of the oldest restorative justice organizations in that country. One of its programs, the Victim–Offender Mediation Program, is used when a serious crime has occurred that warrants at least two years of imprisonment, and includes cases of murder. In one example of the implementation of the program, a woman named Jillian and her parents arranged a victim–offender mediation after her brother was killed by his cellmate while incarcerated in a pretrial correctional facility. Jillian explained how after several meetings with the facilitators, the mediation occurred.

> When it came time to meet "Gordon" (not his real name), the offender, we felt as prepared as we could ever be. We were able to ask him questions about what occurred that day and to receive honest answers. Together with the facilitators who had brought us together and arranged our entry to a federal prison, we sat in a circle and shared our thoughts and feelings in meaningful dialogue with Gordon. Not only did we get answers to some of the heavy questions that had been weighing on our minds for nearly two years, but we also received perspective. We learned a good deal about Gordon: how he grew up, his struggles, his strengths, his hopes and future goals.
>
> Forgiveness is neither a requirement nor an expectation of CJI's RJ processes. However, offering Gordon forgiveness allowed us to see him as a fellow human being, and not as the "monster" our minds may have been trying to convince us he might be. Choosing to forgive him had been our objective from day one. We knew that carrying the guilt and shame of what he had done was already enough for him to bear. We wanted him to know that we would be okay. But, it was not until we offered our forgiveness to him face-to-face that we realized it was really for our own healing. In fact, my father says, "Forgiving him for what he had done to my son changed my whole outlook on life."[18]

Restorative justice practitioners emphasize that forgiveness is not the goal or mandatory in victim–offender mediations or any restorative justice practices. Instead, the goal is to create a dialogue that gives survivors and offenders the chance to ask and answer questions about the offense, explain the impact of the offense, and reach an agreement about how the harm can be repaired and what actions the offender can take to accept accountability and not reoffend.

Research has found that VOM can benefit both victims and offenders. For victims, meeting with the person who harmed them can reduce anger and fear. They are able to discuss what happened, ask why the offender committed the offense, and impart the effect of the harm it caused them. For offenders, they have greater realization of the impact of their actions and the harm they caused as well as increased empathy for the victim. Offenders are also held more accountable for the harm they caused through VOM compared to traditional court procedures.[19]

In the traditional criminal justice system, while offenders are "punished," they often do not accept "accountability" for their actions. From the earliest stages of the legal process—initial arrest—police read those suspected of committing an offense their Miranda Rights and advise them as follows: *"Anything you say can and will be used against you in a court of law."* From that moment on, offenders have little incentive to acknowledge their responsibility in the harm caused. Most defense attorneys and public defenders do not even ask their clients if they committed the crime they are charged with because they are most concerned with whether the district attorney can prove their case—not their client's guilt or innocence.

In *Policing the Black Man*, Angela J. Davis argues that in the criminal legal system, prosecutors wield the most power, yet their role in mass incarceration isn't discussed often enough. While police officers have the power to "stop, search, and arrest," prosecutors "make the most important decisions in the criminal process—whether to charge and offer a plea bargain and what the charge and plea offer should be." Further, the prosecutors "make these decisions behind closed doors and are not required to justify or explain their choices to anyone. The consequences can be life-changing for everyone involved—criminal defendants, crime victims, and the families of both."[20] Unlike in restorative justice practices, where survivors' needs are paramount to the process, survivors of crime have no say in what charges prosecutors bring against the offenders.

Prosecutors have the power to charge an offender with a different charge than the actual crime committed, including a more or less serious charge. Davis explains that if police arrest a person who had a large quantity of cocaine, the prosecutor may charge that person with a more serious felony offense like intent to distribute, which has a mandatory minimum sentence, or charge that person with a misdemeanor offense of simple possession, which does not have a mandatory minimum sentence.

> The difference between a misdemeanor and a felony could be the difference between freedom and imprisonment, a job and unemployment, housing and homelessness, the ability to vote and disenfranchisement. . . . But because prosecutors are not required to justify their decisions, they often make these decisions arbitrarily or for the wrong reasons. And sometimes these choices produce unwarranted disparities—differences in treatment that often appear to be based on class or race.[21]

Prosecutors also control whether they offer a plea bargain, whereby defendants plead guilty to a less serious charge in exchange for the prosecutor dismissing the remainder of charges that are more serious and resolving the case. While that may seem beneficial, in practice "it is frequently an unfair and one-sided process." Defense attorneys often have to advise their clients to accept a plea deal even before they are able to fully investigate the case. According to Davis, "95 percent of all criminal cases are resolved with a guilty plea."[22]

The factors of race and poverty further exacerbate the discrepancies in the criminal legal system. Because people who cannot afford bail are often incarcerated while awaiting trial, they are more likely to accept a plea agreement in order to be freed from incarceration even if they are not guilty. On the other hand, people who have enough money to post bail and secure their freedom, and have the money to afford a private defense attorney, have a better chance at securing a favorable plea bargain or proving their innocence at trial.

Due to the fact the majority of cases are resolved with a plea bargain and no trial occurs, survivors of crimes are often pushed to the sidelines and never have their "day in court." They never have the chance to face their offender and often do not provide a victim impact statement that the offender will read. On the other hand, offenders most often plead to a crime they did not actually commit. Unlike restorative justice, this process does not encourage offenders to be accountable for the actual harm they caused, and offenders often lament they did not have their day in court and feel victimized themselves by the unjust legal process.

Restorative justice attempts to rectify these deficits. A second practice dominant in restorative justice is family group conferences. This conference includes family members or other significant individuals close to those directly involved. Family members of offenders are encouraged to participate to help the offender accept responsibility for the harm they caused and let the offender know how their actions affected the offender's family. The family of the survivors is also invited to support the survivor and to voice how the harm affected everyone close to the survivor. Zehr explains how one early model of family group conferences originated in New Zealand—a model now standardly used for juvenile justice cases in that country.

In 1989, there was a crisis in the New Zealand juvenile welfare and justice system, which was "criticized by the indigenous Māori population for utilizing an imposed, alien, colonial system," and led to the creation of a new restorative justice approach that utilizes family group conferences that "can be seen as both a system of justice and as a mode of encounter in New Zealand." According to the Youth Justice website, the "characteristics of the 'New Zealand model,' acclaimed internationally at the time, are diversion, community-based sanctions, family decision-making and cultural flexibility." The Oranga Tamariki Act 1989 (in English, Children's and Young People's Well-Being Act 1989), lists four principles that guide the children and youth justice system:

(1) the well-being and best interests of the child or young person; and
(2) the public interest (which includes public safety); and
(3) the interests of any victim; and
(4) the accountability of the child or young person for their behavior.[23]

When a child or youth criminal offense happens, a youth justice coordinator convenes the family group conference and offers a formal restorative justice process that families can agree to participate in facilitated by community-based providers after the court-ordered conference. If all the participants come to agreement about what actions the offender will take to repair the harm done, an agreement is entered into that specifies "what the action is; the name of *te tamaiti* [the child] who is to complete it; the person responsible for making sure it is implemented; the timeframe for completion; the person responsible for ensuring the action is completed."[24]

The New Zealand restorative justice approach encompasses serious offenses like theft, robbery, assault, and burglary; and this approach has resulted in decreased youth crime. "The number of children aged 10 to 13 who offended and came to the attention of Police decreased by 61% between the 2010/11 and 2020/21 fiscal years (from 4,760 to 1,860)."[25]

The New Zealand approach to caring for children and youth offenders and those victimized by crime can be seen in stark contrast to the U.S. legal system, which convicts hundreds of thousands of youth as adults, subjecting them to greater risk of sexual abuse and suicide in adult prisons. Yet precharge diversion programs based on New Zealand's family group conferences are increasingly being used in many parts of the United States for both youth and adults.

There are several counties in California that have adopted restorative justice as diversion programs for youth offenders, including Contra Costa, Alameda, San Francisco, and Los Angeles. For example, in Contra Costa since 2019, the county uses "a pre-charge model of restorative justice diversion developed by Impact Justice's Restorative Justice Project."[26] Impact Justice (IJ),[27] a national innovative justice center founded in 2015, undertakes projects that:

(1) reduce the number of people caught up in harmful legal systems by creating alternatives that are responsive, restorative, fair, and effective;
(2) improve living conditions and life outcomes and safeguard fundamental human rights for the millions of people still subject to mass incarceration;
(3) expand opportunities for formerly incarcerated and other system-involved people to heal, fully participate in community life, and reach their potential.

Impact Justice is working "nationally to expand restorative justice as a safe and racially just alternative to neglecting the needs of those harmed and incarcerating people who cause harm." The district attorneys in the counties using the IJ restorative justice model may refer young people arrested for serious misdemeanors or felonies, such as robbery, burglary, or assault, to RYSE Youth Center in Richmond, California, to "hold a facilitated face-to-face meeting with the consent of the person harmed, the responsible youth, respective family members, and other impacted community members. A consensus-based plan to make things right is created, and once the youth completes the plan, no charges are filed."

The San Francisco District Attorney's Office partnered with IJ to launch Make it Right (MIR), a restorative justice approach for youths ages thirteen to seventeen facing prosecution for an array of felony charges in San Francisco. The SFDA teamed with Community Works and Huckleberry Youth, two Bay Area nonprofits, to pilot the MIR program at the end of 2013. Between 2013 and 2019, 143 cases were deemed eligible to participate in the pilot program, with 99 (69.2 percent of study subjects) randomly referred to MIR and 44 (30.8 percent) randomly referred to face traditional prosecution. Results from the pilot study found "juvenile restorative justice community conferencing can reduce recidivism among youth charged with serious offenses and be an effective alternative to traditional juvenile justice practices."

Nearly half of the control group was rearrested within six months of randomization and over 70 percent were rearrested by the end of the four-year period. The rearrest rates are markedly lower for youth in the treatment group (those given the option to participate in MIR): the rearrest rate for the MIR group is approximately 20 percentage points lower than the control group at six months, and this difference continued for four years following the offer to participate.

An offer to participate in MIR reduces the likelihood of rearrest by 18.9 percentage points within the first six months, 18.4 percentage points within the first year, and 14.4 percentage points within the first two years. Relative to young people who were not given an offer to participate in MIR and were prosecuted, these effect sizes imply a 44 percent, 33 percent, and 23 percent reduction in recidivism, respectively. The overall effect sizes persist at three years following the date of program offer (14.7 percentage

points or 20 percent less than youth not given an offer to participate) and widens at four years (26.7 percentage points or 30 percent less than youth not given the offer to participate).

The 12-month rearrest rates among youth who completed is
much lower (19.2 percent) than those who enrolled but did not
complete (57.7 percent). While these substantial differences sug-
gest MIR transforms the outcomes for the youth involved, it's
also possible that youth who complete the program and youth
who do not may be different in other ways that contribute to differences in subsequent arrest rates.[28]

The final restorative justice practice commonly used that I will discuss
are Circles. Zehr explains that Circles consciously enlarge the number of
people who participate to include those "who have been harmed, those
who have caused harm, their family members, and sometime justice officials," and "community members are essential participants as well." The
community members may be invited either because they are connected
to a specific offense or because they are part of a group of volunteers
from the community. The addition of community members broadens the
issues discussed in the Circle and addresses situations in the community
like "obligations that the community have, community norms, or other
related community issues."

Circles are used for many purposes, such as to determine criminal
sentences, healing, address workplace conflict, and facilitate community
dialogue, and they are the predominant restorative justice model used in
educational settings like schools.[29]

In *The Little Book of Circle Processes*, Kay Pranis writes that peacemaking circles "draw directly from the tradition of the Talking Circle,
common among indigenous people of North America." Pranis believes
the practice of gathering in a circle to discuss issues important to a community was likely a part of the "tribal roots of most people," and that practice still exists among Indigenous people throughout the world. The use
of Circles in mainstream public processes like criminal justice originated
in Yukon, Canada, in the early 1990s. The Peacemaking Circle Process
was first used in the United States in Minnesota's criminal justice system
in the mid-'90s and "offered a way to include those harmed by crime,

those who commit crime, and the community in a partnership with the justice system to determine the most effective response to a crime that would promote healing and safety for everyone."

Though the Circles were first used to decide sentences for offenders who committed crimes and help them fulfill the obligations of their sentences, they soon became used to facilitate community reentry for people who were incarcerated and on probation, in schools, workplaces, neighborhoods groups, and families. Pranis outlines how a Circle may be organized:

> Participants sit in a circle of chairs with no tables. Sometimes objects that have meaning to the group are placed in the center as a focal point to remind participants of shared values and common ground. The physical format of the Circle symbolizes shared leadership, equality, connection, and inclusion. It also promotes focus, accountability, and participation from all.
>
> Using very intentional structural elements—ceremony, a talking piece, a facilitator or keeper, guidelines, and consensus decision-making—Circles aim to create a space in which participants are safe to be their most authentic self.[30]

Danielle Sered is the executive director of Common Justice in New York City, which operates the first alternative-to-incarceration and victim-service program in the United States that focuses on violent felonies in the adult court.[31] Sered discussed a Circle process involving a young offender.

> I think often about a young man early in our time in Common Justice who had been gang involved since he was eight years old. He had caused more harm than anyone should. He had survived more harm than anyone should. He had seen more harm than anyone should in a lifetime, let alone in his brief 19 years before we met him. And he sat one day in the circle with the young man he hurt, and with that young man's mother, and faced the pain that he had caused them. And sat through the process of reckoning with it, of reaching agreements of how to repair it. The circle

went for hours and hours. And when it was finally done and everyone was going home, he asked me if he could sit in my office for a while before he left. . . .

And he said, "Can I ask you, for all the harm I've done, for everything I've been through, I don't know if I've ever heard a real apology before. Do you think I did all right?" And, because it was true, I said, "Yes, I think you did great." And he said, "Pardon my language, but that's the scariest shit I've ever done." And he knew there was something in the human process of facing the hurt he had caused. Of facing those impacted by his actions that was harder than any of the violence he sustained. . . . But looking into the mirror, looking into the eyes of those we have hurt is one of the most demanding things that can be asked of us as human beings. And accountability asks that of us in ways prison never will.[32]

The restorative justice community has made strides in its work, but it also has to work consciously to avoid replicating harms in American society and the criminal legal system. Fania Davis's *Little Book of Race and Restorative Justice* importantly states the ways the restorative justice community failed to address race, racism, and inequity during its first forty years. Her book aims to merge restorative justice and racial justice because they can work together to address systemic racism and promote healing and repair for the Black community. Davis believes all restorative justice practitioners must be trained to learn about racism and implicit bias, or else people will bring those views with them in their restorative justice work and perpetuate them.

Racism in the United States is three-dimensional: structural, institutional, and individual, according to Davis. Structural racism is "the normalization and legitimization of white supremacy, enacted from the nation's beginnings, by vast historical, governmental, cultural, economic, educational, institutional, and psychological forces, all working in concert to perpetuate racial inequity." In American society, white skin holds a place of privilege, and black skin is disadvantaged and relegated to the lowest place.

The next dimension of racism that Davis lists is institutional racism, which "involves the ubiquitous practices and policies within schools, workplaces, financial establishments, housing, hospitals, the justice system, and other private and governmental institutions that, intentionally or not, produce outcomes that consistently advantage whites while disadvantaging people of color." Examples this book has discussed are the federal government's segregated-housing policies, the school-to-prison pipeline, and the policies of the war on drugs that have resulted in mass incarceration.

The last dimension of racism, Davis says, is individual racism, which "encompasses the explicit or implicit racial bias that plays out in interpersonal spheres." Individual racism may not be as overt as Dylann Roof's, the man who in 2015 murdered nine Black members of Emanuel African Methodist Episcopal Church in Charleston, South Carolina, or Payton Gendron's, who in 2022 targeted and killed ten people at a grocery store in Buffalo, New York, in a racially motivated attack. Often individual racism today "mostly manifests as implicit bias occurring when a person rejects stereotypes on conscious levels yet holds onto them on unconscious levels." Davis explains how widespread implicit bias is today.

> In general, more than 85 percent of all Americans view themselves as unbiased, yet studies show that most Americans have implicit bias. One study found that 80 percent of whites and 40 percent of blacks have a prowhite bias, consistently showing blacks are associated with such negative stereotypes as bad, lazy, aggressive, and unpleasant. When historically marginalized people have implicit bias, it is often referred to as internalized oppression.[33]

As a result of the pervasiveness of racist structures in American society, Davis believes that restorative justice is also informed by those racist structures even though white people today did not choose or create them. Therefore, Davis states that restorative justice must not just be concerned with healing interpersonal harm but also committed to "transforming the context in which the injury occurs: the socio-historical conditions and institutions that are structured precisely to perpetuate harm."

To combat the lack of racial awareness in the restorative justice community, Davis and a small group of restorative justice practitioners met in 2011 to discuss the "troubling whiteness of the restorative justice movement, and resolved to take action." Out of that dialogue came the first national conference in 2013, which featured "race and restorative justice as the theme and a dialogue between racial and restorative justice advocates." Since then, much more research and many programs have focused on racial equity within the restorative justice movement.[34]

Among the most important places for restorative justice practices to combat early racism are schools in their school-to-prison pipeline, where restorative justice encourages racial equity and supports students on the margins. It was in Queensland, Australia, where restorative justice was first practiced in schools in 1994, and its positive outcomes led to its expansion across Australia and throughout the rest of the world.

Restorative practices have become increasingly utilized in the United States, and studies have established that when practiced in schools, suspensions, expulsions, police referrals, and violence are all reduced while academic performance and results are enhanced. Restorative Justice for Oakland Youth (RJOY) launched the first pilot program in California at a middle school in Oakland in 2006. Due to its success, which included suspension rates dropping by 87 percent during the first two years after implementation, by 2010 the Oakland Unified School District had adopted restorative justice as official policy and committed to funding its implementation with staff and resources. By 2019, nearly forty schools in the district had implemented practices such as "restorative conversations, conferencing and circles, mediation" that had strong student leadership. Davis states its effectiveness:

> For instance, according to a 2015 implementation study of whole-school restorative justice in Oakland that compared schools with restorative justice to schools without, from 2011 to 2014, graduation rates in restorative schools increased by 60 percent compared to a 7 percent increase in nonrestorative schools; reading scores

increased 128 percent versus 11 percent; and the dropout rate decreased 56 percent versus 17 percent. Harm was repaired in 76 percent of conflict circles, with students learning to talk instead of fight through differences at home and at school, and more than 88 percent of teachers said that restorative practices were very or somewhat helpful in managing difficult student behaviors.[35]

Georgetown Law's Center on Poverty and Inequality's "state-by-state analysis found that 21 states and the District of Columbia have adopted laws that support the use of school-based restorative justice."[36]

In 2021, Des Moines, Iowa, became one of the first school districts in the United States that entirely replaced armed police with staff trained in restorative practices. As detailed in this book previously, Des Moines was like many schools throughout the country that employed police as school resource officers. In an investigative report, Andy Kopsa reported on the school district that made changes.[37] After the 2020 racial justice movement, "students, parents and community members spoke out against SROs at Des Moines School Board meetings" and the district decided to terminate its police contract with their schools. When students returned to school campuses after the Covid pandemic shutdowns, staff trained in restorative practices greeted them instead of police. Kopsa highlighted how the activism of students, especially Lyric Sellers and Endí Montalvo-Martinez, propelled the school district to end the use of school police.

The protests and the town halls inspired Sellers, then a junior, and East High School senior Endí Montalvo-Martinez to liberate the city's schools from oppressive systems—which, to them, meant ousting SROs. Sellers and Montalvo-Martinez worked with the Iowa Department of Human Rights to compile racial data about in-school arrests in Des Moines. Those findings were released at an October 2020 school board meeting and revealed that, between 2015 and 2019, the number more than doubled, from 273 annually to 590. What's more, Black students made up 53% of all "complaints" (juvenile justice system terminology for "arrests"), despite accounting for only 20% of the student body.

And, even starker, an ACLU report released that month found that Black girls in Iowa were nine times more likely than white girls to be arrested.

The school district was able to redirect the $750,000 that would have paid school police to fund instead twenty new teacher positions and hire specially trained restorative practitioner staff across the city's five public high schools.

Kopsa notes Des Moines was not the only school district to bow to protests and demands to remove police from schools.

In Los Angeles, under pressure from students, the school district cut its school police force by a third, and the city reinvested tens of millions from the police budget into school mental health counselors and restorative justice-trained "climate coaches." In Chicago, an existing anti-SRO campaign by parents and youth activists got a lift from the protests—and the backing of the teachers' union. The city agreed to empower local school councils to remove SROs, leading to a citywide reduction from 180 to 59, and schools reinvested the money in positions including social workers, security guards and restorative justice coordinators.

Implementing restorative practices in schools does not mean students are not disciplined or have little formal structure. The restorative practices staff at one high school in Des Moines, Roosevelt High School, has created a "Think Tank" where students go if they have violated school rules. It's not a place to hang out and have fun; instead "students cannot talk, have outside meals or snacks and must turn off electronics." Students choose to go to the Think Tank where they must complete assignments, which actually improves students' grades instead of suspensions that can harm students' academic achievement. Staff also makes sure to have check-ins with students to understand how each student is doing and identify any issues that may be affecting them. For students the school determines to be no longer suitable for attending school, there is a deferred expulsion program, which provides "a safe space" for students not attending school where restorative practice facilitators still check in with expelled students.

There are qualitative results for the new restorative practices implementation at the Des Moines schools:

Des Moines Public Schools released the results of the Iowa Department of Education's annual Conditions For Learning survey, administered to students in March (unless opted out by their parents). Broadly, Roosevelt improved its overall score for students' sense of physical safety, from 36% in 2019 to 54% in 2022. Feelings of emotional safety dropped, overall, by ten percentage points from 2019 to 2022, but that's in line with a state-wide downturn during the pandemic. Students also reported improved relationships with peers, from 33% in 2019 to 50% in 2022.

Similarly, districtwide, the quantitative goal to reduce school arrests was met, with arrests falling from 538 to 98.

In spite of the progress made toward a more just and equitable school, some conservative parents and legislatures have criticized the new districtwide policy changes. Kopsa noted that local television news aired a fight that occurred at one of the Des Moines high schools, picked up by right-wing media outlets that criticized the new practices as soft on crime. The Republican governor of Iowa, Kim Reynolds, blamed the school system at a press conference, stating, "The tragedy is our system, our educational system, is letting these kids down." Though restorative justice is a promising alternative to the punitive system in place throughout most of American schools, critics and opponents must also have a change of heart and mind to be open to allowing restorative justice to work over time.

That change of heart involves putting on a restorative justice lens that seeks to emphasize and restore the humanity of all people. This is especially important in a society that has dehumanized Indigenous people and people of African descent since North America was colonized. Part of the process of recognizing the humanity of all people is a greater respect and understanding for people who commit harm.

One Catholic working to recognize and honor the humanity of gang members is Fr. Gregory Boyle. He is an American Jesuit priest and the founder of Homeboy Industries in Los Angeles, which is the largest gang-intervention, rehabilitation, and re-entry program in the world. In 2022, a *Los Angeles Times* article covering the celebration of Fr. Boyle's fifti-eth year quoted a Jesuit priest calling Boyle "the patron saint of second chances and humility."[38] In his work with people with histories of gang activity and incarceration, Fr. Boyle epitomizes what it means to treat all people with respect, dignity, and love. Instead of standing in judgment for the decisions people made that landed them in trouble with the law, Fr. Boyle speaks about the great respect and admiration he has for people who survive in the most difficult situations when living on the margins of American society and seek assistance at Homeboy Ministries.

> There's a great book called *The Deepest Well* by Nadine Burke Harris who's our surgeon general here in the state of California. It's about the ACEs study, the 10 checklist of traumas that if you've experienced them under the age of 18, 18 and under, she says if you're four out of the 10 checklist, four or five, that kid is going to have serious health issues as an adults—and I would add, difficulties in socializing if you are a four or five.
>
> Every man or woman who walks through our doors, 15,000 of them a year, every single one is a nine or a 10 on the ACEs, which is, whoa, that's just so huge. Once folks come to know that, and the 10 are things like physical abuse, sexual abuse, emotional abuse, parent in prison, parent mentally ill, parent addicted to drugs, there are 10 of them.
>
> If you've been exposed to these things and to the tune of nine or 10 out of 10, then that's just staggering. It should lead us not to say, "Wow! How come you're not making better choices?" Well, I mean, not all choices are created equal. I think morality is the least helpful thing when it comes to understanding the gulf that exists between the haves and the have-nots, and those that have access to things, and those who don't, and the great disparity in the difference between everything from healthcare to education to job opportunities, you name it.[39]

Repairing harm is central to restoring right relationships and central to restorative justice, and the call for repair is not only reserved for communities, juvenile incarceration facilities, and schools, but for our country. A broader question, based on the history presented throughout this book, is: What does the United States of America owe to the African American community who descended from people who were enslaved, lived through brutal Jim Crow segregation and racial terror, and is still reeling from the impact of the war on drugs and mass incarceration? How does the government repair the systemic, institutional, and generational harm it has committed against Black people for centuries?

Ta-Nehisi Coates's *Atlantic* article "The Case for Reparations"[40] argued that most white Americans don't want to examine the case for reparations because what might be unearthed would change the narrative of American history. Yet, he believes it is the country's duty to do so.

We invoke the words of Jefferson and Lincoln because they say something about our legacy and our traditions. We do this because we recognize our links to the past—at least when they flatter us. But black history does not flatter American democracy; it chastens it. The popular mocking of reparations as a harebrained scheme authored by wild-eyed lefties and intellectually unserious black nationalists is fear masquerading as laughter. Black nationalists have always perceived something unmentionable about America that integrationists dare not acknowledge—that white supremacy is not merely the work of hotheaded demagogues, or a matter of false consciousness, but a force so fundamental to America that it is difficult to imagine the country without it.

And so we must imagine a new country. Reparations—by which I mean the full acceptance of our collective biography and its consequences—is the price we must pay to see ourselves squarely. . . . Reparations beckons us to reject the intoxication of hubris and see America as it is—the work of fallible humans. . . .

What I'm talking about is more than recompense for past injustices—more than a handout, a payoff, hush money, or a reluctant bribe. What I'm talking about is a national reckoning that would lead to spiritual renewal.

Black people for centuries have been told they must take the high road and forgive the sins of racism committed against them in order to live peaceably in the United States. Examples of African Americans forgiving white people who harmed them are given by government and media as exemplars while Black people resisting racism in any form, including Colin Kaepernick taking a knee, or Black Lives Matter organizers leading marches, are vilified.

"Forgiveness and reconciliation are central themes in Christianity," teaches Pope Francis in *Fratelli Tutti*, but "there is a risk that an inadequate understanding and presentation of these profound convictions can lead to fatalism, apathy, and injustice, or even intolerance and violence." Yet Francis argues people should not call for forgiveness "when it involves renouncing our own rights, confronting corrupt officials, criminals, or those who would debase our dignity."

> We are called to love everyone, without exception; at the same time, loving an oppressor does not mean allowing him to keep oppressing us, or letting him think that what he does is acceptable. On the contrary, true love for an oppressor means seeking ways to make him cease his oppression; it means stripping him of a power that he does not know how to use, and that diminishes his own humanity and that of others. Forgiveness does not entail allowing oppressors to keep trampling on their own dignity and that of others, or letting criminals continue their wrongdoing. Those who suffer injustice have to defend strenuously their own rights and those of their family, precisely because they must preserve the dignity they have received as a loving gift from God. If a criminal has harmed me or a loved one, no one can forbid me from demanding justice and ensuring that this person—or anyone else—will not harm me, or others, again. This is entirely just; forgiveness does not forbid it but actually demands it.[41]

Francis insists the answer is not to "fuel anger, which is unhealthy for our own soul and the soul of our people, or to become obsessed with taking revenge and destroying the other." He admits it's not easy to "overcome the bitter legacy of injustices, hostility, and mistrust left by conflict," and only good can overcome evil by "cultivating those virtues which foster reconciliation, solidarity, and peace." But those who have suffered unjustly cannot be forced by a society that has harmed them to forgive and forget. Similar to Coates's words, Francis states, "Neither must we forget the persecutions, the slave trade, and the ethnic killings that continue in various countries, as well as the many other historical events that make us ashamed of our humanity. They need to be remembered, always and ever anew."

> Nowadays, it is easy to be tempted to turn the page, to say that all these things happened long ago and we should look to the future. For God's sake, no! We can never move forward without remembering the past; we do not progress without an honest and unclouded memory. We need to "keep alive the flame of collective conscience, bearing witness to succeeding generations to the horror of what happened," because that witness "awakens and preserves the memory of the victims, so that the conscience of humanity may rise up in the face of every desire for dominance and destruction."[42]

Nkechi Taifa, a human rights lawyer, founding member of the National Coalition of Blacks for Reparations in America (N'COBRA), and an inaugural commissioner of the National African American Reparations Commission (NAARC), stated, "Reparations is repairing or restoring.... It's a formal acknowledgment and apology, recognition that the injury continues, commitment to redress and actual compensation."[43]

Beginning in 1989, the late Representative John Conyers, a Democratic congressperson from Detroit, Michigan, and ranking member of the House Judiciary Committee, repeatedly introduced H.R. 40, "a bill that would establish a commission to examine the institution of slavery in the U.S. and its early colonies, and recommend appropriate remedies." In 2017, before he retired from Congress, Conyers stated, "I'm not giving up.... Slavery is a blemish on this nation's history, and until it is formally addressed, our country's story will remain marked by this blight."

> The "40" in H.R. 40 is a reference to an order signed in the waning days of the Civil War aimed at helping newly freed Black people survive and make a fresh start after 200 years in bond-

age. The government would take land that was confiscated from Confederates and redistribute it, with each Black family receiving 40 acres. However, after President Abraham Lincoln was assassinated, the order was rescinded and the land was returned to White Confederates.[44]

John Conyers first introduced the legislation after President Ronald Reagan signed the Civil Liberties Act of 1988, "which granted reparations to Japanese Americans who had been interned by the U.S. government during World War II." The $1.6 billion reparations program made $20,000 payments to 82,210 Japanese Americans and their heirs interned in American camps during World War II.[45]

After Conyers's retirement, Texas Representative Sheila Jackson Lee took the mantel and continued to champion the bill. Thirty years later, in 2021, H.R. 40 made it out of committee for the first time and was "approved by the House Judiciary Committee in a 25-to-17 vote along party lines." In early 2022, Jackson Lee said there were enough votes to pass the bill that would create a commission to study reparations. Given its likelihood of failing in the Senate, democratic legislatures urged President Biden to issue an executive order. "Reparations," Jackson Lee stated, "is about repair and when you repair the damage that has been done, you do so much to move a society forward. This commission can be a healing process. Telling the truth can heal America."[46]

Even with the optimism, support from major civil rights organizations, and congressional activism, the bill did not result in a vote. And Republicans taking control of the House in 2023 made the vote unlikely. A 2021 *Washington Post* poll found "that 65 percent of Americans opposed paying cash reparations to the descendants of enslaved Black people. While 46 percent of Democrats favored the idea, 92 percent of Republicans opposed it. Two-thirds of Black respondents supported the idea, but only 18 percent of White respondents did." While the majority of Americans oppose reparations, the number who support it—two-thirds of Black respondents and 46 percent of Democrats—has increased from the 19 percent supporting it in 1999. Advocates of the bill believe a commission educating the public on the need for reparations will create more public support.[47]

The idea of H.R. 40 is to respond to those who say, "My family didn't have enslaved people, it's not my fault," Jackson Lee said. "What I say to them is be very assured, we will not be knocking on individual White people's doors demanding money for African Americans. But for slavery, for the hanging of thousands of Black people, for Jim Crow laws, for the horrible segregation laws of the 20th century, for the segregation of the United States military, for redlining, your government has a responsibility because it was all government-sanctioned. Your government has a debt.[48]

Described by the *New Yorker* as "perhaps the country's leading scholar on the economics of racial inequality," professor and economist William A. Darity Jr., along with Kirsten Mullen, a writer and lecturer married to Darity, co-authored *From Here to Equality: Reparations for Black Americans in the Twenty-First Century*, which not only lays out a detailed economic plan for reparations but also makes the historical case for why it is needed.

Darity and Mullen's work "draws a thick line from the nation's origins to the present" and argues that reparations are owed to African American descendants of people who were enslaved "based on all three tiers or phases of injustice: slavery, American apartheid (Jim Crow), and the combined effects of present-day discrimination and the ongoing deprecation of black lives."[49]

Though many critics of any form of reparations argue slavery has long past, Darity and Mullen explain that many Black Americans "are only three generations removed from slavery." Take Bryan Stevenson, founder and executive director of the Equal Justice Initiative. He was born in 1959, and two of his great-grandparents on his mother's side were "born into slavery in Virginia in the late 1840s and early 1850s." As this book has explained, the injury did not end with slavery. It extended through Jim Crow and continues today. Apartheid-like segregation ended only about fifty years ago, and Black baby boomers alive today experienced it and all the racialized terror and oppression endured during that time, including the assassination of beloved African American leaders like Martin Luther King Jr.[50]

In the *New York Times*, Darity states the debt the American government owes to African Americans includes that for housing discrimination and for GI Bill discrimination that prevented Black people from buying homes and accumulating wealth, which was discussed in chapter 5. White Americans today continue to reap the benefits of government programs that were denied to Black people. There are more than forty-six million white Americans today (25 percent of the population) who are beneficiaries of the 1868 Homestead Act. Millions more white people still benefit from the overtly racist federal housing policies begun after the New Deal. Ninety-eight percent of the loans insured by the Federal Housing Administration from 1934 through 1962 went to white borrowers.[51]

As a result of over four hundred years of oppression and inequality, and persistent structural, institutional, and interpersonal racism, African American households in 2016 had a median net worth of $17,600, which is only one-tenth of white household net worth of $171,000. "That means, on average, that for every dollar the middle white household holds in wealth—measured by assets like homes, cash savings, and retirement funds—the middle black household possesses a mere ten cents."[52]

According to a 2019 McKinsey & Company report on income inequality,

> Black Americans can expect to earn up to $1 million less than white Americans over their lifetimes. This discrepancy is the product of a lifetime of diverging circumstances. For instance, without a resource-rich community or family of origin, individual families may improve their economic positions with their earnings. A family can increase its earning potential by attaining more education to develop its store of human capital. However, black families face serious obstacles on the journey through the education system and converting education to stable employment that provides rising incomes. Obstacles that reduce lifetime earning potential come in the form of poor school quality, differential treatment in the criminal-justice system, workplace discrimination, career selection, and a lack of role models who can guide professionals' career advancement.[53]

Darity refutes the idea that the breakdown of Black families is the main reason for racial income inequality. Take, for example, single Black women over the age of sixty with a bachelor's degree. They have a median net worth of about $11,000 compared to single white women over the age of sixty with a college degree that have a $384,000 median net worth. For younger women ages twenty to twenty-nine years old who have completed college, white women have a median net worth of $3,400 while Black women have a median net worth of negative $11,000. "The greatest socio-economic disparities for most women of color are rooted in racial inequality, which is then worsened by smaller but significant gendered disparities."[54]

The belief that blacks lack motivation and effort is contradicted by the evidence on racial differences in educational attainment. For comparable levels of family socioeconomic status, black youth obtain more years of schooling and credentials, including college degrees, than white youth. Moreover, unfortunately, motivation and effort are not enough to close the black-white wealth gap. Data from both the Survey of Income and Program Participation and the Survey of Consumer Finances provides the facts. Black household heads with a college or university degree have about $10,000 less in median net worth than white household heads who never completed high school. Blacks who are working full-time have a lower median net worth than whites who are unemployed. Blacks in the third quintile of the income distribution have similar levels of median wealth as whites in the lowest quintile. That means that, on average, blacks whose incomes were about $60,000 in 2014 had a level of median wealth of about $22,000, while whites whose incomes were less than $26,000 had a median wealth of about $18,000. Blacks in the lowest quintile had a median wealth of a paltry $200.[55]

Though there are other proposals for reparations, and the state of California has its own reparations taskforce, Darity's is the most comprehensive plan that would secure reparations for African Americans who qualify. The plan Darity supports would provide reparations only to U.S. citizens who can establish they had at least one ancestor enslaved in the country after it was founded and that those persons can prove they have self-identified as Black or African American for at least twelve years before the reparations program is enacted.[56] To establish a financial figure to be provided as reparations, Darity looks to the wealth disparity between whites and Black, which he believes is a better measure of economic well-being than income. "The gap in mean household wealth by race derived from the 2016 Survey of Consumer Finances was about $795,000." For ten million Black households with an average household of 3.31 persons, the total reparations estimate is $7.95 trillion.[57]

Darity argues the money must come from the federal government, whose policies since slavery have stolen wealth from Black Americans—not taxpayers, states, or municipalities. The payment could be made partly as "direct payouts to eligible recipients," as were given to Japanese Americans forced into internment camps and 9/11 victims' family members. They may also be paid in incremental amounts over an allocated amount of time no longer than ten years, similar to how the German government paid some victims of the Nazi Holocaust $100 a month.

Reparations could also be paid in the form of "establishment of a trust fund to which eligible blacks could apply for grants for various asset-building projects, including home-ownership, additional education, or start-up funds for self-employment" or "even vouchers for the purchase of financial assets." Endowments to historically Black colleges and universities are also an option of payment.[58]

Darity argues the government has demonstrated it can come up with that type of money in other instances such as the response to the Great Recession when the Federal Reserve transferred $1 trillion overnight to investment banks and provided "monthly outlays of $45 to $55 billion to conduct 'quantitative easing.'"[59] In September 2021, Darity wrote, "the Covid-19 pandemic demonstrated that the federal government can rapidly mobilize resources and spend huge sums without raising taxes. Federal expenditures to mitigate the economic impact of Covid-19 now exceed $6 trillion."[60]

The McKinsey & Company report found that doing nothing about racial economic inequality will not only continue to hurt African Americans but will cost the entire country—white, Black, and all citizens—over a trillion dollars:

> The widening racial wealth gap disadvantages black families, individuals, and communities and limits black citizens' economic power and prospects, and the effects are cyclical. Such a gap contributes to intergenerational economic precariousness: almost 70 percent of middle-class black children are likely to fall out of the middle class as adults. Other than its obvious negative impact on human development for black individuals and communities, the racial wealth gap also constrains the US economy as a whole. It is estimated that its dampening effect on consumption and investment will cost the US economy between $1 trillion and $1.5 trillion between 2019 and 2028—4 to 6 percent of the projected GDP in 2028.[61]

In a video clip from 1964 of him being questioned about whether progress has been made in the United States, Malcolm X answered, "If you stick a knife in my back nine inches and pull it out six inches, there's no progress. If you pull it all the way out that's not progress. Progress is healing the wound that the blow made. And they haven't even pulled the knife out much less healed the wound. They won't even admit the knife is there."[62]

Mass incarceration and overpolicing are the proverbial knives still in the back of the African American community. In spite of the racial justice reckoning of 2020 that decried the atrocities committed against African Americans such as George Floyd, Ahmaud Arbery, and Breonna Taylor and demanded money be diverted from the police state to low-income communities and social services and violence prevention programs, in 2022 President Biden's Safer America Plan directed funding to hire one hundred thousand more police officers throughout the country.[63] The U.S. Justice Department has conducted decades' worth of investigations of police departments, jails, and prisons throughout the United States to know that race-based human rights abuses are committed against African Americans in cities and states across the country every day; yet it has not committed to policies to rectify holistically the injustices. Until the war on drugs is ended, until convictions are expunged and formerly incarcerated people are able to fully reenter society after serving time, until police end their occupation of low-income Black neighborhoods and surveillance of Black American motorists, there will be no racial equality, repair, or progress.

In *Redemption and Restoration*, Timothy W. Wolfe writes:

> The effects of involvement with the criminal justice system can be devastating and long-lasting, persisting over generations, and they can even drag down entire neighborhoods. Every dollar spent on the war on drugs and the attendant aggressive policing, harsh sentences, and reliance on incarceration is a dollar that cannot be spent on victim support, crime prevention, housing, education, health care, job training, and infrastructure needs. "Million-dollar blocks" refer to census units where the cost of incarceration for residents of that block exceeds a million dollars. Mapping software allows researchers to match inmates with their home addresses to show how much money we spend in a wasteful cycle of arrests, convictions, stints of incarceration, release, rearrests again and again for technical, nonviolent offenders in our poorest communities. As a result of this powerful visualization tool, policy makers and others have begun to think differently about how finite resources are used. . . .
>
> While there is growing awareness of the economic waste and human suffering that result from our ill-conceived war on drugs, the problems in our criminal justice system are still massive; the prison industrial complex built over decades is still largely intact; and the need to dismantle and replace it is staring us in the face. . . .
>
> Related problems—from erroneous convictions and clear racial disparities in the application of the death penalty, to plea bargaining that has gone awry, inadequate funding of public defense, and the privatization and commercialization of prisons—persist and need to be addressed as well. Because all of these problems are interrelated and symptomatic of larger under-

lying problems, simply addressing one or even a few aspects of our broken criminal justice system will not be sufficient.[64]

For over two hundred years during the horrific institution of slavery in the United States the majority of white Americans were indifferent to the suffering inflicted upon African Americans held in bondage. In the years that followed until now, the majority of Americans have been complicit in the face of the unjust policing, incarceration, and postconviction discrimination that has locked up millions of people in cages and subjugated millions of Black Americans to permanent second-class status. The call for restorative justice, reparations, and repair is a call for Americans to become conscious and then outraged enough to demand—and be part of—the change that needs to happen. Answering the call will cost people: their comfort, their security, their privilege, maybe even some wealth. But the moral and spiritual toll of doing nothing exacts a greater price on our collective humanity. Without justice there is no restoration; without change there is no repair.

Conclusion
A Catholic Call for Justice

When he [Jesus] came to Nazareth, where he had been brought up, he went to the synagogue on the sabbath day, as was his custom. He stood up to read, and the scroll of the prophet Isaiah was given to him. He unrolled the scroll and found the place where it was written: "The Spirit of the Lord is upon me, because he has anointed me to bring good news to the poor. He has sent me to proclaim release to the captives and recovery of sight to the blind, to let the oppressed go free, to proclaim the year of the Lord's favor." And he rolled up the scroll, gave it back to the attendant, and sat down. The eyes of all in the synagogue were fixed on him. Then he began to say to them, "Today this scripture has been fulfilled in your hearing."

Luke 4:16–21

The story and fate of Jordan Neely encapsulates so much of what has been discussed in this book. Thirty-year-old Neely was a Black man, a man with an extensive arrest history, who suffered childhood trauma when his mother was murdered, who struggled with a serious mental health disorder, and who was homeless. On May 1, 2023, he was on a subway train full of New Yorkers. Neely, exasperated and at his wit's end, asked for money and said to those in the car that he didn't have food, didn't have a drink, was fed up, and didn't mind if he went to prison or died. He then threw his jacket on the floor.

A twenty-four-year-old white man named Daniel Penny, claiming he was acting to protect himself and others on the train, put Neely in a chokehold and strangled the life out of him. Two other train riders also subdued the agitated Neely as he struggled for his life.

Penny was questioned by the police and then released. Only after protests and calls for his arrest did the district attorney's office file charges of second-degree murder. Penny turned himself in, was booked, and released after posting bail. The National Police Association shared Penny's fundraiser for his defense fees and called him a "Good Samaritan," a claim Ron DeSantis, governor of Florida, echoed. Nearly $3 million has been raised for Penny's legal defense.

Jordan Neely's murder and the overwhelming support of it by a large segment of white America demonstrate the moral and spiritual crisis our nation faces in the wake of slavery, Jim Crow segregation, and mass incarceration. In the Catholic tradition, and many other faith traditions, human life is considered sacred in and of itself. In *Harm, Healing, and Human Dignity*, author Caitline Morneau writes, "Because of this inherent truth, every person deserves to be treated with dignity, no matter the harm they have suffered or caused."[1] To resist a culture of death that sees a Black, homeless man as a threat deserving of white vigilante murder involves the call to affirm the inviolable dignity and worth of every person regardless of skin color, socioeconomic status, and health status.

In the introduction to this book I referenced the words of Jesus from the Gospel of Matthew 25:31–46:

> Then the king will say to those at his right hand, "Come, you who are blessed by my Father, inherit the kingdom prepared for you from the foundation of the world, for I was hungry and you gave me food, I was thirsty and you gave me something to drink, I was a stranger and you welcomed me, I was naked and you gave me clothing, I was sick and you took care of me, I was in prison and you visited me." Then the righteous will answer him, "Lord, when was it that we saw you hungry and gave you food or thirsty and gave you something to drink? And when was it that we saw you a stranger and welcomed you or naked and gave you clothing? And when was it that we saw you sick or in prison and visited you?" And the king will answer them, "Truly I tell you, just as

you did it to one of the least of these brothers and sisters of mine, you did it to me."

Too many Christians, too many who claim a spiritual and moral compass in America, have failed to honor the dignity of others. When encountering those suffering on the margins of society, they turn away. Cesar Chavez, the great advocate for the rights of farmworkers, said, "History will judge societies and governments—and their institutions— not by how big they are or how well they serve the rich and powerful but by how effectively they respond to the needs of the poor and helpless."[2]

As a nation that many claim as "Christian," the United States failed Jordan Neely and countless other people throughout the nation's history who have been—and are—discarded and treated as less than human.

The same country that has nearly one million homeless people is also the country whose tax policy directly benefits the ultra wealthy and corporations. According to the U.S. Senate Committee on the Budget, "the Bush and Trump tax cuts for the wealthy and corporations have driven recent and projected federal deficits. They have been the largest driver of deficits over the past two decades and account for 57% of the increase in the debt-to-GDP ratio since 2001." A May 2023 report released by the nonpartisan Congressional Budget Office (CBO) found that if the Republicans extend the Trump tax cuts as they've proposed, it would add $3.5 trillion to the deficit over the next decade. That means the top 5 percent of earners would receive nearly 40 percent of the benefit in the first year alone. "For every penny they give in tax handouts to the rich, down the road they're going to demand equivalent cuts that boot people off their health care, increase child hunger, and raise the cost of living for typical Americans."[3]

Added to that, Charles Rettig, the Internal Revenue Service commissioner, estimated in 2021 that the United States is losing $1 trillion every year in unpaid taxes, and that "most of the unpaid taxes are the result of evasion by the wealthy and large corporations." Biden's administration proposed increasing levels of funding for the tax collection agency in order to increase oversight of tax returns of high-income earners and companies,[4] which Congress approved in 2022. Republican politicians, however, responded by calling to "defund the IRS," and the first bill they passed in 2023 after gaining narrow control of the House was the Family and Small Business Taxpayer Protection Act, which would repeal $80 billion approved for the IRS. Though the Republican bill most likely won't pass the Democrat-controlled Senate, if it did, the "measure would increase the budget deficit by more than $114 billion through 2032, according to the Congressional Budget Office."[5]

Over the past decade, "the percentage of the largest companies being audited fell from 93 percent to 38 percent."[6] To add insult to injury, according to a 2023 letter sent by IRS commissioner Daniel Werfe to the U.S. Senate, recent research indicates it is Black taxpayers who are "between three and five times more likely to be audited."[7]

In the richest nation on earth, Jordan Neely, instead of receiving compassion and assistance for his human needs, was brutally murdered. To American society, Neely transgressed a barrier by expressing his frustration with being homeless, hungry, and thirsty. Most Americans have become accustomed to ignoring the plight of the poor, homeless, exploited, incarcerated, shunned, and outcast in our society—and others like Daniel Penny, who don't respond by ignoring the person in front of them, respond instead with violence. As mainstream media fails to highlight the unjust and exploitive actions by wealthy Americans, corporations, and lawmakers, they focus blame on and highlight Black and brown people who face the results of the exploitation of that same government, those same corporations who benefit through the harm of others. The faces of people who evade taxes are not plastered on the nightly news. The CEOs and shareholders of companies polluting our environment and Black and brown communities are not named every night in the headlines. Instead, Americans are trained by the media to fear and despise the people who have the *least* in our society, who have been the most harmed and marginalized. The media organizations owned by billionaires want their consumers to fear people who want their basic needs met to survive: food, clothing, and shelter. Americans respond by saying, How dare people who have nothing ask for that much!

The great theologian James Cone, who in his book *God of the Oppressed* declared a truly Christian approach to the dignity of others, offers an approach that is focused on justice. Only a Jesus who is "Black" can truly identify with and liberate African Americans. He wrote,

Christ's blackness is both literal and symbolic. His blackness is literal in the sense that he truly becomes One with the oppressed blacks, taking their suffering as his suffering and revealing that he is found in the history of our struggle, the story of our pain, and the rhythm of our bodies. . . . The least in America are literally and symbolically present in black people. . . .

To say that Christ is black means that God, in his infinite wisdom and mercy, not only takes color seriously, he also takes it upon himself and discloses his will to make us whole—new creatures born in the spirit of divine blackness and redeemed through the blood of the Black Christ. Christ is black, therefore, not because of some cultural or psychological need of black people, but because and only because Christ really enters into our world where the poor, the despised, and the black are, disclosing that he is with them, enduring their humiliation and pain and transforming oppressed slaves into liberated servants.[8]

For the majority of non-Black Christians in America, calling Jesus Black is blasphemous. Despite Jesus's being born in Bethlehem, in present-day Palestine, of a people with brown skin, America depicts Jesus as a white man whose mother and disciples, along with church fathers, are also white. Yet, Jesus himself, an ethnic Jew, lived in a region under Roman occupation. Jesus was a member of a minority who in his ministry subverted the status quo and ministered to the poor, marginalized, unclean, outcasts, and sinners.

The Gospel of Luke outlines Jesus's ministry of salvation and liberation for those who suffer in the world, and its companion book of Acts demonstrates how that mission is continued through Jesus's followers. In the central text that opens this conclusion, Jesus proclaims he was anointed "to bring good news to the poor" and sent "to proclaim release to the captives and recovery of sight to the blind, to let the oppressed go free."

In *Jesus before Christianity*, Albert Nolan argues that Jesus did not identify with the outcasts of society or seek to "save" people in order to prove his importance. Instead, Jesus was motivated by compassion.

Anyone who thinks that Jesus' motive for performing miracles of healing was a desire to prove something, to prove that he was the Messiah or Son of God, has thoroughly misunderstood him. His one and only motive for healing people was compassion. His only desire was to liberate people from their suffering and their fatalistic resignation to suffering. He was deeply convinced that this could be done, and the miraculous success of his efforts must be attributed to the power of his faith. Nor did he think that he had any monopoly on compassion, faith, and miraculous cures. What he wanted to do most of all was to awaken the same compassion and the same faith in the people around him. That alone would enable the power of God to become effective in their midst.[9]

Americans who claim a Christian identity must answer the questions: Will you let compassion guide your lives and actions more than your comfort and fear? Can you as Christians be true followers of Christ if you ignore the plight of African Americans overly incarcerated in inhumane conditions, locked out of society because of earlier criminal convictions, segregated in neighborhoods marked by poverty and high unemployment, police occupation, substandard segregated schools, and unconscionable levels of gun violence?

Like America postslavery, the majority of Americans view the issues overwhelmingly faced by Black Americans as "a Black problem" that needs to be solved by "Black Americans" or with a return to "traditional Black marriage." That refusal to view Black Americans first as "Americans" plays a role in why issues facing Black communities aren't priorities of the American government, and why predominately Black neighborhoods and institutions aren't provided with proper investments in community-initiated solutions, but instead police and incarceration are funded.

As Nolan stated, "Without compassion all religious practices and beliefs are useless and empty. . . . Without compassion all politics will be oppressive, even the politics of revolution."[10]

Saint Paul VI, in his 1967 encyclical *Populorum Progressio*, taught societies the need to build a "human community where men can live truly human lives, free from discrimination on account of race, religion or nationality, free from servitude to other men." He said it is an unacceptable "less than human condition" to have "oppressive political structures resulting from the abuse of ownership or the improper exercise of power."[11] The American criminal legal system from policing to prosecution, sentencing and imprisonment, to surveillance and postincarceration social exile is an oppressive political structure that improperly targets and improperly exercises its power against African Americans.

The systems and structures that allow caging, torture, assault, rape, and dehumanization must be abolished. People who caused harm must be healed. And people who survived harm must be made whole. Both as a people and as a nation, the oppressed must be set free.

There are actions people can take to work toward justice individually, in their local and faith communities, states, and nationally. In the last chapter of the book, I outlined calls for restorative justice in schools, diversion programs, and prisons, and I looked at advocating for restitution and repair. And there are organizations to join where you can add your resources and time. Another action—that is simple and profound—is to build a friendship with a person who is incarcerated. In a social media post, the Innocence Project recommended Abolition Apostles, Wire of Hope, Prison Correspondence Project, and Black and Pink. Becoming pen pals with people who are incarcerated through Abolition Apostles and working with their collective has not only helped me better understand the reality of incarceration but also put me in proximity with people on the outside (family members and supporters of those who are incarcerated), people I can learn from and support.

Another outlet for action and support is encouraging legislation change around limiting those formerly incarcerated as well as encouraging employers to hire formerly incarcerated people. Or you may wish to invest in businesses, organizations, or nonprofits created and run by formerly incarcerated people. I recommend to people to start with this goal: become an ally of people who are incarcerated or formerly incarcerated in order to support their self-determination.

And make it local. Vote! One of the most important actions people can take is to vote in elections for the district attorney. I wrote about the role of prosecutors in maintaining mass incarceration in the last chapter. According to an ACLU survey, 89 percent of voters prefer a district attorney candidate who supports ending mass incarceration; 77 percent support reducing racial bias; and 79 percent support holding police accountable. Reflecting on the survey's results, Taylor Pendergrass, senior campaign strategist for the ACLU Campaign for Smart Justice, said, "Prosecutors are the most powerful, unaccountable, and least transparent actors in the criminal justice system. They hold the keys to ending mass incarceration. They just have to use them."[12]

Both locally and nationally, it's also important to support candidates who believe in funding programs that aid the most vulnerable in society such as SNAP, Social Security, affordable housing, health care, mental health care, substance use disorder treatment, public schools, community violence prevention programs, and job training and creation. It's essential to divert money from bloated police department budgets to social programs. Police are being tasked with being first responders and performing jobs they are not equipped to do, such as responding to people experiencing housing insecurity, mental health crises, substance use disorders, student discipline, and traffic violations. Trained professionals such as mental health clinicians, housing advocates, addiction counselors, teachers, social workers, and unarmed traffic responders must begin to alleviate the burden placed on police, which will lead to the protection of Americans in crisis from armed police who are trained to kill.

One immediate action that can greatly reduce the number of people incarcerated is advocating for the elimination of cash bail. According to the Prison Policy Initiative, more than four hundred thousand people, and about 75 percent of people held in jails, are incarcerated in this country who have not been convicted of a crime and are being held simply because they cannot pay bail. That number has almost quadrupled since the 1980s, when the war on drugs gained steam. It costs $13.6 billion annually to detain people pretrial even though studies have shown that people who are released on their own recognizance and those who post bail are just as statistically likely to appear in court. Just three days in jail can have a devastating impact on a person's life in the areas of "employment, housing, financial stability, and family wellbeing." Like almost every aspect of mass incarceration, Black people make up a disproportionate number of those held pretrial, 43 percent,[13] one reason the NAACP has called for the elimination of cash bail.[14]

Other actions that call for our advocacy: reducing the number of people incarcerated and ending mandatory minimum sentences. In the Sentencing Project's report "Counting Down: Paths to a 20-Year Maximum Prison Sentence," the authors provide evidence that mandatory minimum sentences "do not improve public safety" but "increase racial disparities, incarceration rates, and coercive plea bargains." Many organizations like "the Judicial Conference of the United States, the American Law Institute's Model Penal Code, and the American Bar Association" have called for the end of minimum sentences.[15] The vast majority of people "age out" of criminal behavior. Abolishing life sentences altogether and greatly reducing lengths of prison sentences not only make sense but can also save the government, taxpayers, and justice-involved families billions of dollars every year, while liberating people from prisons and giving them another opportunity at freedom.

Advocating for universal basic income is essential for aiding poor people and especially formerly incarcerated people returning home. This is something that Pope Francis has spoken of and written in support of. In *Let Us Dream*, Francis states:

> Recognizing the value to society of the work of nonearners is a vital part of our rethinking in the post-Covid world. That's why I believe it is time to explore concepts like the universal basic income (UBI), also known as "the negative income tax": an unconditional flat payment to all citizens, which could be dispersed through the tax system.
>
> The UBI could reshape relations in the labor market, guaranteeing people the dignity of refusing employment terms that trap them in poverty. It would give people the basic security they need, remove the stigma of welfarism, and make it easier to move between jobs as technology-driven labor patterns increasingly demand. Policies like the UBI can also help free people to combine earning wages with giving time to the community.[16]

In the article "Universal Basic Income Has Been Tested Repeatedly. It Works. Will America Ever Embrace It?," Megan Greenwell explains that since the nation's first guaranteed income program in Stockton,

California, which has spread to pilot programs throughout the country, "a growing body of research based on the experiments shows that guaranteed income works—that it pulls people out of poverty, improves health outcomes, and makes it easier for people to find jobs and take care of their children."[17] While the U.S. government may not be ready to guarantee basic income, individuals who want to donate to such causes have options like the Fund for Guaranteed Income.

The story of Jordan Neely is not only one that shows us the devastating result of broken, racist systems that privilege white and wealthy citizens while harming the poor and people of color. His is also a story within which I realize my own story. I could have been Jordan Neely. I'm Black; I experienced childhood trauma; I was a victim of a crime; I had a mental breakdown, followed by a brief period of homelessness. I know what it's like to lose everything. If it weren't for my family, resources, and (expensive) health care providers—which Neely didn't have—I would have been on the street begging for food and drink. I have people in my extended family who are incarcerated. I'm not a theologian or lawyer engaging in an academic exercise writing this book. Instead, I am telling the story of Black Americans, past and present, who have gone through unspeakable tragedies and still experienced joy and triumph.

My eldest child is now a college student studying criminal justice. For most of his life, I had a gnawing fear that he would become incarcerated. He had a lot of energy, a big personality, difficulty conforming in the K–12 academic settings, and liked to push boundaries and take risks. While his statistical risk of incarceration will continue to drop after he graduates college and grows older, there are far too many mothers of Black boys across the country who will have their worst fears realized. For me, for those women, for our sons, for anyone struggling as a Black person in America, this book is my prayer, my offering, and my hope: that all Americans are able to live in a society free from the fear of incarceration as the primary response to Blackness, poverty, unemployment, trauma, mental illness, and addiction; that America, and Americans, may turn from racism and punitiveness toward justice that restores, repairs, and reconciles. As African Americans, we should never be ashamed of what we or our ancestors have endured. Even Jesus's resurrected body still had his wound marks after his resurrection.

Endnotes

Introduction

1. U.S. Department of Education Office for Civil Rights, "Civil Rights Data Collection Data Snapshot: Early Childhood Education," March 2014, https://www2.ed.gov/about/offices/list/ocr/docs/crdc-early-learning-snapshot.pdf.

2. Jason P. Robey, Michael Massoglia, and Michael T. Light, "A Generational Shift: Race and the Declining Lifetime Risk of Imprisonment," *Demography* 2023; 10863378, doi: https://doi.org/10.1215/00703370-10863378.

3. James Forman Jr., *Locking Up Our Own: Crime and Punishment in Black America* (New York: Farrar, Straus and Giroux, 2017), 13.

4. Bryan N. Massingale, *Racial Justice and the Catholic Church* (Maryknoll, NY: Orbis Books, 2010), 15.

5. Loic Wacquant, "From Slavery to Mass Incarceration: Rethinking the 'Race Question' in the US," *New Left Review* (January/February 2002), https://loicwacquantorg.files.wordpress.com/2019/03/lw-2002-from-slavery-to-mass-incarceration-rethinking-the-race-question-in-the-us.pdf.

6. "Fact Sheet: Trends in U.S. Corrections," The Sentencing Project, May 2021, https://www.sentencingproject.org/wp-content/uploads/2021/07/Trends-in-US-Corrections.pdf.

7. Ashley Nellis, "Mass Incarceration Trends," The Sentencing Project, January 25, 2023, https://www.sentencingproject.org/reports/mass-incarceration-trends.

8. Robey et al., "A Generational Shift."

9. Anna R. Haskins, Wade C. Jacobsen, and Joes Mittleman, "Optimism and Obstacles: Racialized Constraints in College Attitudes and Expectations among Teens of the Prison Boom," *Sociology of Education* 2023, 96:3, 211–33, https://doi.org/10.1177/00380407231167412open_in_new.

10. Rebecca Neusteter and Megan O'Toole, "Every Three Seconds—Emerging Findings," Vera Institute of Justice, January 2019, https://www.vera.org/publications/arrest-trends-every-three-seconds-landing/arrest-trends-every-three-seconds/findings#:~:text=The%20data%20shows%20that%20non,than%20five%20percent%20of%20arrests.

11. Criminalization of People with Mental Illness, NAMI: National Alliance on Mental Illness, 2022, https://www.nami.org/Advocacy/Policy-Priorities/Stopping-Harmful-Practices/Criminalization-of-People-with-Mental-Illness.

12. Brandy F. Henry, "Typologies of Adversity in Childhood & Adulthood as Determinants of Mental Health & Substance Use Disorders of Adults Incarcerated in US Prisons," *Child Abuse & Neglect* 99 (2020), https://doi.org/10.1016/j.

chiabu.2019.104251, https://www.sciencedirect.com/science/article/pii/S01452134 19304284.

13. Prison Policy Initiative, "Rates of Mental Illness and Substance Use Disorder Are Much Higher among 'Frequent Utilizers' of Jails," 2019, https://www.prisonpolicy.org/graphs/frequent_utilizers_mh_sud.html.

14. R. C. Heter and J. L. Eberhardt, "Racial Disparities in Incarceration Increase Acceptance of Punitive Policies," *Psychological Science* 25, no. 10 (1949–1954), https://doi.org/10.1177/0956797614540307.

15. Allison L. Skinner-Dorkenoo, Apoorva Sarmal, Kasheena G. Rogbeer, Chloe J. André, Bhumi Patel, and Leah Cha, "Highlighting COVID-19 Racial Disparities Can Reduce Support for Safety Precautions among White U.S. Residents," *Social Science & Medicine* 301 (2022), https://www.sciencedirect.com/science/article/pii/S027795362200257X.

16. House Committee on Oversight and Reform. "Committee Releases Documents Showing Sackler Family Wealth Totals $11 Billion," April 20, 2021, https://oversight.house.gov/news/press-releases/committee-releases-documents-showing-sackler-family-wealth-totals-11-billion.

17. "A Proclamation on Second Chance Month, 2022" (April 2022), The White House, https://www.whitehouse.gov/briefing-room/presidential-actions/2022/03/31/a-proclamation-on-second-chance-month-2022.

18. Ericka Taylor, "'Halfway Home' Make Case That the Formerly Incarcerated Are Never Truly Free," NPR, February 2, 2021, https://www.npr.org/2021/02/02/962722415/halfway-home-makes-case-that-the-formerly-incarcerated-are-never-truly-free.

19. MacArthur Foundation, "Reuben Jonathan Miller," 2022, https://www.macfound.org/fellows/class-of-2022/reuben-jonathan-miller#searchresults.

20. David W. Blight, "The Civil War and Reconstruction Era, 1845-1877," Open Course, Yale University, Spring 2008, https://oyc.yale.edu/history/hist-119.

21. *The 1619 Project: Episode 106 "Justice,"* directed by Roger Ross-Williams and Jonathan Clasberry, Lionsgate Production, 2023.

22. "Ten Years after 'The New Jim Crow,'" *The New Yorker*, January 17, 2020, https://www.newyorker.com/news/the-new-yorker-interview/ten-years-after-the-new-jim-crow.

23. Robert P. Long, *White Too Long: The Legacy of White Supremacy in American Christianity* (New York: Simon & Schuster, 2020), 10.

24. Rachel L. Swarns, *The 272: The Families Who Were Enslaved and Sold to Build the American Catholic Church* (New York: Random House, 2023), xvi.

25. Sandra Pavelka and Anne Seymour, "Guiding Principles and Restorative Practices for Crime Victims and Survivors," *Corrections Today*, January/February 2019, https://www.aca.org/common/Uploaded%20files/Publications_Carla/Docs/Corrections%20Today/2019%20Articles/Guiding-Principles-and-Restorative-Practices-for-Crime_Victims-and-Survivors.pdf.

26. Yotam Shem-Tov, Steven Raphael, and Alissa Skog, "Can Restorative Justice Conferencing Reduce Recidivism? Evidence from the Make-It-Right Program," NBER—National Bureau of Economic Research, August 12, 2021, https://www.nber.org/papers/w29150.

27. Fania E. Davis, *The Little Book of Race and Restorative Justice: Black Lives, Healing, and US Social Transformation* (New York: Good Books, 2019), 52–54.

Chapter 1: Slavery and Neoslavery

1. Dwight N. Hopkins and Edward P. Antonio, *The Cambridge Companion to Black Theology* (New York: Cambridge University Press, 2012), 3.

2. Carl Wise and David Wheat, "Pope Nicolas V and the Portuguese Slave Trade; African Laborers for a New Empire: Iberia, Slavery, and the Atlantic World," Lowcountry Digital History Initiative, ldhi.library.cofc.edu, https://ldhi.library.cofc.edu/exhibits/show/african_laborers_for_a_new_emp/pope_nicolas_v_and_the_portugu.

3. Hopkins et al., *The Cambridge Companion to Black Theology*, 4.

4. Ibid., 5.

5. Howard W. French, *Born in Blackness: Africa, Africans, and the Making of the Modern World, 1471 to the Second World War* (New York: Liveright Publishing Company, 2021), 280–83.

6. Ibid., 283–84.

7. Ibid., 285–86.

8. Cyprian Davis, O.S.B., *The History of Black Catholics in the United States* (New York: Crossroad Publishing Company, 1990), 16; *Correspondance de Dom Afonso, roi du Congo, 1506–1543*, ed. Louis Jadin and Mireille Dicorato (Brussels, 1974).

9. French, *Born in Blackness*, 286–90.

10. Ibid., 295.

11. Davis, *The History of Black Catholics*, 17; "Dom Joao III au Roi Dom Afonso," in *Correspondance de Dom Afonso*, 176.

12. French, *Born in Blackness*, 299.

13. Ibid., 312.

14. Beth Austin, "1619: Virginia's First Africans," Hampton History Musuem, December 2019, https://hampton.gov/DocumentCenter/View/24075/1619-Virginias-First-Africans?bidId=.

15. Davis, *The History of Black Catholics*, 18. For more information, see W. G. L. Randles, *L'ancien royaume du Congo des origines à la fin du XIX siècle* (Paris: Mouton, 1968), 87–104. See also Basil Davidson, *The African Slave Trade* (Boston: Little, Brown, 1980).

16. Jamie T. Phelps, O.P., *Black and Catholic: The Challenge and Gift of Black Folk: Contributions of African American Experience and Thought to Catholic Theology* (Milwaukee: Marquette University Press, 1997), 23.

17. French, *Born in Blackness*, 175.

18. "Guns Germs & Steel: Variables. Smallpox," PBS, www.pbs.org, https://www.pbs.org/gunsgermssteel/variables/smallpox.html.

19. Oliver Milman, "European Colonization of Americas Killed So Many It Cooled Earth's Climate," *The Guardian*, January 31, 2019, http://www.theguardian.

com/environment/2019/jan/31/european-colonization-of-americas-helped-cause-climate-change.

20. Henry Louis Gates, "How Many Slaves Landed in the U.S.? The African Americans: Many Rivers to Cross," PBS, The African Americans: Many Rivers to Cross, www.pbs.org, https://www.pbs.org/wnet/african-americans-many-rivers-to-cross/history/how-many-slaves-landed-in-the-us/.

21. French, *Born in Blackness*, 8.

22. Nikole Hannah-Jones, Caitlin Roper, Ilena Silverman, and Jake Silverstein, *The 1619 Project* (New York: One World, 2021), 9–10; Austin, "1619: Virgina's First Africans."

23. Phelps, *Black and Catholic*, 22–23.

24. Hannah-Jones et al., *The 1619 Project*, 11.

25. Pearl M. Graham, "Thomas Jefferson and Sally Hemings," *The Journal of Negro History* 46, no. 2 (1961): 89–103.

26. Michael Harriot, "What to the Slave Is the Fourth of July," *The Root*, www.theroot.com, https://www.theroot.com/what-to-the-slave-is-the-fourth-of-july-1836083536.

27. Douglas A. Blackmon, *Slavery by Another Name: The Re-Enslavement of Black Americans from the Civil War to World War II* (New York: Anchor Books, 2009), 40.

28. Dorothy Roberts, "Race," in Hannah-Jones et al., *The 1619 Project*, 50.

29. Roberts, "Race," 53; Rachel A. Feinstein, *When Rape Was Legal: The Untold History of Sexual Violence during Slavery* (New York: Routledge, 2019), 2.

30. Roberts, "Race," 53; Christine Kenneally, "Large DNA Study Traces Violent History of American Slavery," *New York Times*, July 23, 2020, https://www.nytimes.com/2020/07/23/science/23andme-african-ancestry.html; Steven J. Micheletti, Kaisa Bryc, Ancona Esselmann, Samantha Go, William A. Freyman, Meghan E. Moreno, G. David Poznik, Anjali J. Shastri, and 23andMe Research Team, "Genetic Consequences of the Transatlantic Slave Trade in the Americas," *American Journal of Human Genetics* 107, no. 2 (2020): 265–77.

31. Delores S. Williams, *Sisters in the Wilderness: The Challenge of Womanist God-Talk* (Maryknoll, NY: Orbis Books, 1993, 2013), 52.

32. Hannah-Jones et al., *The 1619 Project*, 11.

33. Larry H. Spruill, "Slave Patrols, 'Packs of Negro Dogs' and Policing Black Communities," *Phylon* 53, no. 1 (2016): 42–66.

34. Ibid.

35. Harriot, "What to the Slave Is the Fourth of July."

36. Hannah-Jones et al., *The 1619 Project*, 55.

37. Wilma King, "'Mad' Enough to Kill: Enslaved Women, Murder, and Southern Courts," *Journal of African American History* 92, no. 1 (2007): 37–56; *State of Missouri v. Celia*, FCCC, MO.

38. Ibid.

39. Equal Justice Initiative, "Slavery in America," eji.org, June 15, 2021, https://eji.org/reports/slavery-in-america.

40. Gregory D. Smithers, *Slave Breeding: Sex, Violence, and Memory in African American History* (Gainesville: University Press of Florida, 2012), 27.

41. Robert P. Long, *White Too Long: The Legacy of White Supremacy in American Christianity* (New York: Simon & Schuster, 2020), 77.

42. Ibid., 88.

43. Nathaniel Hunter, "Pray for Justice with Our Lady of Stono," *U.S. Catholic,* uscatholic.org, September 1, 2020, https://uscatholic.org/articles/202009/pray-with-our-lady-of-stono-to-heal-the-wounds-of-slavery.

44. Ibid.

45. Nat Turner, *The Confessions of Nat Turner, the Leader of the Late Insurrections in Southampton, Va. As Fully and Voluntarily Made to Thomas R. Gray, in the Prison Where . . . Account of the Whole Insurrection* (2011), 19.

46. Christopher Klein, "10 Things You May Not Know about Nat Turner's Rebellion," History, www.history.com, February 5, 2020, https://www.history.com/news/10-things-you-may-not-know-about-nat-turners-rebellion.

47. Turner, *The Confessions of Nat Turner,* 23–24.

48. Ibid., 25–26.

49. Klein, "10 Things You May Not Know about Nat Turner's Rebellion."

50. Davis, *The History of Black Catholics,* 39–40.

51. Ibid., 36–58.

52. "Slavery in the Upper South (AR, NC, TN, VA), Encyclopedia.Com," www.encyclopedia.com, https://www.encyclopedia.com/humanities/applied-and-social-sciences-magazines/slavery-upper-south-ar-nc-tn-va.

53. Equal Justice Initiative, "Slavery in America."

54. Blackmon, *Slavery by Another Name,* 41.

55. Ibid., 44.

56. Ibid., 45.

57. Smithers, *Slave Breeding,* 20.

58. Ibid.

59. Equal Justice Initiative, "Slavery in America."

60. Missouri State Archives, https://www.sos.mo.gov/archives/resources/africanamerican/scott/scott.asp.

61. Ibid.

62. Ibid.

63. "Dred Scott, Plaintiff in Error v. John F. A. Sandford, Supreme Court, US Law, LII, Legal Information Institute," www.law.cornell.edu, December 1, 1856, https://www.law.cornell.edu/supremecourt/text/60/393.

64. Hannah-Jones et al., *The 1619 Project,* 22–23.

65. Ibid., 23.

66. The Abraham Lincoln Association, *Collected Works of Abraham Lincoln, vol. 5* (2006), https://quod.lib.umich.edu/l/lincoln/lincoln5/1:812?rgn=div1;view=fulltext.

67. Hannah-Jones et al., *The 1619 Project,* 24.

68. "Frederick Douglass Project Writings: The President and His Speeches, RBSCP," River Campus Libraries, https://rbscp.lib.rochester.edu/4387.

69. Ibid.

70. Hannah-Jones et al., *The 1619 Project,* 24.

71. Sydney Trent, "Abraham Lincoln's Disastrous Effort to Get Black People to Leave the U.S.," *Washington Post*, February 19, 2023, https://www.washingtonpost.com/history/2023/02/19/abraham-lincolns-disastrous-effort-get-black-people-leave-us.

72. "America's Reconstruction: People and Politics after the Civil War," Gilder Lehrman Institute of American History, www.digitalhistory.uh.edu, https://www.digitalhistory.uh.edu/exhibits/reconstruction/section1/section1_soldiers.html.

73. Hannah-Jones et al., *The 1619 Project*, 233.

74. "The 13th Amendment of the U.S. Constitution," National Constitution Center—The 13th Amendment of the U.S. Constitution, constitutioncenter.org, https://constitutioncenter.org/interactive-constitution/amendment/amendment-xiii.

75. Blackmon, *Slavery by Another Name*, 41.

76. Bryan Stevenson, "Slavery in America and the Ideology of White Supremacy" in Angela Davis, *Policing the Black Man* (New York: Pantheon Books, 2017).

77. Blackmon, *Slavery by Another Name*, 7.

78. Ibid., 73.

79. French, *Born in Blackness*, 419.

80. Blackmon, *Slavery by Another Name*, 7.

81. Ellen Terrell, "The Convict Leasing System: Slavery in Its Worst Aspects, Inside Adams," Library of Congress, June 17, 2021, https://blogs.loc.gov/inside_adams/2021/06/convict-leasing-system.

82. Ibid.

83. Clarissa Olds Keeler, *The Crime of Crimes; or The Convict System Unmasked*, Library of Congress, African American Pamphlet Collection: Washington, DC, 1907, https://www.loc.gov/item/07026922/?loclr=blogadm.

84. Ibid.

85. Ibid.

86. Blackmon, *Slavery by Another Name*, 57.

87. Ibid., 8.

88. Ibid., 274–77, 375–83.

89. Stevenson, "Slavery in America," 12.

Chapter Two: *The Evolution from Lynching to the Death Penalty*

1. Julie Buckner Armstrong, *Mary Turner and the Memory of Lynching* (Athens: University of Georgia Press, 2011), 32–57.

2. Ibid.

3. Aaryn Urell, "EJI's Reconstruction in America Report Changes Picture of Lynching in America," Equal Justice Initiative, https://eji.org/news/reconstruction-in-america-report-changes-picture-of-lynching-in-america.

4. Douglas A. Blackmon, *Slavery by Another Name: The Re-Enslavement of Black Americans from the Civil War to World War II* (New York: Anchor Books, 2009), 18.

5. Nikole Hannah-Jones, Caitlin Roper, Ilena Silverman, and Jake Silverstein, *The 1619 Project* (New York: One World, 2021), 297–98.

6. Blackmon, *Slavery by Another Name*, 18.

7. Hannah-Jones et al., *The 1619 Project*, 260–61.

8. Ibid., 92, 157.

9. James H. Cone, *The Cross and the Lynching Tree* (Maryknoll, NY: Orbis Books, 2013), 4.

10. Ibid., 5–6.

11. "Plessy v. Ferguson," Oyez, https://www.oyez.org/cases/1850-1900/163us537.

12. Plessy v. Ferguson, 163 U.S. 537 (1896), Justia, https://supreme.justia.com/cases/federal/us/163/537/#tab-opinion-1917401.

13. Ibid.

14. Alfreda M. Duster, *Crusade for Justice: The Autobiography of Ida B. Wells* (Chicago: University of Chicago Press, 1970), 32.

15. Ibid., 42–44.

16. "History of Lynching in America," February 11, 2022, https://naacp.org/find-resources/history-explained/history-lynching-america.

17. "W. E. B. Du Bois," naacp.org, May 11, 2021, https://naacp.org/find-resources/history-explained/civil-rights-leaders/web-du-bois.

18. Cone, *The Cross and the Lynching Tree*, 103.

19. Buckner Armstrong, *Mary Turner and the Memory of Lynching*, 70–71.

20. "The Great Migration (1910–1970)," National Archives, www.archives.gov, May 20, 2021, https://www.archives.gov/research/african-americans/migrations/great-migration#:~:text=The%20Great%20Migration%20was%20one,the%201910s%20until%20the%201970s.

21. Cone, *The Cross and the Lynching Tree*, 9. See James Allen, *Without Sanctuary: Lynching Photography in America* (Santa Fe, NM: Twin Palms, 2003), front and back postcard photos 25 and 26, the burnt corpse of William Stanley, August 1915, Temple, Texas.

22. Cone, *The Cross and the Lynching Tree*, 7. Cited in Adam Gussow, *Seems Like Murder Here: Southern Violence and the Blues Tradition* (Chicago: University of Chicago Press, 2002), 49.

23. BucknerArmstrong, *Mary Turner and the Memory of Lynching*, 58.

24. Amistad Digital Resource, "President Woodrow Wilson's Proclamation of July 26, 1918, Denouncing Lynching," https://www.amistadresource.org/documents/document_07_06_030_wilson.pdf.

25. "Red Summer: When Racist Mobs Ruled, American Experience," PBS, https://www.pbs.org/wgbh/americanexperience/features/t-town-red-summer-racist-mobs.

26. Bryan Stevenson, "Slavery in America and the Ideology of White Supremacy," in Angela Davis, *Policing the Black Man* (New York: Pantheon Books, 2017), 16.

27. Ibid., 37.

28. Cone, *The Cross and the Lynching Tree*, 12.

29. Chris M. Messer, "The Tulsa Race Riot of 1921: Toward an Integrative Theory of Collective Violence," *Journal of Social History* 44, no. 4 (2011): 1217–32.

30. Kweku Crowe and Thabiti Lewis, "The 1921 Tulsa Massacre," The National Endowment for the Humanities, Winter 2021, https://www.neh.gov/article/1921-tulsa-massacre.

31. Messer, "The Tulsa Race Riot of 1921," 1217–32.

32. Crowe and Lewis, "The 1921 Tulsa Massacre."

33. "1921 Tulsa Race Massacre," Tulsa Historical Society & Museum, www.tulsahistory.org, May 11, 2021, https://www.tulsahistory.org/exhibit/1921-tulsa-race-massacre/#flexible-content.

34. Hannah-Jones et al., The 1619 Project, 299.

35. Messer, "The Tulsa Race Riot of 1921," 1217–32.

36. Ibid.

37. Cone, The Cross and the Lynching Tree, 63.

38. Jamie T. Phelps, O.P, Black and Catholic: The Challenge and Gift of Black Folk: Contributions of African American Experience and Thought to Catholic Theology (Milwaukee: Marquette University Press, 1997), 28.

39. Stevenson, "Slavery in America," 16.

40. Ibid., 18.

41. Lincoln Caplan, "Racial Discrimination and Capital Punishment: The Indefensible Death Sentence of Duane Buck," The New Yorker, April 20, 2016, https://www.newyorker.com/news/news-desk/racial-discrimination-and-capital-punishment-the-indefensible-death-sentence-of-duane-buck.

42. Cone, The Cross and the Lynching Tree, 49.

43. Ibid.

44. U.S. Reports: Furman v. Georgia, 408 U.S. 238 (1972), https://www.loc.gov/item/usrep408238.

45. Stevenson, "Slavery in America," 19.

46. Anthony G. Amsterdam, "Opening Remarks: Race and the Death Penalty before and after McCleskey," Columbia Human Rights Law Review 39, no. 1 (2007): 34–58.

47. NAACP Legal Defense and Educational Fund, "The Legacy and Importance of McCleskey v. Kemp," April 22, 1987, https://www.naacpldf.org/case-issue/landmark-mccleskey-v-kemp.

48. U.S. Reports: McCleskey v. Kemp, Superintendent, Georgia Diagnostic and Classification Center, 481 U.S. 279 (1987), https://www.loc.gov/item/usrep481279.

49. "The Legacy and Importance of McCleskey v. Kemp."

50. Amsterdam, "Opening Remarks," 34–58.

51. "The Legacy and Importance of McCleskey v. Kemp."

52. Steven F. Shatz and Terry Dalton, "Challenging the Death Penalty with Statistics: Furman, McCleskey, and a Single County Case Study," Cardozo Law Review 34, no. 4 (April 2013): 1227–82.

53. Legacy Museum and National Memorial for Peace and Justice, "Memorial," museumandmemorial.eji.org, October 31, 2017, https://museumandmemorial.eji.org/memorial.

54. Helen Prejean, C.S.J., Dead Man Walking: The Eye Witness Account of the

Death Penalty That Sparked a National Debate (New York: Vintage Books, 1993, 2013), vii.

55. Ibid., 21.

56. Ibid., 116.

57. Death Penalty Information Center, "Botched Executions," deathpenalty info.org, https://deathpenaltyinfo.org/executions/botched-executions.

58. Noah Caldwell, Ailsa Chang, and Jolie Myers, "Inmate Autopsies Reveal Troubling Effects of Lethal Injection," NPR, September 21, 2020, https://www.npr.org/2020/09/21/793177589/gasping-for-air-autopsies-reveal-troubling-effects-of-lethal-injection.

59. Ibid.

60. Death Penalty Information Center, "Innocence, Death Penalty Information Center," February 18, 2021, https://deathpenaltyinfo.org/policy-issues/innocence.

61. "The National Registry of Exoneration 2021 Annual Report," April 12, 2022, https://www.law.umich.edu/special/exoneration/Pages/mission.aspx.

62. Samuel R. Gross, Maurice Possley, and Klara Stephens, "Race and Wrongful Convictions in the United States," March 7, 2017, https://www.law.umich.edu/special/exoneration/Pages/mission.aspx.

63. Pew Research Center, "How Black, White Americans Differ in Views of Criminal Justice System," May 21, 2019, https://www.pewresearch.org/fact-tank/2019/05/21/from-police-to-parole-black-and-white-americans-differ-widely-in-their-views-of-criminal-justice-system.

64. Pew Research Center—U.S. Politics & Policy, "Most Americans Favor the Death Penalty Despite Concerns about Its Administration," June 2, 2021, https://www.pewresearch.org/politics/2021/06/02/most-americans-favor-the-death-penalty-despite-concerns-about-its-administration.

65. U.S. Catholic Church, *Catechism of the Catholic Church* (Washington, DC: Libreria Editrice Vaticana, 2nd ed., 2019), 546.

66. Pope Francis, *Fratelli Tutti: On Fraternity and Social Friendship* (Huntington, IN: Our Sunday Visitor Publishing Division, 2020), 150–51.

67. Amnesty International, "Death Penalty 2021: Facts and Figures," May 24, 2022, https://www.amnesty.org/en/latest/news/2022/05/death-penalty-2021-facts-and-figures.

68. Author interview with Krisanne Vallencourt Murphy, May 19, 2023.

Chapter Three: From the War on Crime to the War on Drugs: The Creation of Mass Incarceration

1. Tana Ganeva, "Fate Winslow, Freed in December from a One-Time Life Sentence for Pot, Has Been Murdered," *The Intercept*, May 10, 2021, https://theintercept.com/2021/05/10/fate-winslow-murder.

2. Ibid.; Tana Ganeva, "How a Man Serving Life without Parole for $20 of Weed Gained His Freedom," *The Intercept*, July 11, 2023. https://theintercept.com/2020/12/25/fate-winslow-louisiana-law.

3. The Sentencing Project, *No End In Sight: America's Enduring Reliance on Life Imprisonment* (2020), https://www.sentencingproject.org/wp-content/uploads/2021/02/No-End-in-Sight-Americas-Enduring-Reliance-on-Life-Imprisonment.pdf.

4. ACLU, "A Living Death: Life without Parole for Nonviolent Offense" (2019), https://www.aclu.org/sites/default/files/field_document/111813-lwop-complete-report.pdf.

5. Lila Kazemian, "An International Perspective—Task Force on Long Sentences," Council on Criminal Justice, December 2022, https://counciloncj.foleon.com/tfls/long-sentences-by-the-numbers/an-international-perspective.

6. "Fact Sheet: Trends in U.S. Corrections," The Sentencing Project, May 2021, https://www.sentencingproject.org/wp-content/uploads/2021/07/Trends-in-US-Corrections.pdf.

7. Prison Policy Initiative, "States of Incarceration: The Global Context 2021," https://www.prisonpolicy.org/global/2021.html.

8. Prison Policy Initiative, "Visualizing the Racial Disparities in Mass Incarceration," https://www.prisonpolicy.org/blog/2020/07/27/disparities.

9. Kazemian, "An International Perspective."

10. Bruce Western and Christopher Wildeman, "The Black Family and Mass Incarceration," *The Annals of the American Academy of Political and Social Science* 621 (January 2009); "The Moynihan Report Revisited: Lessons and Reflections after Four Decades" (January 2009), 221–42, Sage Publications, in association with the American Academy of Political and Social Science Stable, https://www.jstor.org/stable/40375840.

11. David Garland, "Introduction: The Meaning of Mass Imprisonment," *Punishment & Society* 3, no. 1, 5–7, https://doi.org/10.1177/14624740122228203.

12. Pope Francis, *Fratelli Tutti: On Fraternity and Social Friendship* (Vatican City, 2020), 61.

13. Nikole Hannah-Jones, Caitlin Roper, Ilena Silverman, and Jake Silverstein, *The 1619 Project* (New York: One World, 2021), 32–33.

14. Martin Luther King Jr., *I Have a Dream: Writings and Speeches That Changed the World* (New York: HarperCollins, 1992), x.

15. Marc Mauer, "The Endurance of Racial Disparity in the Criminal Justice System," in Angela J. Davis, *Policing the Black Man* (New York: Pantheon Books, 2017), 31.

16. King Jr., *I Have a Dream*, x–xi.

17. Ibid., x–xxv.

18. Michelle Alexander, *The New Jim Crow: Mass Incarceration in the Age of Colorblindness, Tenth Anniversary Edition* (New York: New Press, 2020), 47.

19. Ibid., 89.

20. Ibid., 35.

21. Richard Rothstein, *The Color of Law: A Forgotten History of How Our Government Segregated America* (New York: Liveright Publishing Corporation, 2017), 155–56.

22. Ibid., 158–60.

23. Elizabeth Hinton, *From the War on Poverty to the War on Crime: The Making of Mass Incarceration in America* (Cambridge, MA: Harvard University Press, 2016), 28–31.

24. The Martin Luther King Jr. Research and Education Institute, "March on Washington for Jobs and Freedom," July 6, 2017, https://kinginstitute.stanford.edu/encyclopedia/march-washington-jobs-and-freedom.

25. Hinton, *From the War on Poverty*, 28.

26. Alexander, *The New Jim Crow*, 48.

27. National Archives, "Civil Rights Act (1964)," October 5, 2021, https://www.archives.gov/milestone-documents/civil-rights-act.

28. Hinton, *From the War on Poverty*, 52–55.

29. Blackmon, *Slavery by Another Name*, 383.

30. Encyclopedia of Alabama, "Bloody Sunday," http://encyclopediaofalabama.org/article/h-1876.

31. Ibid.

32. Ibid.

33. Hinton, *From the War on Poverty*, 55.

34. Ibid., 27.

35. Ibid., 57–58.

36. Daniel Geary, "The Moynihan Report: An Annotated Edition," *The Atlantic*, www.theatlantic.com, September 14, 2015, https://www.theatlantic.com/politics/archive/2015/09/the-moynihan-report-an-annotated-edition/404632.

37. Hinton, *From the War on Poverty*, 59–61.

38. Report of the National Advisory Commission on Civil Disorders, Washington, DC: Kerner Commission, U.S. G.P.O., 1968.

39. Ibid.

40. Othering & Belonging Institute, "Key Kerner Commission Recommendations," https://belonging.berkeley.edu/key-kerner-commission-recommendations.

41. Report of the National Advisory Commission on Civil Disorders.

42. Ibid.

43. Terence McArdle, "The 'Law and Order' Campaign That Won Richard Nixon the White House 50 Years Ago," *Washington Post*, https://www.washingtonpost.com/history/2018/11/05/law-order-campaign-that-won-richard-nixon-white-house-years-ago.

44. Alexander, *The New Jim Crow*, 51.

45. Hinton, *From the War on Poverty*, 141.

46. Ibid., 163–71.

47. Ibid., 175.

48. Mauer, "The Endurance of Racial Disparity," 36.

49. J. D. Kasarda, "Urban Industrial Transition and the Underclass," *Annals of the American Academy of Political and Social Science* 501, no. 1 (1989), https://doi.org/10.1177/0002716289501001002.

50. Hinton, *From the War on Poverty*, 255–56.

51. L. Quillian, "Migration Patterns and the Growth of High Poverty Neighborhoods, 1970–1990," *American Journal of Sociology* 105, no. 1 (1999): 1–37.

52. Hinton, *From the War on Poverty*, 256.

53. Alexander, *The New Jim Crow*, 60, 51.

54. James Forman Jr., *Locking Up Our Own: Crime and Punishment in Black America* (New York: Farrar, Straus and Giroux, 2017), 35.

55. Ibid., 57.

56. Ibid., 67.

57. Alexander, *The New Jim Crow*, 62.

58. Forman, *Locking Up Our Own,* 156–57.

59. Alexander, *The New Jim Crow*, 63.

60. Forman, *Locking Up Our Own*, 156.

61. Alexander, *The New Jim Crow*, 7.

62. Donna M. Hartman and Andrew Golub, "The Social Construction of the Crack Epidemic in the Print Media," *Journal of Psychoactive Drugs* 31, no. 4 (1999): 423–33.

63. Ibid.

64. Ibid.

65. Forman, *Locking Up Our Own*, 164.

66. Alexander, *The New Jim Crow*, 68.

67. Radley Balko, *Rise of the Warrior Cop: The Militarization of America's Police Forces* (New York: Public Affairs, 2021), 151–53.

68. Ibid.

69. Hartman and Golub, "The Social Construction of the Crack Epidemic," 31:4, 423–33.

70. Alexander, *The New Jim Crow*, 76.

71. Forman, *Locking Up Our Own*, 17–20.

72. ACLU, "Report: The War on Marijuana in Black and White: Billions of Dollars Wasted on Racially Biased Arrests," June 2013, https://www.aclu.org/report/report-war-marijuana-black-and-white.

73. ACLU. "A Tale of Two Countries: Racially Targeted Arrests in the Era of Marijuana Reform," 2020, https://www.aclu.org/report/tale-two-countries-racially-targeted-arrests-era-marijuana-reform.

74. Katya Schwenk, "Phoenix Man Serving 16-Year Pot Sentence Denied Clemency," *Phoenix New Times*, August 10, 2022, https://www.phoenixnewtimes.com/news/board-denies-clemency-for-phoenix-man-serving-16-year-pot-sentence-14190098.

75. Human Rights Watch, "United States: Stark Race Disparities in Drug Incarceration," June 7, 2000, https://www.hrw.org/news/2000/06/07/united-states-stark-race-disparities-drug-incarceration.

76. National Institute of Drug Abuse, *Drug Use among Racial/Ethnic Minorities (2003),* https://archives.drugabuse.gov/sites/default/files/minorities03_1.pdf.

77. Western and Wildeman, "The Black Family and Mass Incarceration," 221–42.

78. Lauren J. Krivo and Ruth D. Peterson, "Extremely Disadvantaged Neighborhoods and Urban Crime," *Social Forces* 75, no. 2 (December 1996): 619–48, https://doi.org/10.1093/sf/75.2.619.

79. Ibid.

80. Western and Wildeman, "The Black Family and Mass Incarceration," 221–42.

81. Helen Prejean, C.S.J., *Dead Man Walking: The Eye Witness Account of the Death Penalty That Sparked a National Debate* (New York: Vintage Books, 1993, 2013), 9.

82. Ibid., 302.

83. ACLU, *The War on Marijuana in Black and White* (2013), https://www.aclu.org/sites/default/files/field_document/1114413-mj-report-rfs-rel1.pdf.

84. Bruce Western, "Incarceration and Invisible Inequality," May 2004, https://www.russellsage.org/sites/all/files/u4/Western_Incarceration.pdf.

85. Alexander, *The New Jim Crow*, 72.

86. Forman, *Locking Up Our Own*, 161.

87. Premilla Nadasen, "Welfare Reform and the Politics of Race," https://www.historians.org/publications-and-directories/perspectives-on-history/summer-2016/welfare-reform-and-the-politics-of-race-20-years-later.

88. Bryan Stevenson, *Just Mercy* (New York: One World/Ballantine, 2015), 16.

89. Ashley Nellis, "Mass Incarceration Trends," The Sentencing Project, January 25, 2023, https://www.sentencingproject.org/reports/mass-incarceration-trends.

90. Anna R. Haskins, Wade C. Jacobsen, Joes Mittleman, "Optimism and Obstacles: Racialized Constraints in College Attitudes and Expectations among Teens of the Prison Boom," *Sociology of Education* 96, no. 3 (2023): 211–33.

91. Sara Wakefield and Christopher Uggen, "Incarceration and Stratification," *Annual Review of Sociology* 36 (2010): 387–406.

92. R. Kelley Raley, Megan M. Sweeney, and Danielle Wondra, "The Growing Racial and Ethnic Divide in U.S. Marriage Patterns," *Future Child* 25, no. 2 (2015): 89–109.

93. "Births: Final Data for 2012," National Vital Statistics Reports, December 30, 2013, cdc.gov/nchs/data/nvsr62/nvrs62_09.pdf.

94. Pew Research Center's Social & Demographic Trends Project, "Facts about the U.S. Black Population," March 2, 2023, https://www.pewresearch.org/social-trends/fact-sheet/facts-about-the-us-black-population.

95. The White House—President Barack Obama, "Progress of the African-American Community during the Obama Administration," October 14, 2016, https://obamawhitehouse.archives.gov/the-press-office/2016/10/14/progress-african-american-community-during-obama-administration.

96. United States Sentencing Commission, "Report to the Congress: Impact of the Fair Sentencing Act of 2010," August 2015, https://www.ussc.gov/sites/default/files/pdf/news/congressional-testimony-and-reports/drug-topics/201507_RtC_Fair-Sentencing-Act.pdf.

97. Jason P. Robey, Michael Massoglia, and Michael T. Light, "A Generational Shift: Race and the Declining Lifetime Risk of Imprisonment," *Demography* 2023; 10863378, doi: https://doi.org/10.1215/00703370-10863378.

98. "A Proclamation on Second Chance Month, 2022" (April 2022), The White House, https://www.whitehouse.gov/briefing-room/presidential-actions/2022/03/31/a-proclamation-on-second-chance-month-2022.

99. Kate Cimini, "Black People Disproportionately Homeless in California–CalMatters," *CalMatters,* October 5, 2019. https://calmatters.org/california-divide/2019/10/black-people-disproportionately-homeless-in-california/.

100. "Barriers to Progress," *Invisible People,* December 2021, https://invisiblepeople.tv/research/2021/invisible-people-2021-research.pdf.

101. Alexander, *The New Jim Crow*, 3.

102. Stevenson, *Just Mercy*, 15.

103. Algernon Austin, "The Jobs Crisis for Black Men Is a Lot Worse Than You Think," Center for Economic and Policy Research, December 8, 2012, https://cepr.net/report/the-jobs-crisis-for-black-men-is-a-lot-worse-than-you-think; Brian L. Levy, Nolan E. Phillips, and Robert J. Sampson, "Triple Disadvantage: Neighborhood Networks of Everyday Urban Mobility and Violence in U.S. Cities," *American Sociological Review* 85, no. 6 (2020): 925–56.

Chapter Four: Waging War

1. ABC News, "Ferguson Police's Show of Force Highlights Militarization of America's Cops," April 14, 2014, https://abcnews.go.com/US/ferguson-police-small-army-thousands-police-departments/story?id=24977299.

2. Gallup Inc., "Martin Luther King Jr.: Revered More after Death Than Before," January 16, 2006, https://news.gallup.com/poll/20920/martin-luther-king-jr-revered-more-after-death-than-before.aspx.

3. Elizabeth Hinton, "The War on Crime, LBJ and Ferguson: Time to Reassess the History," *Time,* March 20, 2015, https://time.com/3746059/war-on-crime-history.

4. Michelle Alexander, *The New Jim Crow: Mass Incarceration in the Age of Colorblindness, Tenth Anniversary Edition* (New York: The New Press, 2020), 53.

5. Charles E. Jones and Judson L. Jeffries, "Don't Believe the Hype: Debunking the Panther Mythology," in Charles E. Jones, *The Black Panther Party [Reconsidered]* (Baltimore: Black Classic Press, 1998), 25.

6. Elizabeth Hinton, *From the War on Poverty to the War on Crime: The Making of Mass Incarceration in America* (Cambridge, MA: Harvard University Press, 2016), 97.

7. Ibid., 111–12.

8. Ibid., 97–99.

9. Ibid., 27.

10. Ibid., 30–32.

11. Ibid., 38.

12. Alex S. Vitale, *The End of Policing* (Brooklyn: Verso, 2018), 14.

13. Hinton, *From the War on Poverty*, 94.

14. Ibid., 145–46

15. Elizabeth Hinton, *America on Fire: The Untold History of Police Violence and Black Rebellion since the 1960s* (New York: Liveright Publishing Corporation, 2021), 9.

16. Hinton, *From the War on Poverty*, 94.

17. Hinton, *America on Fire*, 178.

18. Betty Medsger, *The Burglary: The Discovery of J. Edgar Hoover's Secret FBI* (New York: Vintage Books, 2014), 88.

19. Ibid., 17–18.

20. Ibid., 18–19.

21. Ibid., 38–39.

22. Ibid., 169–70.

23. Ibid., 226.

24. Hinton, *From the War on Poverty*, 204–5.

25. Mckay Bolden, "Malcolm X's Family Reveals Letter Implicating FBI and NYPD in His Assassination," CBS News, February 22, 2021, https://www.cbsnews.com/news/malcolm-x-conspiracy-assassination-fbi-nypd.

26. Medsger, *The Burglary*, 346–47.

27. Hinton, *From the War on Poverty*, 204–5.

28. Alexander, *The New Jim Crow*, 53.

29. National Archives. "Fred Hampton (August 30, 1948–December 4, 1969)," https://www.archives.gov/research/african-americans/individuals/fred-hampton.

30. Alicia Maynard, "The Assassination of Fred Hampton; Digital Chicago," Lake Forest College in partnership with the Chicago History Museum, https://digitalchicagohistory.org/exhibits/show/fred-hampton-50th/the-assassination.

31. Hinton, *From the War on Poverty*, 205–6.

32. Matthew Fleischer, "50 Years Ago, SWAT Raided the L.A. Black Panthers. It's Been Targeting Black Communities Ever Since," *Los Angeles Times,* December 8, 2019, https://www.latimes.com/opinion/story/2019-12-08/50-years-swat-black-panthers-militarized-policinglos-angeles.

33. Hinton, *From the War on Poverty*, 206.

34. Fleischer, "50 Years Ago."

35. Hinton, *From the War on Poverty*, 206.

36. Alexander, *The New Jim Crow*, 95.

37. Fleischer, "50 Years Ago."

38. ACLU, "War Comes Home: The Excessive Militarization of American Police," American Civil Liberties Union, June 2004, https://www.aclu.org/report/war-comes-home-excessive-militarization-american-police.

39. Fleischer, "50 Years Ago."

40. Radley Balko, *Rise of the Warrior Cop: The Militarization of America's Police Forces* (New York: Public Affairs, 2021), 133.

41. Ibid., 146–47.

42. Alexander, *The New Jim Crow*, 93–94.

43. Ibid., 89.

44. Renée McDonald Hutchins, "Racial Profiling: The Law, the Policy, and the Practice," in Angela J. Davis, *Policing the Black Man* (New York: Pantheon Books, 2017), 98.

45. Deborah Ramirez, Jack McDevitt, and Amy Farrell, "A Resource Guide on Racial Profiling Data Collection Systems: Promising Practices and Lessons Learned," https://www.ojp.gov/pdffiles1/bja/184768.pdf.

46. Alexander, *The New Jim Crow*, 71.

47. Ibid.

48. McDonald Hutchins, "Racial Profiling," 98.

49. E. Pierson, C. Simoiu, J. Overgoor et al., "A Large-Scale Analysis of Racial Disparities in Police Stops across the United States," *Nature Human Behavior* 4 (2020): 736–45.

50. David D. Kirkpatrick, Steve Eder, Kim Barker, and Julie Tate, "Why Many Police Traffic Stops Turn Deadly," *New York Times*, October 31, 2021, https://www.nytimes.com/2021/10/31/us/police-traffic-stops-killings.html.

51. "Mapping Police Violence," November 2022, https://mappingpolice violence.us.

52. Hinton, *From the War on Poverty*, 327.

53. Ramirez et al., "A Resource Guide on Racial Profiling."

54. Marc Mauer, "The Endurance of Racial Disparity in the Criminal Justice System," in Angela J. Davis, *Policing the Black Man* (New York: Pantheon Books, 2017), 43.

55. U.S. Department of Justice Civil Rights Division, "Investigation of the Ferguson Police Department," https://www.justice.gov/sites/default/files/opa/press-releases/attachments/2015/03/04/ferguson_police_department_report.pdf.

56. Charlotte Lawrence and Cyrus J. O'Brien, "Federal Militarization of Law Enforcement Must End," May 12, 2021, https://www.aclu.org/news/criminal-law-reform/federal-militarization-of-law-enforcement-must-end.

57. Tom Gjelten, "Peaceful Protesters Tear-Gassed to Clear Way for Trump Church Photo-Op," NPR, June 1, 2020, https://www.npr.org/2020/06/01/867532070/trumps-unannounced-church-visit-angers-church-officials.

58. ACLU, "Congress: End Police Militarization and Over-Policing in Our Communities Now," https://action.aclu.org/send-message/congress-end-police-militarization-and-over-policing-our-communities-now.

59. Alexander, *The New Jim Crow*, 71.

Chapter Five: The Opioid Crisis

1. Patrick Radden Keefe, *Empire of Pain: The Secret History of the Sackler Dynasty* (New York: Doubleday, 2021), 320.

2. Beth Macy, *Dopesick: Dealers, Doctors, and the Drug Company That Addicted America* (New York: Little, Brown, 2018), 87–89.

3. Ibid., 57–58.

4. Ed Bisch, "My Son Died of an Oxy Overdose. Drug Company Execs Who Are Responsible Should Be Sent to Jail," STAT, July 13, 2022, https://www.statnews.com/2022/07/13/opioid-pushing-executives-should-get-jail-time-not-fines.

5. Keefe, *Empire of Pain*, 4.

6. Keith Humphreys et al., "Responding to the Opioid Crisis in North America and Beyond: Recommendations of the Stanford–Lancet Commission," *The Lancet*, February 5, 2022, https://www.thelancet.com/journals/lancet/article/PIIS0140-6736(21)02252-2/abstract.

7. The U.S. Attorney's Office, District of Nevada, "Heroin and Opioid Awareness," January 29, 2015, https://www.justice.gov/usao-nv/heroin-and-opioid-awareness.

8. Centers for Disease Control and Prevention, "U.S. Overdose Deaths in 2021 Increased Half as Much as in 2020—But Are Still Up 15%," May 11, 2022, https://www.cdc.gov/nchs/pressroom/nchs_press_releases/2022/202205.htm.

9. Humphreys et al., "Responding to the Opioid Crisis."

10. Mengyao Feijun Luo and Florence Curtis, "State-Level Economic Costs of Opioid Use Disorder and Fatal Opioid Overdose—United States, 2017," Centers for Disease Control and Prevention, April 15, 2021, https://www.cdc.gov/mmwr/volumes/70/wr/mm7015a1.htm.

11. Macy, *Dopesick*, 45.

12. Barry Meier, "3 Executives Spared Prison in OxyContin Case," *New York Times*, July 2007, https://www.nytimes.com/2007/07/21/business/21pharma.html.

13. House Committee on Oversight and Reform, "Committee Releases Documents Showing Sackler Family Wealth Totals $11 Billion," April 20, 2021, https://oversightdemocrats.house.gov/news/press-releases/committee-releases-documents-showing-sackler-family-wealth-totals-11-billion.

14. Kelsey Vlamis, "Trump Called On Lawmakers to Institute the 'Death Penalty for Drug Dealers' Despite the Fact That He Pardoned People Convicted of Selling Drugs," *Business Insider*, September 2022, https://www.businessinsider.com/trump-calls-for-death-penalty-drug-dealers-despite-pardoning-some-2022-9.

15. U.S. Census Bureau, "Quick Facts Idaho," July 6, 2022, https://www.census.gov/quickfacts/fact/table/ID/PST045221.

16. E. Ann Carson, "Prisoners in 2020—Statistical Tables," December 2021, https://bjs.ojp.gov/content/pub/pdf/p20st.pdf.

17. "Race and Ethnicity in Prison," The Sentencing Project, May 2022, https://www.sentencingproject.org/app/uploads/2022/11/Incarcerated-Women-and-Girls.pdf.

18. Carson, "Prisoners in 2020."

19. William Sabol and Thaddeus Johnson, "National Trends—Racial Disparities," September 2022, https://counciloncj.foleon.com/reports/racial-disparities/national-trends.

20. Appalachian Regional Commission, "About the Appalachian Region," https://www.arc.gov/about-the-appalachian-region.

21. Pam Fessler, "Kentucky County That Gave War on Poverty a Face Still Struggles," NPR, January 8, 2014, https://www.npr.org/2014/01/08/260151923/kentucky-county-that-gave-war-on-poverty-a-face-still-struggles.

22. Macy, *Dopesick*, 16.

23. Ibid., 18.

24. Ibid., 45.

25. Keefe, *Empire of Pain*, 52.

26. Ibid., 63–64.

27. Ibid., 159–64.

28. Ibid., 162.

29. Ibid., 181–82.

30. Ibid., 193–96.

31. Art Van Zee, "The Promotion and Marketing of Oxycontin: Commercial Triumph, Public Health Tragedy," *American Journal of Public Health* 99, no. 2 (February 2009): 221–27.

32. Ibid., 18–19.

33. Keefe, *Empire of Pain*, 227.

34. Ibid., 208.

35. Macy, *Dopesick*, 31.

36. Van Zee, "The Promotion and Marketing of Oxycontin."

37. Keefe, *Empire of Pain*, 226.

38. Macy, *Dopesick*, 36–39.

39. Barry Meier, "A Nun, a Doctor and a Lawyer—and Deep Regret over the Nation's Handling of Opioids," *New York Times*, August 2019, https://www.nytimes.com/2019/08/18/health/opioids-purdue-pennington-gap.html.

40. Macy, *Dopesick*, 49.

41. Meier, "A Nun, a Doctor and a Lawyer."

42. Macy, *Dopesick*, 50.

43. Ibid., 51.

44. Hearing before the Subcommittee on Oversight and Investigations of the Committee on Energy and Commerce House of Representatives, "OxyContin: Its Use and Abuse," August 28, 2001, https://www.govinfo.gov/content/pkg/CHRG-107hhrg75754/pdf/CHRG-107hhrg75754.pdf.

45. Barry Meier and Eric Lipton, "Under Attack, Drug Maker Turned to Giuliani for Help," *New York Times*, December 28, 2007, https://www.nytimes.com/2007/12/28/us/politics/28oxycontin.html.

46. Ibid.

47. Meier and Lipton, "Under Attack."

48. Keefe, *Empire of Pain*, 262–68.

49. Ibid., 272–73.

50. Emily Chasan, "Purdue Frederick Pleads Guilty in OxyContin Case," May 2007, https://www.reuters.com/article/us-oxycontin-misbranding-idUSWBT00695020070510.

51. Meier and Lipton, "Under Attack."

52. Keefe, *Empire of Pain*, 283.

53. Ibid., 275–77.

54. Ibid., 283.

55. Meier, "A Nun, a Doctor and a Lawyer."

56. Brian Mann, "4 U.S. Companies Will Pay $26 Billion to Settle Claims They Fueled the Opioid Crisis," NPR, February 25, 2022, https://www.npr.org/2022/02/25/1082901958/opioid-settlement-johnson-26-billion.

57. Jonathan Stempel, "Johnson & Johnson Charged by New York with Civil Insurance Fraud over Opioid Claims," September 17, 2020, https://www.reuters.com/article/us-johnson-johnson-new-york-opioids-idUSKBN2682HF.

58. Mann, "4 U.S. Companies."

59. Pew Charitable Trusts, "Drug Arrests Stayed High Even as Imprisonment Fell from 2009 to 2019," February 15, 2022, https://www.pewtrusts.org/en/research-and-analysis/issue-briefs/2022/02/drug-arrests-stayed-high-even-as-imprisonment-fell-from-2009-to-2019.

60. Joan Oleck, "With 40,000 Americans Incarcerated for Marijuana Offenses, the Cannabis Industry Needs to Step Up, Activists Said This Week," *Forbes,* June 26, 2020.

61. William N. Evans, Ethan M. J. Lieber, and Patrick Power, "How the Reformulation of OxyContin Ignited the Heroin Epidemic," National Bureau of Economic Research (April 2018), https://www.nber.org/papers/w24475.

62. Keefe, *Empire of Pain*, 314–15.

63. Centers for Disease Control and Prevention, "Opioid Data Analysis and Resources," June 2022, https://www.cdc.gov/opioids/data/analysis-resources.html.

64. Courtney Kan, Nick Miroff, Scott Higham, Steven Rich, and Tyler Remmel, "Overview: From Mexican Labs to U.S. Streets, a Lethal Pipeline," *Washington Post,* December 12, 2022, https://www.washingtonpost.com/investigations/interactive/2022/fentanyl-crisis-mexico-cartel.

65. Liz Essley Whyte, Geoff Mulvihill, and Ben Wieder, "Politics of Pain: Drugmakers Fought State Opioid Limits amid Crisis," Center for Public Integrity, September 18, 2016, http://publicintegrity.org/politics/state-politics/politics-of-pain-drugmakers-fought-state-opioid-limits-amid-crisis.

66. Keefe, *Empire of Pain*, 314–15.

67. Tyler N. A. Winkelman, Virginia W. Chang, and Ingrid A. Binswanger, "Health, Polysubstance Use, and Criminal Justice Involvement among Adults with Varying Levels of Opioid Use," *JAMA Network Open* 1, no. 3 (2018): e180558. doi:10.1001/jamanetworkopen.2018.0558.

68. Natalie Hemsing, Lorraine Greaves, Nancy Poole, and Rose Schmidt, "Misuse of Prescription Opioid Medication among Women: A Scoping Review," *Pain Research and Management* (2016), Article ID 1754195, https://doi.org/10.1155/2016/1754195.

69. The Sentencing Project, "Incarcerated Women and Girls," May 12, 2022, https://www.sentencingproject.org/fact-sheet/incarcerated-women-and-girls.

70. Wendy Sawyer and Wanda Bertram, "Prisons and Jails Will Separate Millions of Mothers from Their Children in 2022," Prison Policy Initiative, May 4, 2022, https://www.prisonpolicy.org/blog/2022/05/04/mothers_day.

71. Keefe, *Empire of Pain*, 380–82.

72. Ibid., 383–85.

73. Soo Youn, "New York Adds Owners of Company That Makes OxyContin to Lawsuit against Opioid Makers, Distributors," ABC News, March 28, 2019, https://abcnews.go.com/US/york-adds-owners-company-makes-oxycontin-lawsuit-opioid/story?id=62012633.

74. Berkeley Lovelace, "Nearly Every US State Is Now Suing OxyContin Maker Purdue Pharma," CNBC, June 4, 2019, https://www.cnbc.com/2019/06/04/nearly-every-us-state-is-now-suing-oxycontin-maker-purdue-pharma.html.

75. Keefe, *Empire of Pain*, 400–405.

76. Ibid., 418–19.

77. Ibid., 420–21.

78. Jan Hoffman, "Purdue Pharma Is Dissolved and Sacklers Pay $4.5 Billion to Settle Opioid Claims," *New York Times*, September 1, 2021, https://www.nytimes.com/2021/09/01/health/purdue-sacklers-opioids-settlement.html.

79. "Data Overview," June 1, 2022, https://www.cdc.gov/opioids/data/index.html.

80. Kan et el., "Overview: From Mexican Labs to U.S. Streets."

81. Julie Vitkovskaya and Courtney Kan, "Why Is Fentanyl So Dangerous?," *Washington Post*, November 3, 2022, https://www.washingtonpost.com/nation/2022/11/03/fentanyl-opioid-epidemic.

82. Nick Miroff, Scott Higham, Steven Rich, Salwan Georges, and Erin Patrick O'Connor, "Cause of Death: Washington Faltered as Fentanyl Gripped America," *Washington Post*, December 12, 2022, https://www.washingtonpost.com/investigations/interactive/2022/dea-fentanyl-failure.

83. Ibid.

84. Tessie Catillo, "What Do Prosecutors and District Attorneys Say about 911 Good Samaritan Laws?" HuffPost, April 16, 2014, https://www.huffpost.com/entry/what-do-prosecutors-and-d_b_5159938.

85. Miroff et al., "Cause of Death."

86. Melba Newsome and Gioncarlo Valentine, "The Opioid Epidemic Is Surging among Black People Because of Unequal Access to Treatment," *Scientific American*, December 1, 2022, https://www.scientificamerican.com/article/the-opioid-epidemic-now-kills-more-black-people-than-white-ones-because-of-unequal-access-to-treatment/.

87. Oleck, "With 40,000 Americans Incarcerated."

Chapter Six: Prison Pipelines

1. Khalil Gibran Muhammad, *The Condemnation of Blackness: Race, Crime, and the Making of Modern Urban America* (Cambridge, MA: Harvard University Press, 2019), 128.

2. Corbin Carson, "KFI News Presents: This Sand Is My Sand: The Stolen Legacy of Bruce's Beach," October 10, 2021, https://kfiam640.iheart.com/content/2021-09-29-kfi-news-special-this-sand-is-my-sand-the-stolen-legacy-of-bruces-beach.

3. Ibid.

4. Sam Levin, "California Returns Beachfront Property Taken from Black Couple in 1920s," *The Guardian*, June 29, 2022, https://www.theguardian.com/us-news/2022/jun/29/california-returns-beachfront-property-taken-black-couple-bruces-beach.

5. Bill Chappell, "The Black Family Who Won the Return of Bruce's Beach Will Sell It Back to LA County," NPR, January 4, 2023, https://www.npr.org/2023/01/04/1146879302/bruces-beach-la-county-california.

6. Richard Rothstein, *Color of Law: A Forgotten History of How Our Government Segregated America* (New York: Liveright Publishing Corporation, 2017), Introduction.

7. Ibid., 21.

8. Ibid., 24.

9. Ibid., 30–31.

10. Ibid., 32.

11. Ibid., 34.

12. Ibid., 64.

13. Ibid.

14. Ibid., 70.

15. Ibid., 88.

16. Emily Badger, "Why a Housing Scheme Founded in Racism Is Making a Resurgence Today," *Washington Post*, May 13, 2016, https://www.washingtonpost.com/news/wonk/wp/2016/05/13/why-a-housing-scheme-founded-in-racism-is-making-a-resurgence-today.

17. Raymond Mohl, "The Interstates and the Cities: Highways, Housing, and the Freeway Revolt," Poverty and Race Research Action Council, 2002, https://www.prrac.org/pdf/mohl.pdf.

18. Ibid.

19. Michele Lerner, "Black Homeownership Continues to Lag in 50 Largest U.S. Cities," *Washington Post*, April 26, 2022, https://www.washingtonpost.com/business/2022/04/26/black-share-homeownership-disproportionately-low.

20. U.S. Department of Housing and Urban Development, "Unequal Burden: Income and Racial Disparities in Subprime Lending in America," February 22, 2008, https://archives.hud.gov/reports/subprime/subprime.cfm.

21. Courtney Connley, "Why the Homeownership Gap between White and Black Americans Is Larger Today Than It Was over 50 Years Ago," CNBC, August 21, 2020, https://www.cnbc.com/2020/08/21/why-the-homeownership-gap-between-white-and-black-americans-is-larger-today-than-it-was-over-50-years-ago.html.

22. Rothstein, *Color of Law*, 132.

23. Jacob Kang-Brown, Jennifer Trone, Jennifer Fratello, and Tarika Daftary-Kapur, "A Generation Later: What We've Learned about Zero Tolerance in Schools," Vera Institute, December 2013, https://www.vera.org/downloads/publications/zero-tolerance-in-schools-policy-brief.pdf.

24. Ibid.

25. Russell W. Rumberger and Daniel J. Losen, "School Suspensions Cost Taxpayers Billions," The Civil Rights Project at UCLA, June 1, 2016, https://www.civilrightsproject.ucla.edu/news/press-releases/featured-research-2016/school-suspensions-cost-taxpayers-billions.

26. U.S. Department of Education Office for Civil Rights, "Civil Rights Data Collection Data Snapshot: Early Childhood Education," March 2014, https://www2.ed.gov/about/offices/list/ocr/docs/crdc-early-learning-snapshot.pdf.

27. U.S. Department of Education Office for Civil Rights, "Discipline Practices in Preschool," July 2021, https://www2.ed.gov/about/offices/list/ocr/docs/crdc-DOE-Discipline-Practices-in-Preschool-part1.pdf.

28. U.S. Department of Education Office for Civil Rights, "Suspensions and Expulsions in Public Schools," August 2022, https://www2.ed.gov/about/offices/list/ocr/docs/suspensions-and-expulsion-part-2.pdf.

29. Anna Simonton, "New School Year, Same School-to-Prison Pipeline," The Appeal, September 14, 2022, https://theappeal.org/new-school-year-same-school-to-prison-pipeline.

30. Kristin Henning, "Boys to Men: The Role of Policing in the Socialization of Black Boys," in Angela J. Davis, *Policing the Black Man* (New York: Pantheon Books, 2017), 65–66.

31. Alex S. Vitale, *The End of Policing* (Brooklyn: Verso, 2018), 61.

32. *J. W. v. Birmingham Board of Education,* September 30, 2015, https://www.splcenter.org/sites/default/files/documents/findings_of_fact_and_conclusions_of_law.pdf.

33. *J. W. v. Birmingham Board of Education*, United States Court of Appeals for the Eleventh Circuit, September 24, 2018, https://casetext.com/case/through-his-next-friend-tammy-williams-g-s-by-v-birmingham-bd-of-educ.

34. *J. W. v. Birmingham Board of Education*, September 30, 2015.

35. *J. W. v. Birmingham Board of Education*, United States Court of Appeals for the Eleventh Circuit, September 24, 2018.

36. *J. W. v. Birmingham Board of Education,* September 30, 2015.

37. Amir Whitaker, Sylvia Torres-Guillén, Michelle Morton, Harold Jordan, Stefanie Coyle, Angela Mann, and Wei-Ling Sun, "Cops and No Counselors: How the Lack of School Mental Health Staff Is Harming Students," ACLU, March 2019, https://www.aclu.org/sites/default/files/field_document/030419-acluschooldisciplinereport.pdf.

38. Jeremy Travis and Bruce Western, "Poverty, Violence, and Black Incarceration," in Angela J. Davis, *Policing the Black Man* (New York: Pantheon Books, 2017), 294.

39. Rothstein, *Color of Law*, 186.

40. Ibid., 187.

41. Malika Saada Saar, Rebecca Epstein, Lindsay Rosenthal, and Yasmin Vafa, "The Sexual Abuse to Prison Pipeline: A Girl's Story," Center on Poverty and Inequality, Georgetown Law, February 2015, https://genderjusticeandopportunity.georgetown.edu/trauma-and-mental-health-for-girls/sexual-abuse-to-prison-pipeline.

42. Ibid.

43. Ibid.

44. Ibid.

45. The Sentencing Project, "Incarcerated Women and Girls," May 2022, https://www.sentencingproject.org/wp-content/uploads/2016/02/Incarcerated-Women-and-Girls.pdf.

46. Danielle Sered, *Until We Reckon: Violence, Mass Incarceration, and a Road to Repair* (New York: New Press, 2019), 74.

47. Brandy F. Henry, "Typologies of Adversity in Childhood & Adulthood as Determinants of Mental Health & Substance Use Disorders of Adults Incarcerated in US Prisons," *Child Abuse & Neglect* 99 (2020), https://doi.org/10.1016/j.chiabu.2019.104251, https://www.sciencedirect.com/science/article/pii/S0145213419304284.

48. Ibid.

49. Edward Lyon, "Imprisoning America's Mentally Ill," Prison Legal News, February 2019, https://www.prisonlegalnews.org/news/2019/feb/4/imprisoning-americas-mentally-ill.

50. Jessica Placzek, "Did the Emptying of Mental Hospitals Contribute to Homelessness?," KQED, December 8, 2016, https://www.kqed.org/news/11209729/did-the-emptying-of-mental-hospitals-contribute-to-homelessness-here.

51. Ibid.

52. Lyon, "Imprisoning America's Mentally Ill."

53. Criminalization of People with Mental Illness, National Alliance on Mental Illness, 2022, https://www.nami.org/Advocacy/Policy-Priorities/Stopping-Harmful-Practices/Criminalization-of-People-with-Mental-Illness.

54. Ibid.

55. Ibid.

56. Sered, *Until We Reckon*, 71.

57. U.S. Department of Justice Civil Rights Division, "Investigation of Alameda County, John George Psychiatric Hospital, and Santa Rita Jail," April 22, 2021, https://www.justice.gov/crt/case-document/file/1388891/download.

58. Ibid.

59. Ibid.

60. Ibid.

61. Michelle Alexander, *The New Jim Crow: Mass Incarceration in the Age of Colorblindness, Tenth Anniversary Edition* (New York: New Press, 2020), xxix.

62. Rebecca Neusteter and Megan O'Toole, "Every Three Seconds—Emerging Findings," Vera Institute of Justice, January 2019, https://www.vera.org/publications/arrest-trends-every-three-seconds-landing/arrest-trends-every-three-seconds/findings#:~:text=The%20data%20shows%20that%20non,than%20five%20percent%20of%20arrests.

63. Alexander, *The New Jim Crow*, xxv.

64. FBI, "FBI Releases 2020 Incident-Based (NIBRS) Data," December 6, 2021, https://www.fbi.gov/news/press-releases/press-releases/fbi-releases-2020-incident-based-data.

65. Pew Research Center. "What the Data Says about Gun Deaths in the U.S.," February 3, 2022, https://www.pewresearch.org/fact-tank/2022/02/03/what-the-data-says-about-gun-deaths-in-the-u-s.

66. CDC, "Suicide Data and Statistics," June 28, 2022, https://www.cdc.gov/suicide/suicide-data-statistics.html.

67. James H. Cone, *God of the Oppressed* (Maryknoll, NY: Orbis Books, 2018), 200.

68. Elizabeth Hinton, LeShae Henderson, and Cindy Reed, "An Unjust Burden: The Disparate Treatment of Black Americans in the Criminal Justice System," Vera Institute for Justice, May 2018, https://www.vera.org/downloads/publications/for-the-record-unjust-burden-racial-disparities.pdf.

69. "Gun Homicide: What to Know and Where to Go," The Center for Just Journalism, 2022, https://justjournalism.org/page/gun-homicide.

70. "Invisible Wounds: Gun Violence and Community Trauma among Black Americans," Everytown for Gun Safety Support Fund, May 27, 2022, https://everytownresearch.org/report/invisible-wounds-gun-violence-and-community-trauma-among-black-americans/.

71. Ibid.

72. Ibid.

73. Ibid.

74. Ibid.

75. Pew Research Center, "What We Know about the Increase in U.S. Murders in 2020," October 27, 2021, https://www.pewresearch.org/fact-tank/2021/10/27/what-we-know-about-the-increase-in-u-s-murders-in-2020.

76. FBI UCR, "2019 Crime in the United States," Criminal Justice Information Services Division, https://ucr.fbi.gov/crime-in-the-u.s/2019/crime-in-the-u.s.-2019/topic-pages/clearances.

77. Ali Bauman, "A Closer Look at Disparities in NYPD's Homicide Clearance Rates: 'It Made Me Feel Like They Didn't Care,'" CBS, June 30, 2022, https://www.cbsnews.com/newyork/news/crime-without-punishment-new-york.

78. "Homicide Database: Mapping Unsolved Murders in Major U.S. Cities," *Washington Post*, July 2018, https://www.washingtonpost.com/graphics/2018/investigations/unsolved-homicide-database.

79. FOX13 News Memphis, "New Details Surrounding the Death of Eliza Fletcher Released," September 7, 2022, https://www.fox13memphis.com/news/local/new-details-surrounding-death-eliza-fletcher-released/LSJPMCV44 NGGLNYUQHMBOLOYGY/.

80. Meaghan Ybos, "After Eliza Fletcher's Murder, Authorities Don't Have Their Priorities Right," *Commercial Appeal*, September 2022, https://www.commercialappeal.com/story/opinion/2022/09/28/after-eliza-fletchers-murder-authorities-dont-have-priorities-right/69523010007/.

81. Elizabeth Hinton, *America on Fire: The Untold History of Police Violence and Black Rebellion since the 1960s* (New York: Liveright Publishing Corporation, 2021), 230.

82. Ibid., 231–33.

83. Ibid., 243–44.

84. Ibid., 247.

85. Ibid., 253–254.

86. Lois Beckett, "How the Gun Control Debate Ignores Black Lives," November 24, 2015, ProPublica, https://www.propublica.org/article/how-the-gun-control-debate-ignores-black-lives.

87. Ibid.

88. Sered, *Until We Reckon*, 67.
89. Danielle Sered, "Accounting for Violence: How to Increase Safety and Break Our Failed Reliance on Mass Incarceration," Vera Institute for Justice, 2017, https://d3n8a8pro7vhmx.cloudfront.net/commonjustice/pages/82/attachments/original/1506608259/accounting-for-violence.pdf.

Chapter Seven: From Subhuman to Superpredator

1. Danielle Sered, *Until We Reckon: Violence, Mass Incarceration, and a Road to Repair* (New York: New Press, 2019), 11.
2. Howard W. French, *Born in Blackness: Africa, Africans, and the Making of the Modern World, 1471 to the Second World War* (New York: Liveright Publishing Company, 2021), 102.
3. Ibid., 117.
4. M. Shawn Copeland, *Enfleshing Freedom: Body, Race, and Being* (Minneapolis: Fortress Press, 2010), 12.
5. Ibid., 10.
6. Katherine Bankole, "The Human/Subhuman Issue and Slave Medicine in Louisiana," *Race, Gender & Class* 5, no. 3 (1998): 3–11.
7. Sered, *Until We Reckon*, 55.
8. Copeland, *Enfleshing Freedom*, 24.
9. Cyprian Davis, O.S.B., *The History of Black Catholics in the United States* (New York: Crossroad Publishing Company, 1990), 44–45.
10. Ibid., 46–47.
11. Ibid., 51–52.
12. Copeland, *Enfleshing Freedom*, 36.
13. Ibid., 34.
14. Ibid., 37.
15. Davis, *The History of Black Catholics*, 59–61.
16. Khalil Gibran Muhammad, *The Condemnation of Blackness: Race, Crime, and the Making of Modern Urban America* (Cambridge, MA: Harvard University Press, 2010, 2019), xiv.
17. Ibid., 20.
18. Megan J. Wolff, "The Myth of the Actuary: Life Insurance and Frederick L. Hoffman's Race Traits and Tendencies of the American Negro," *Public Health Reports* 121, no. 1 (2006): 84–91, https://www.ncbi.nlm.nih.gov/pmc/articles/PMC1497788.
19. Ibid.
20. Gibran Muhammad, *The Condemnation of Blackness*, 40.
21. Wolff, "The Myth of the Actuary," 84–91.
22. Gibran Muhammad, *The Condemnation of Blackness*, 43.
23. Ibid., 47.
24. Ibid., 90.
25. Ibid., 109.
26. Ibid., 52.

27. Carroll Bogert and LynNell Hancock, "Superpredator: The Media Myth That Demonized a Generation of Black Youth," The Marshall Project, November 2020, https://www.themarshallproject.org/2020/11/20/superpredator-the-media-myth-that-demonized-a-generation-of-black-youth.

28. John DiIulio, "The Coming of the Super-Predators," *Washington Examiner*, November 27, 1995, https://www.washingtonexaminer.com/weekly-standard/the-coming-of-the-super-predators.

29. Ibid.

30. Ibid.

31. Ibid.

32. John J. DiIulio Jr., "My Black Crime Problem, and Ours," *City Journal*, Spring 1996, https://www.city-journal.org/article/my-black-crime-problem-and-ours.

33. DiIulio, "The Coming of the Super-Predators."

34. Kristin Henning, "Boys to Men: The Role of Policing in the Socialization of Black Boys," in Angela J. Davis, *Policing the Black Man: Arrest, Prosecution, and Imprisonment* (New York: Pantheon Books, 2017), 59.

35. Bogert and Hancock, "Superpredator."

36. Elizabeth Becker, "An Ex-Theorist on Young 'Superpredators,' Bush Aide Has Regrets," *New York Times*, February 2001, https://www.nytimes.com/2001/02/09/us/as-ex-theorist-on-young-superpredators-bush-aide-has-regrets.html?referringSource=articleShare.

37. Liz Ryan and Nancy La Vigne, "Trends in Youth Arrests for Violent Crimes," U.S. Department of Justice, August 2022, https://ojjdp.ojp.gov/publications/trends-in-youth-arrests.pdf.

38. Jill Tucker and Joaquin Palomino, "Vanishing Violence: Tracking California's Remarkable Collapse in Youth Crime," *San Francisco Chronicle*, March 2019, https://projects.sfchronicle.com/2019/vanishing-violence.

39. Becker, "An Ex-Theorist on Young 'Superpredators.'"

40. Ibid.

41. Ibid.

42. Bogert and Hancock, "Superpredator."

43. Henning, "Boys to Men," 61.

44. Sylvia Wynter, "'No Humans Involved': An Open Letter to My Colleagues," Forum N.H.I.: Knowledge for the 21st Century 1, no. 1 (Fall 1994), https://people.ucsc.edu/~nmitchel/sylvia.wynter_-_no.humans.allowed.pdf.

45. Ibid.

46. Ibid.

47. Fania E. Davis, *The Little Book of Race and Restorative Justice: Black Lives, Healing, and US Social Transformation* (New York: Good Books, 2019), 69.

48. Bogert and Hancock. "Superpredator."

49. "California Sent Thousands of Juveniles to Prison. Laws Have Softened, but Fallout Remains," *San Francisco Chronicle*, October 3, 2019, https://www.sfchronicle.com/bayarea/article/California-once-sent-thousands-of-juveniles-to-14480958.php.

50. National Juvenile Justice Network, "Keep Youth Out of Adult Prisons," 2022, https://www.njjn.org/about-us/keep-youth-out-of-adult-prisons.

51. Ram Subramanian, "How Some European Prisons Are Based on Dignity Instead of Dehumanization," Brennan Center for Justice, November 2021, https://www.brennancenter.org/our-work/analysis-opinion/how-some-european-prisons-are-based-dignity-instead-dehumanization.

52. Emily Gallagher, September 14, 2021, https://twitter.com/EmilyAssembly/status/1437787192903049238?s=20&t=rTIjSg1WD7f3oH3Cnmjszw.

53. Jan Ransom and Bianca Pallaro, "Behind the Violence at Rikers, Decades of Mismanagement and Dysfunction," *New York Times*, December 31, 2021, https://www.nytimes.com/2021/12/31/nyregion/rikers-island-correction-officers.html.

54. Ibid.

55. Erica Bryant, "18 People Have Died from New York City Jails in 2022." Vera Institute, November 2022, https://www.vera.org/news/nyc-jail-deaths-2022.

56. *Norbert v. City of San Francisco*, 10 F.4th 918 (9th Cir. 2021), https://casetext.com/case/norbert-v-city-of-san-francisco.

57. Sered, *Until We Reckon*, 76.

58. Vera Institute for Justice, "Incarceration Trends in Alabama," December 2019, https://www.vera.org/downloads/pdfdownloads/state-incarceration-trends-alabama.pdf.

59. U.S. Department of Justice Civil Rights Division, United States Attorney's Offices for the Northern, Middle, and Southern Districts of Alabama, "Investigation of Alabama's State Prisons for Men," April 2, 2019, https://www.justice.gov/opa/press-release/file/1150276/download.

60. U.S. Department of Justice Civil Rights Division, United States Attorney's Offices for the Northern, Middle, and Southern Districts of Alabama, "Investigation of Alabama's State Prisons for Men," July 23, 2020, https://www.justice.gov/crt/case-document/file/1297031/download.

61. U.S. Department of Justice Civil Rights Division, United States Attorneys' Offices for the Northern, Middle, and Southern Districts of Alabama, "Investigation of Alabama's State Prisons for Men," April 2, 2019, https://www.justice.gov/opa/press-release/file/1150276/download.

62. Ibid.

63. Ibid.

64. Ibid.

65. Ibid.

66. Ibid.

67. Ibid.

68. Ibid.

69. Ibid.

70. Mike Cason, "U.S. Department of Justice Sues Alabama over Unsafe Prison Conditions," December 9, 2020, https://www.al.com/news/2020/12/us-department-of-justice-sues-alabama-over-unsafe-prison-conditions.html.

71. Aaryn Urell, "Alabama Prison Crisis Continues with Homicide at Elmore," Equal Justice Initiative, November 8, 2022, https://eji.org/news/alabama-prison-crisis-continues-with-marquis-hatcher-homicide-at-elmore.

72. Michael Sainato, "Alabama Prisoners Strike over 'Horrendous' Conditions," *The Guardian*, October 6, 2022, https://www.theguardian.com/us-news/2022/oct/06/alabama-prison-strike-work-conditions.

73. ACLU and the University of Chicago, the Law School Global Human Rights Clinic, "Captive Labor: Exploitation of Incarcerated Workers," 2022, https://www.aclu.org/sites/default/files/field_document/2022-06-15-captive laborresearchreport.pdf.

74. Sam McCann, "What You Need to Know about the Alabama Prison Strike," Vera Institute, October 2022, https://www.vera.org/news/what-you-need-to-know-about-the-alabama-prison-strike.

75. Ibid.

76. Ibid.

77. Zoltan Lucas, "Senate Inquiry Documents Widespread Sexual Abuse in Federal Prisons," *The Crime Report*, December 14, 2022, https://thecrimereport.org/2022/12/14/senate-inquiry-documents-widespread-sexual-abuse-in-federal-prisons/.

78. "The Beauty Products 4 Women Bought after They Were Released from Prison," *Allure*, October 13, 2022, https://www.allure.com/story/beauty-products-formerly-incarcerated-women-buy.

79. Laura Gotti Tedeschi, "No Cell Can Keep Prisoners from God, Says Pope," *Catholic Herald*, October 24, 2013, https://catholicherald.co.uk/no-cell-can-keep-prisoners-from-god-says-pope.

Chapter Eight: Restorative Justice, Reparations, and Repair

1. The Discovery Deposition of George Powell, United States District Court for the Northern District of Illinois Eastern District, *Leroy Orange v. City of Chicago*, May 10, 2006 (George Powell, witness).

2. Chicago Torture Justice Center, "History of Chicago's Reparations Movement," https://www.chicagotorturejustice.org/history.

3. Sam Charles, "New 'Chicago Police Torture Archive' Details Acts of Jon Burge and Underlings," *Chicago Sun-Times*, February 3, 2021, https://chicago.suntimes.com/2021/2/3/22263444/new-chicago-police-torture-archive-details-acts-of-jon-burge-and-underlings.

4. Mariame Kaba, "Public Torture, Reparations, and Echoes from the 'House of Screams,'" in *We Do This 'Til We Free Us: Abolitionist Organizing and Transforming Justice* (Chicago: Haymarket Books, 2021), 107–9.

5. Democracy Now!, "As Torture Victims Win $5.5M in Reparations, Could Chicago Be a Model for Police Abuses Nationwide?," May 15, 2015, http://www.democracynow.org/2015/5/15/as_torture_victims_win_55m_in_reparations.

6. Flint Taylor, "Commentary: Burge Torture Taxpayer Tab Eclipses $210M—and Counting," *Injustice Watch*, June 14, 2022, https://www.injusticewatch.org/commentary/2022/burge-torture-taxpayer-tab-210-million.

7. Fania E. Davis, *The Little Book of Race and Restorative Justice: Black Lives, Healing, and US Social Transformation* (New York: Good Books, 2019), 10.

8. Davis, *The Little Book of Race and Restorative Justice*, 25.

9. Howard Zehr, Lorraine S. Amstutz, Allan Macrae, and Kay Pranis, *The Big Book of Restorative Justice: Four Classic Justice & Peacebuilding Books in One Volume* (New York: Good Books, 2015), 55.

10. Ibid., 29–30.

11. Randi Hagi, "Howard Zehr: Pioneer of Restorative Justice," *Crossroads Magazine–Eastern Mennonite University*, July 20, 2015, https://emu.edu/now/crossroads/2015/07/20/howard-zehr-pioneer-of-restorative-justice.

12. Zehr et al., *The Big Book of Restorative Justice*, 15–16.

13. Ibid., 30–32.

14. Catholic Mobilizing Network (CMN), "Restorative Justice," October 9, 2018, https://catholicsmobilizing.org/restorative-justice.

15. Trudy D. Conway, David Matzko McCarthy, and Vicki Schieber, *Redemption and Restoration* (Collegeville, MN: Liturgical Press, 2017), 25–26.

16. Zehr et al., *The Big Book of Restorative Justice*, 15–16.

17. Conway et al., *Redemption and Restoration*, 34.

18. Community Justice Initiatives, "Care of the Soul," June 19, 2019, https://cjibc.org/victim-offender-mediation-stories/care-of-the-soul.

19. Jiska Jonas, Svan Zebel, Jacques Claessen, and Hans Nelen, "The Psychological Impact of Participation in Victim-Offender Mediation on Offenders: Evidence for Increased Compunction and Victim Empathy," *Frontiers in Psychology* 12 (2002), https://www.frontiersin.org/articles/10.3389/fpsyg.2021.812629/full, DOI=10.3389/fpsyg.2021.812629.

20. Angela J. Davis, "The Prosecution of Black Men," in Angela J. Davis, *Policing the Black Man* (New York: Pantheon Books, 2017), 178–79.

21. Ibid., 179–80.

22. Ibid., 181–82.

23. Oranga Tamariki–Ministry of Children, "Oranga Tamariki Act 1989 No 24 (as at 1 September 2022), Public Act 4A Well-Being and Best Interests of Child or Young Person–New Zealand Legislation," New Zealand Legislation, September 1, 2022, https://www.legislation.govt.nz/act/public/1989/0024/latest/LMS216298.html#LMS216298.

24. Oranga Tamariki–Ministry of Children, "Restorative Justice and the Family Group Conference–Section 258(2), Practice Centre, Oranga Tamariki," https://practice.orangatamariki.govt.nz/our-work/interventions/family-group-conferencing/youth-justice-family-group-conference/restorative-justice-and-the-family-group-conference-section-2582/.

25. P. Spier, Children Arrested by Police in 2020/21, Wellington, New Zealand: Oranga Tamariki—Ministry for Children, https://www.orangatamariki.govt.nz/assets/Uploads/About-us/Research/Latest-research/Children-arrested-by-Police-in-2020/21/Children-arrested-by-Police-in-F2021.pdf.

26. Alex Busansky, "Contra Costa Becomes 4th County in California to Adopt Restorative Justice Diversion for Youth," Impact Justice, May 6, 2019, https://impactjustice.org/contra-costa-becomes-4th-county-in-california-to-adopt-restorative-justice-diversion-for-youth.

27. Impact Justice, https://impactjustice.org.

28. Yotam Shem-Tov, Steven Raphael, and Alissa Skog, "Can Restorative Justice Conferencing Reduce Recidivism? Evidence from the Make-It-Right Program," National Bureau of Economic Research, August 12, 2021, https://www.nber.org/papers/w29150.

29. Zehr et al., *The Big Book of Restorative Justice*, 66–67.

30. Ibid., 289–93.

31. Common Justice, "Our Work," 2022, https://www.commonjustice.org/our_work.

32. Encounters with Dignity Podcast, "Danielle Sered—Redefining Accountability," May 25, 2022, https://encounters-with-dignity.captivate.fm/episode/danielle-sered-redefining-accountability.

33. Davis, *The Little Book of Race and Restorative Justice*, 37–38.

34. Ibid., 39–42.

35. Ibid., 52–54.

36. The Georgetown Law Center on Poverty and Inequality, "School-Based Restorative Justice: State-by-State Analysis," 2020, https://genderjusticeand opportunity.georgetown.edu/restorative-justice-practices/rj-trends.

37. Andy Kopsa, "The City That Kicked Cops Out of Schools and Tried Restorative Practices Instead," *In These Times*, December 12, 2022, https://inthesetimes.com/article/the-city-that-kicked-cops-out-of-schools-and-tried-restorative-practices-instead.

38. Steve Lopez, "50 Years as a Jesuit Priest on a Mission of Redemption, and the Homies Say Thanks to Father Greg," *Los Angeles Times*, November 2, 2022, https://www.latimes.com/california/story/2022-11-02/lopez-column-father-greg-boyle-homeboy-industries-50-years-jesuit-priest.

39. Encounters with Dignity Podcast, "Fr. Greg Boyle, S.J.—Leading with Tenderness," July 26, 2022, https://encounters-with-dignity.captivate.fm/episode/fr-greg-boyle-leading-with-tenderness.

40. Ta-Nehisi Coates, "The Case for Reparations," *The Atlantic,* May 22, 2014, https://www.theatlantic.com/magazine/archive/2014/06/the-case-for-reparations/361631.

41. Pope Francis, *Fratelli Tutti: On Fraternity and Social Friendship* (Huntington, IN: Our Sunday Visitor Publishing Division, 2020), 135–38.

42. Ibid., 138–41.

43. Donna M. Owens, "Rep. John Conyers Hopes Americans Are Finally Ready to Talk about Reparations," NBC News, February 19, 2017, https://www.nbcnews.com/news/nbcblk/rep-john-conyers-still-pushing-reparations-divided-america-n723151.

44. Emmanuel Felton, "Supporters Say They Have the Votes in the House to Pass a Reparations Bill after Years of Lobbying," *Washington Post*, February 25, 2022,

https://www.washingtonpost.com/nation/2022/02/25/reparations-bill-congress-support/.

45. Democracy Now!, "WW II Reparations: Japanese-American Internees," February 18, 1999, http://www.democracynow.org/1999/2/18/wwii_reparations_japanese_american_internees.

46. Ibid.

47. Ibid.

48. Ibid.

49. William A. Darity Jr. and Kristen A. Mullen, *From Here to Equality: Reparations for Black Americans in the Twenty-First Century* (Chapel Hill: University of North Carolina Press, 2020), 37.

50. Ibid., 374–75.

51. *The 1619 Project: Episode 106 "Justice,"* directed by Roger Ross-Williams and Jonathan Clasberry, Lionsgate Production, 2023.

52. Darity and Mullen, *From Here to Equality*, 74.

53. Nick Noel and Duwain Piner, "The Economic Impact of Closing the Racial Wealth Gap," McKinsey & Company, August 13, 2019, https://www.mckinsey.com/industries/public-and-social-sector/our-insights/the-economic-impact-of-closing-the-racial-wealth-gap.

54. Darity and Mullen, *From Here to Equality*, 74–77.

55. Ibid., 77–78.

56. Ibid., 397.

57. Ibid., 404–5.

58. Ibid., 406–7.

59. Darity and Mullen, *From Here to Equality*, 408–9.

60. William Darity Jr., "Why Reparations Are Needed to Close the Racial Wealth Gap," *New York Times,* September 24, 2021, https://www.nytimes.com/2021/09/24/business/reparations-wealth-gap.html.

61. Nick and Piner, "The Economic Impact of Closing the Racial Wealth Gap."

62. Mateo Askaripour, "Falling in Love with Malcolm X—and His Mastery of Metaphor," Literary Hub, April 10, 2019, https://lithub.com/falling-in-love-with-malcolm-x-and-his-mastery-of-metaphor.

63. White House, "Fact Sheet: President Biden's Safer America Plan," August 1, 2022, https://www.whitehouse.gov/briefing-room/statements-releases/2022/08/01/fact-sheet-president-bidens-safer-america-plan-2.

64. Conway et al., *Redemption and Restoration*, 45–46.

Conclusion: A Catholic Call for Justice

1. Caitlin Morneau, *Harm, Healing, and Dignity: A Catholic Encounter with Restorative Justice* (Collegeville, MN: Liturgical Press, 2019), 5.

2. Richard Kreitner, "We Are Judged by How We Treat the Helpless and the Poor," *The Nation*, March 31, 2016, https://www.thenation.com/article/archive/we-are-judged-by-how-we-treat-the-helpless-and-the-poor.

3. U.S. Senate Committee on the Budget, "Extending Trump Tax Cuts Would Add \$3.5 Trillion to the Deficit, According to CBO," May 16, 2023, https://www.budget.senate.gov/chairman/newsroom/press/extending-trump-tax-cuts-would-add-35-trillion-to-the-deficit-according-to-cbo.

4. Alan Rappeport, "Tax Cheats Cost the U.S. \$1 Trillion per Year, I.R.S. Chief Says," *New York Times*, October 13, 2023, https://www.nytimes.com/2021/04/13/business/irs-tax-gap.html.

5. Kate Dore, "House Republicans Vote to Strip IRS Funding, Following Pledge to Repeal Nearly \$80 Billion Approved by Congress," CNBC, January 10, 2023, https://www.cnbc.com/2023/01/10/house-republicans-have-voted-to-cut-irs-funding-.html.

6. Philip Bump, "McCarthy's Sales Pitch for His Deal: Less Money for Law Enforcement," *Washington Post*, May 30, 2023, https://www.washingtonpost.com/politics/2023/05/30/debt-ceiling-republicans-mccarthy-irs.

7. "Black Taxpayers More Likely to Be Audited, IRS Admits," BBC News, May 17, 2023, https://www.bbc.com/news/world-us-canada-65617128.

8. James H. Cone, *God of the Oppressed, Revised Edition* (Maryknoll, NY: Orbis Books, 2018), 125–26.

9. Albert Nolan, *Jesus before Christianity, Twenty-Fifth Anniversary Edition* (Maryknoll, NY: Orbis Books, 2001), 43.

10. Ibid., 120.

11. Pope Paul IV, "Populorum Progressio," https://www.vatican.va/content/paul-vi/en/encyclicals/documents/hf_p-vi_enc_26031967_populorum.html.

12. ACLU, "Americans Overwhelmingly Support Prosecutorial Reform, Poll Finds," http://www.aclu.org/press-releases/americans-overwhelmingly-support-prosecutorial-reform-poll-finds.

13. Prison Policy Initiative, "Pretrial Detention," https://www.prisonpolicy.org/research/pretrial_detention; Prison Policy Initiative, "Releasing People Pretrial Doesn't Harm Public Safety," November 17, 2020, https://www.prisonpolicy.org/blog/2020/11/17/pretrial-releases.

14. NAACP, "Resolution Elimination of Cash Bail," 2022, https://naacp.org/resources/elimination-cash-bail.

15. Liz Komar, Ashley Nellis, and Kristen M. Budd, "Counting Down: Paths to a 20-Year Maximum Prison Sentence," The Sentencing Project, February 15, 2023, https://www.sentencingproject.org/reports/counting-down-paths-to-a-20-year-maximum-prison-sentence.

16. Pope Francis, *Let Us Dream: The Path to a Better Future* (New York: Simon & Schuster, 2020), 131–32.

17. Megan Greenwell, "Universal Basic Income Has Been Tested Repeatedly. It Works. Will America Ever Embrace It?," *Washington Post*, October 24, 2022, https://www.washingtonpost.com/magazine/2022/10/24/universal-basic-income.

Acknowledgments

I would like to thank God for lighting the fire within me to write this book and helping me to actually complete it. Thank you to my husband, Israel, who is always my first reader, biggest supporter, and took on many of my parental duties over the course of the year it took me to write it. My children, who are all growing up, motivate me to want to make the world a better place for them. Thank you to my spiritual director, Fr. Brian, who helped me work through the spiritual and emotional issues that *In the Shadow of Freedom* brought up. I was not prepared for how I would embody the pain, trauma, and suffering of so many African Americans whose stories I told in this book. I went to very deep and dark places spiritually and emotionally, and I do not think I would have been able to go through that without spiritual direction. Thank you to Maria Fuentes, who is the only friend/extended family member who has read all three of my books! Your support and encouragement mean everything. Thank you to Robert Ellsberg, who accepted my proposal and gave me the opportunity to write and publish this book. And thank you to my editor, Lillian Copan, whose editorial insights helped take *In the Shadow of Freedom* to the next level.